Emerging Social Issues

Emerging Social Issues

A Sociological Perspective

Edited by James A. Inciardi
and Harvey A. Siegal

PRAEGER PUBLISHERS
New York

Published in the United States of America in 1975
by Praeger Publishers, Inc.
111 Fourth Avenue, New York, N.Y. 10003

Library of Congress Cataloging in Publication Data

Inciardi, James A   comp.
  Emerging social issues.

  CONTENTS: Hauser, P. M. The chaotic society.—
Reich, C. A. Consciousness III: the new generation.—
Roszak, T. Technocracy's children. [etc.]
  Includes bibliographical references.
  1. United States—Social conditions—1960– —Addresses, essays, lectures.
2. Social change—Addresses, essays, lectures. 3. Social problems—Addresses,
essays, lectures. I. Siegal, Harvey A., joint comp. II. Title.
HN65.I6   309.1'73'092   73-19437
ISBN 0-275-52290-3
ISBN 0-275-85090-0 pbk.

Printed in the United States of America

for BROOKS, CRAIG, KAREN, and SHARI
. . . children of technology and
inheritors of the future

CONTENTS

INTRODUCTION

Sociology emerged as a discipline during the late eighteenth and early nineteenth centuries as a result of numerous changes in perceptions of society. It began as an attempt to answer long-standing philosophical questions concerning man's political and civil nature, and to study the phenomena of social interaction. As in other new disciplines, the spirit of rational inquiry or "science" provided the over-all direction. Thus, many of sociology's founding fathers were committed to the application of scientific method to the study of social phenomena.

As sociology matured, however, many of its basic questions remained unanswered. It became apparent that it was no easy matter to explain social processes, collective action, social deviance, or the nature of social institutions. But it became clear that sociology, as a scientific and scholarly field of endeavor, offered a perspective on the world that contributed useful insights into social processes and problems. By emphasizing both perspective and method, sociology provided an intellectual mechanism through which seemingly unrelated events and impressions could be combined into a meaningful synthesis. And it was within this frame that the sociological enterprise burgeoned.

As the development of sociology progressed, the major focus of the discipline shifted from abstract speculation and synthetic philosophical achievement to a concern with the structure and composition of human groups and their relationship to society. Sociologists, searching for the underlying social and social psychological processes that sustained society, began to view the world as a complex social organization. In order to discover these underlying processes, sociologists attempted to dissect society and examine through systematic research each of the pieces separately.

One of the *contemporary* interests of sociology is in study of human beings as they interact—attempting to understand the elements, properties, and rules of interaction as well as the nature of social change and its impact on behavior. The formulation of sociological knowledge results not only from the investigation of social processes but also from the systematic analysis of behavior or activity that is of an economic, political, historical, cultural, psychological, environmental, or technological nature. Therefore, all of man's activities, past and present, can be subjected to some form of sociological analysis.

Within this context, modern sociological inquiry appears to be well suited to examine and interpret the structure, progress, and directional changes that have formed the "American experiment" in contemporary society. The short history of American sociology reflects a notable effort in its specialized analysis of this experience. From the early community studies done at the University of Chicago during the 1920s to the large-scale empirical investigations of the past two decades, sociologists have greatly contributed to our understanding of community, rural and urban life, race relations, poverty and dependence, crime and delinquency, and the industrial order.

Yet recent events demonstrate that as the century and the American social complex have become more mature, the main concerns of sociology have been pushed beyond the traditional analysis of small units to deal with the challenges presented by new and even more complex social issues: technological growth at an unprecedented rate, exploitation of the environment, demographic transition, intergenerational conflict, political discontinuity, social alienation, and organizational revolution. It is the purpose of this volume to focus on these social issues as they have emerged since the 1960s and early 1970s, and as they may affect American social patterns during the last third of the twentieth century. American civilization is viewed within the context of an emerging postindustrial culture * characterized by technological revolution; by drastic transformations within the industrial enterprise, occupational structure, and political system; and by increased geographical mobility and widespread "cybernation."

Selections in this volume from the works of Reich, Roszak, and Slater discuss the changes in American social and psychological life during the last third of the twentieth century. Each, from a different perspective, chooses the contrast between generations as the central theme. The excerpt from Charles A. Reich's *The Greening of America* highlights these differences, whereas both Roszak and Slater demonstrate how today's "real" (or "manifest" in the anthropological sense) has evolved from one generation to the next from a long tradition of the "ideal." Taken collectively, the authors suggest that nothing is the same today as it was even a single generation ago. Reich's *The Greening of*

* Daniel Bell, *The Coming of Post-industrial Society: A Venture in Social Forecasting* (New York: Basic Books, 1973).

America provides a manifesto for new life-styles. His essay "Consciousness III" describes how young Americans are involved in a search for new forms of behavior that will be responsive to their individual needs in our rapidly changing society. The tone of his work is essentially optimistic—a new era is dawning for mankind, one that will surpass what has gone before.

Theodore Roszak's "Technocracy's Children," from his *The Making of a Counter Culture,* is concerned more with alternative political forms. Social dissent is calling forth new coalitions, causing the older political activists to leave their traditional working-class cohorts and unite with the new generation of dissidents.

Philip Slater's *The Pursuit of Loneliness,* from which "I Only Work Here" is excerpted, is a sociocultural look at American society, suggesting that our essential human needs for community, engagement, and dependence have been frustrated by efforts to attain efficiency and technological rationality. One of the major factors affecting society as a result of the increase in the scale of technology suggests that man is essentially a nontechnological being, who is forced to match a machine-like pattern—one he only minimally understands. His attempts to adapt to this pattern are costing him dearly.

In a different frame, Philip M. Hauser's "The Chaotic Society" suggests that the chaotic and anachronistic society of today is experiencing unprecedented tensions and strains as a result of the "social morphological revolution." This revolution involves changes in the size, density, and heterogeneity of the human population and the impact of these changes on the individual and society. Hauser offers further commentary on the fact that, in response to the acceleration of technological and social change, American society has developed a greater capacity for change.

In the excerpts from *Technological Man,* Victor C. Ferkiss offers a summary of prophecies based on the notions that modern technology has made human society a seamless web and that humankind must take new directions to meet the challenges of increased technological change. Central to his thesis is his commentary on what he calls "existential revolution and social inertia," in which he suggests that humanity is on the threshold of self-transfiguration, of attaining new powers over itself and its environment that can fundamentally alter its very nature; yet he acknowledges the paradoxical truth that certain patterns of human institutional and personal behavior are as resistant to change as lower forms of life.

Scott Greer's "Urbanization and Social Character" discusses the attempt by the people of America to invent a social being able to live in a large-scale society and claims that by means of this effort they may be laying the foundations for the first truly democratic civilization in the history of mankind.

Offering an enlightened perspective on crime in America, Richard Quinney's "The Future of Crime" focuses on the changing character of crime and shows how crime both initiates and reflects significant social changes.

The future is, of course, nebulous. It is clear, though, that almost all of our basic institutions are being called into question and examined from perspectives unthinkable even ten years ago. Social interaction, human groups, and even society are phenomena *sui generis*—meaning that the observable whole is greater than the sum of its parts. The real strength of the sociological method is that it never loses sight of this complexity. As the selections that follow will illustrate, one need not necessarily designate himself a "sociologist" to be imbued with what has come to be known as the "sociological imagination."

JAMES A. INCIARDI
Miami, Florida

HARVEY A. SIEGAL
Coral Gables, Florida

October 1974

Emerging Social Issues

CHAPTER 1

THE CHAOTIC SOCIETY

PHILIP M. HAUSER

Among the fundamental issues facing those concerned with long-term historical trends, past and future, has been the question of social continuity and discontinuity. Continuity was innocently reflected in the comparatively quiet years of the early 1960s. Social and political forecasters then conjectured that American society was going through a period of transition, but the spirit of change, they argued, echoed the confidence and optimism that any emergent problems could readily be solved by American energy and know-how. This assumption was clearly reflected in the comments inspired by President Eisenhower's Commission on National Goals, established in 1960. Columnist Walter Lippmann, in a *Life* magazine series on national goals, worried that the nation needed challenges to keep it strong. The late Adlai Stevenson also noted in the same *Life* series that "for the first time in history the engine of social progress has run out of the fuel of discontent."

Clearly, the opinion-makers of the Eisenhower years were naïve in their assumptions, for the 1960s rapidly evolved into a decade of protest. There was protest against racial inequality, poverty in the midst of plenty, inflation and taxes, and the government's inability to deal with the problems of urban decay, environmental pollution, and crime. The nation was shocked by the murders of John F. Kennedy, Martin Luther King, Robert Kennedy, and Medgar Evers; and there was worry and discontent over the increasing use of drugs and the decline in traditional moral standards. Many of our contemporary writers continue to offer conjectures as to the simplicity of current social transitions. They are echoing the same archaic ring that was heard at the onset of the 1960s, when, in fact, the nature and impact of our current change may be as vital and important in world history as was the European movement from a feudal to a bourgeois civilization.

Philip M. Hauser, in his essay "The Chaotic Society," goes well beyond mere conjecture and the notions of transition and discontinuity to describe how contemporary society is in a state of revolution that will continue to manifest the essential elements of chaos for years to come. Professor Hauser's central thesis is that our contemporary social system is experiencing unprecedented strains because of the social morphological revolution, a revolution characterized by rapid changes in the size, density, and heterogeneity of the population, and by the varying impacts of these changes on human behavior and the social order. He further maintains that the social morphological revolution is the product of three developments energized by, and interacting with, a fourth. The three dramatic developments are the "population explosion," the "population implosion," and "population diversification." The fourth, and interrelated, development is the acceleration of technological and social change.

The "population explosion" refers to the remarkable increase in the rate of world population growth, especially during the last three centuries of the modern era. The "population implosion" refers to the increasing concentration of the world's peoples on a small proportion of the earth's surface because of urbanization and metropolitanization. "Population diversification" alludes to the growing heterogeneity of populations not only sharing the same geographical area but also, increasingly, the same life space— economic, social, and political activity. Finally, technological change has both preceded and necessitated social change, and the difference between the rates of technological change and social change has generated great cultural strains and dissonance.

Professor Hauser documents the growth of these four developments, points to why it is likely to continue, and demonstrates how the United States presents the world's most dramatic examples of those developments. Furthermore, he describes clearly how the combined effects of the population explosion, the population implosion, population diversification, and rapid technological change have produced mutation in the American social order. Finally, he discusses the role of the social sciences in attempting to solve the problems of the social morphological revolution.

Ironically, when Philip Hauser first outlined the social morphological revolution in his presidential address to the American Sociological Association on August 28, 1968, his commentary was even more timely than he may have anticipated. During the very moments of his delivery, a new and unprecedented eruption in the American order had begun. For while Hauser spoke in Boston, more than a thousand miles away Mayor Richard J. Daley's Chicago was the scene of angry youth confronting police with clubs and fixed bayonets at and around the site of the Democratic National Convention.

Philip M. Hauser is currently a professor in the Department of Sociology at the University of Chicago, where he earned his Ph.D. degree in 1938. He has occupied the presidential chair of both the American Sociological Association and the American Statistical Association. Professor Hauser, who is highly prominent in the fields of demography and urban sociology, has published a wealth of scholarly material in the literature of various disciplines.

Society as a whole has been viewed historically from many perspectives. It has been envisaged among other ways as "the great society" (Wallas, 1916), "the acquisitive society" (Tawney, 1920), and "the affluent society" (Galbraith, 1958). Contemporary society, whether observed globally, nationally, or locally, is realistically characterized as "the chaotic society" and best understood as "the anachronistic society."

Contemporary society is realistically characterized as chaotic because of its manifest confusion and disorder—the essential elements of chaos. On the international scene, to draw upon a few examples, consider the situation in Vietnam, Czechoslovakia, the Middle East, and Nigeria. On the national level consider the United States, France, the United Kingdom, China, and almost any country in Asia, Latin America or Africa. On the local level, in the United States, consider New York, Chicago, Los Angeles, Detroit, Cleveland, Memphis, Miami, and over 100 other cities which have been wracked by violence.

Contemporary society can be best understood when it is viewed as an anachronistic society. To be sure, society at any time, at least during the period of recorded history, has been an anachronistic society. For throughout the millennia of the historical era, society, at any instant in time, comprised layers of culture which, like geological strata, reflected the passage and deposits of time. Confusion and disorder, or chaos, may be viewed in large part as the resultant of the dissonance and discord among the various cultural strata, each of which tends to persist beyond the set of conditions, physical and social, which generated it.

In some ways chaos in contemporary society differs from that in earlier societies only in degree. But there are a number of unique factors in contemporary chaos which make it more a difference in kind. First contemporary society, as the most recent, contains the greatest number of

"The Chaotic Society: Product of the Social Morphological Revolution" by Philip M. Hauser, pp. 1–19 in Vol. 34, February, 1969, *The American Sociological Review,* reprinted by permission of the author and publisher. This paper was initially prepared as a presidential address before the 63d annual meeting of the American Sociological Association, Boston, August 28, 1968.

cultural layers, and, therefore, the greatest potential for confusion and disorder. Second, contemporary society, by reason of the social morphological revolution, possesses cultural layers much more diverse than any predecessor society and, therefore, much greater dissonance. Third, contemporary society, unlike any predecessor, contains the means of its own destruction, the ultimate weapon, the explosive power of nuclear fusion. Fourth, fortunately, contemporary society possesses the knowledge, embodied in the emerging social sciences, including sociology, that affords some hope for the dissipation of confusion and the restoration of order before the advent of collective suicide. It is a moot question, however, as to whether society yet possesses the will and the organization to utilize available knowledge to this end.

. . . Sociology, as well as the other social sciences, provides knowledge, even though limited, permitting an understanding of society, contemporary and historical, and, in consequence, offers some hope for rational action towards the resolution of the chaos which afflicts us (Hauser, 1946).

It is my central thesis that contemporary society, the chaotic and anachronistic society, is experiencing unprecedented tensions and strains by reason of the social morphological revolution. The key to the understanding of contemporary society lies, therefore, in an understanding of the social morphological revolution. Moreover, it is a corollary thesis that comprehension of the social morphological revolution points to the directions social engineering must take for the reduction or elimination of the chaos that threatens the viability of contemporary society.

I am mindful of the fact that "the social morphological revolution" is not a familiar rubric to the sociological fraternity—nor to anyone else. It is a neologism, albeit with a legitimate and honorable ancestry, for which I must plead guilty. I offer two justifications for injecting this abominable rhetoric into the literature. First, I am convinced that it contains useful explanatory power that has not yet been fully exploited in macro-social considerations, or in empirical research, or in social engineering activities. Second, it is appropriate that the discipline of sociology possess a revolution of its own. After all, the agronomists have the "agricultural revolution"; economists, the "commercial" and "industrial" revolutions; natural scientists, the "scientific revolution"; engineers, the "technological revolution"; and demographers, the "vital revolution." Each of these revolutions is obviously the invention of scholars seeking a short and snappy chapter for a book title to connote complex and highly significant patterns of events. Sociologists, even if they have not formally recognized it, have the "social morphological revolution," and perhaps it is in order formally to acknowledge and to christen it.

THE SOCIAL MORPHOLOGICAL REVOLUTION

What is this social morphological revolution and what are its antecedents?

To answer the second of these questions first, I must repeat that its ancestry is legitimate and honorable. Durkheim (1897–1898), encapsulating earlier literature, provided in a focused way insight into the implications of the most abstract way of viewing a society, namely, by size and density of its population. In his consideration of the structure of the social order Durkheim (1938:81) used the term "social morphology." Wirth (1956) in his classical article "Urbanism as a Way of Life," drawing on Aristotle, Durkheim, Tonnies, Sumner, Willcox, Park, Burgess and others, explicitly dealt with the impact of size, density and heterogeneity of population on human behavior and on the social order.

The social morphological revolution refers to the changes in the size, density and heterogeneity of population and to the impact of these changes on man and society. As far as I know, the term was first published in my Presidential Address to the American Statistical Association (Hauser, 1963). It was used in conjunction with my explication of the "size-density model." This model provides a simplistic demonstration of the multiplier effect on potential human interaction of increased population density in a fixed land area and, therefore, can appropriately be described as an index of the size and density aspects of the social morphological revolution.

The essence of the size-density model, drawing on my earlier writing, is briefly given as follows (Hauser, 1965:11–12):

Let us consider the implications of variation in size and density of population, confining our attention to a fixed land area. For purposes of convenience, consider a circle with a radius of 10 miles. Such a circle would have a total area of approximately 314 square miles. The size of the total population in such a circle under different density conditions is shown below:

Assumed Population Density (persons per square mile)	Area with Approximate Density Assumed	Number of Persons in Circle of 10-Mile Radius
1	U.S. in 1500	314
50	World in 1960	15,700
8,000	Average central city in metropolitan area in U.S.	2,512,000
17,000	Chicago	5,338,000
25,000	New York	7,850,000
75,000	Manhattan	23,550,000

The population densities shown are not unrealistic ones. The population density of 1 may be taken as an approximation of the density of the United States prior to European occupancy. Actually, the Indian population was approximately one-third as dense as this, but 1 is a convenient figure with which to work. The density of 50 is approximately that of the United States in 1960, and approximately the population density of the world as a whole. The density of 8,000 in round numbers is not too far from the density of the average central city in metropolitan areas of the United States in 1960. The density figure 17,000 is approximately that of Chicago, the figure of 25,000 approximately the density of New York, and the figure of 75,000 approximately the density of Manhattan Island.

In aboriginal America a person moving within the ten-mile circle could potentially make only 313 different contacts with other human beings. In contrast, the density of the United States as a whole today would make possible 15,699 contacts in the same land area. The density of the average central city in the United States would permit over 2.5 million contacts, the density of Chicago over 5.3 million contacts, the density of New York City over 7.0 million contacts, and the density of Manhattan over 23.5 million contacts in the same land area. The potential number of contacts, when considered as a measure of potential human interaction, provides, in a simplistic way to be sure, a basis for understanding the difference that city living makes.

This explication is not only simplistic but greatly curtailed, for it does not consider the effects on potential human interaction of contacts in diads, triads and other size groupings which, obviously, would generate high orders in exponentials. Nor does the size-density model encompass the impact of heterogeneity, which is affected by population size and density as well as human migration.

Elements

The social morphological revolution is the product of three developments, energized by, and in interaction with, a fourth. The three developments may be described in dramatic terms as the "population explosion," the "population implosion," and "population diversification." The fourth, and interrelated development, is the acceleration in the tempo of technological and social change.

The "population explosion" refers to the remarkable increase in the rate of world population growth, especially during the three centuries of the modern era. In the long view world population growth rates have increased from perhaps two percent per millennium during the Paleolithic Period to two percent per annum at the present time—a thousandfold increase (Wellemeyer and Lorimer, 1962).

Since [the] mid-seventeenth century, world population has increased over six-fold, from about one-half billion to 3.4 billion at the present time. In quick summary, it took most of the two to 2½ million years man, or a close relative, has occupied the earth to generate a world population of one billion persons—a number not achieved until about 1825. It required only 105 years more to reach a population of 2 billion, by 1930; and only 30 years more to reach a total population of 3 billion, by 1960 (United Nations, 1953:11 and 1966:15).

The population explosion is still under way and, in fact, has achieved a greater magnitude since the end of World War II with its extension to the two-thirds of mankind in the developing areas of the world—in Asia, Africa and Latin America. Despite growing efforts to dampen rates of population growth, and contrary to the wishful thinking of some family planners, the facts indicate continuing acceleration of world population. Certainly, short of the catastrophic, there is little prospect of significant reduction in world population growth between now and the end of this century. Present fertility and mortality trends would beget a world population of 7.5 billion by the year 2000, and even the relatively optimistic preferred projection of the United Nations gives a world total of 6.1 billion by the century's end (United Nations, 1966: 15). Despite efforts to reduce fertility, then, the realistic prospect is that continuing mortality declines, as well as stubbornly high birth rates, will continue to produce explosive world population growth for at least the next two human generations.

The "population implosion" refers to the increasing concentration of the world's peoples on a small proportion of the earth's surface—the phenomenon of urbanization and metropolitanization. Again, in the long view, this is a relatively recent development. Permanent human plants and animals, the proliferation of the crafts, and forms of collective organizational, of the Neolithic Revolution—including domesticated settlement was not achieved until the Neolithic Period. Such permanent settlement had to await the great inventions, technological and social behavior and social organization (Turner, 1941; Childe, 1941; Braidwood and Willey, 1962; Mumford, 1961). Clumpings of population large enough to be called towns or cities did not emerge until after about 3500 B.C., and mankind did not achieve the technological and social organizational development to permit cities of 100,000 or more until as recently as Greco-Roman civilization. With the collapse of the Roman Empire, the relatively large urban agglomerations in the Roman sphere of influence diminished in size to small towns providing services to rural hinterlands together with which they constituted almost autonomous subsistence economies.

With the emergence of Europe from the Dark Ages and the series of "revolutions"—the Agricultural Revolution, the Commercial Revolution, the Industrial Revolution, the Scientific Revolution, and the Technological Revolution—man achieved levels both of technological and social organizational development that permitted ever larger agglomerations of people and economic activities. In consequence, the proliferation of cities of 1,000,000 or more inhabitants became possible during the nineteenth century, and the emergence of metropolitan areas and megalopolis, the coalescence of metropolitan areas, during the second half of the twentieth century. In 1800 only 2.4 percent of the world's people resided in places of 20,000 or more; and only 1.7 percent in places of 100,000 or more. By 1960, 27.1 percent were located in places of 20,000 or more, and 19.9 percent in places of 100,000 or more (Davis, 1955; Breese, 1966).

The trend towards increased urban and metropolitan concentration of population is likely to continue. The reasons for this are to be found in the advantages of clumpings of population and economic activities. As Adam Smith noted, the greater the agglomeration, the greater is the division of labor possible; and this permits increased specialization, easier application of technology and the use of non-human energy, economies of scale, external economies, and the minimization of the frictions of space and communication. In brief, the population implosion is likely to continue because clumpings of people and economic activities constitute the most efficient producer and consumer units yet devised. Moreover, such population agglomerations generate a social milieu of excitement and lure which add to the forces making for larger aggregations. Projections of world urban population indicate that by the end of the century 42 percent of the world's peoples may be resident in places of 100,000 or more, as contrasted with 20 percent in 1960, 5.5 percent in 1900, and 1.7 percent in 1800 (Davis, 1955; Breese, 1966).

"Population diversification" alludes to the increasing heterogeneity of populations not only sharing the same geographic area but also, increasingly, the same life space—economic, social and political activity. And the "same geographic area" and "the same life space," with accelerating technological and social organizational developments, have expanded during the twentieth century virtually to embrace the entire world. Population heterogeneity involves diversity in culture, language, religion, values, behavior, ethnicity and race. These characteristics are obviously not mutually exclusive categories, but they constitute foci of problems of communication, conflicts of interest, and frictions of interaction. Population diversification connotes not only the physical presence of a heterogeneous human aggregation but also social interaction among the diverse elements. It involves not only physical density but also "moral density," as used by Durkheim—social contact and social interaction (Durkheim, 1933, Book II, Ch. 2).

Finally, the accelerated tempo of technological and social change requires little elaboration. Suffice it to say that technological change has, in general, preceded and necessitated social change, and that the difference between rates of technological and social change and differential rates of social change have originated great cultural strains and dissonance (Ogburn, 1922).

The four developments discussed are, needless to say, highly interrelated and constitute the important elements of the social morphological revolution. The population explosion has fed the population implosion. Both have fed population diversification. And the accelerated tempo of technological and social change has operated as both antecedent to, and consequent of, the other three developments. Each in its own way, and all four in concert, have precipitated severe problems: chronic and acute; physical, economic, social and political; domestic and international.

The social morphological revolution incorporates the vital revolution and is closely interrelated with the other revolutions—agricultural, commercial, scientific, technological, and industrial. It is both antecedent to, and consequent of, the other revolutions and, as such, should be, on the one hand, better understood when considered in relation to them and, on the other hand, should be helpful in explaining them.

THE SOCIAL MORPHOLOGICAL REVOLUTION IN THE UNITED STATES

The United States constitutes the world's most dramatic example of all four of the developments described. These developments are reaching climactic proportions, have precipitated major crises, and constitute a framework for comprehending and dealing with America's urban difficulties. Virtually all of the urban problems which are increasingly and urgently requiring national attention, whether they be physical, personal, social, ethnic and racial, economic or governmental problems, may be viewed as frictions of the social morphological revolution which is still under way—frictions in the transition from an agrarian to an urban and metropolitan order.

The Population Explosion

In 1790, when the first Decennial Census of the United States was taken, the United States had a total population of less than 4 million persons. By 1960 the population of the nation numbered more than 180 million; during 1967 it reached 200 million.

The U.S. Bureau of the Census has from time to time made projections of U.S. population on varying assumptions about the future course of fertility and mortality. Such projections made in 1967 indicate that, despite the declining crude birth rate, the United States will continue to experience large absolute population increase in the decades which lie ahead. These projections show that by 1990 . . . the population of the

U.S. may reach a level of from 256 to 300 million. One of these projections, based on a fertility assumption that takes the current slump in the birth rate into account, would produce a population of 206 million by 1970, 232 million by 1980, and 267 million by 1990. The same projection gives a population of 308 million by the year 2000 and 374 million by 2015 (U.S. Bureau of the Census, 1957, 1962, 1967).

The Population Implosion

In 1790, 95 percent of the population of the United States lived in rural areas, on farms, or in places having fewer than 2,500 persons. The 5 percent of the population which lived in cities were concentrated in 24 such places, only two of which (New York and Philadelphia) had populations of 25,000 or more. By 1850, population in urban places was still as low as 15 percent. By 1900, however, almost two-fifths of the population lived in cities. But it was not until as recently as 1920 that the U.S. became an urban nation in the sense that more than half of the population (51 percent) lived in cities.

The speed of the population implosion becomes clear in an examination of developments since the turn of the century. In the first sixty years of this century the increase in urban population absorbed 92 percent of the total population growth in the nation. In the decade 1950 to 1960, the increase in urban population absorbed more than 100 percent of total national growth; that is, total rural population, including nonfarm as well as farm, actually diminished for the first time.

The increase in the population of metropolitan areas is equally dramatic. The increase in the population of the Standard Metropolitan Statistical Areas (SMSA's) absorbed 79 percent of total national growth between 1900 and 1960; and the 24 largest SMSA's, those with 1,000,000 or more, absorbed 43 percent in the first sixty years of this century.

The population implosion in this nation is still under way. Recent projections I have made with a colleague indicate that if present trends continue the metropolitan population, between 1960 and 1985, will increase by some 58 percent, while the non-metropolitan population increases by less than 12 percent (Hodge and Hauser, 1968). By 1985, then, 71 percent of the people in this nation would reside in metropolitan areas as compared with 63 percent in 1960.

Population Diversification

The United States has been one of history's most dramatic examples of population diversification as well as of the population explosion and the population implosion. Although the original European settlers were predominantly from the United Kingdom, the infusion of African Negro population began during the seventeenth century and was followed by waves of diverse European stocks during the nineteenth and early twentieth centuries.

The Census of Population first counted "foreign born" whites in 1850. At that time they constituted 9.7 percent of the total population. Although successive waves of immigration were heavy, the foreign-born whites never exceeded 14.5 percent of the total, a level reached in 1890 and again in 1910; they have been a dwindling proportion of the total ever since. By reason of restrictions on immigration, the foreign-born will become a decreasing proportion of the population of the nation in the decades which lie ahead.

In 1850, native whites made up 74.6 percent of the population of the nation, and "nonwhites," mainly Negroes, 15.7 percent. By 1900, the proportion had changed little, 75.5 percent being native white and 12.1 percent nonwhite. As recently as 1900, however, little more than half the American people were native whites of native parentage. That is, about one-fifth of the population was "second generation" white, or native whites born of foreign or mixed parentage.

By 1960, native whites constituted 83 percent, foreign whites 5.2 percent, and Negroes 10.6 percent of the total. Native whites of native parentage made up 70 percent of the total, the remaining 13 percent of native whites being second generation. Thus, in 1960 "foreign white stock," foreign born plus second generation, still made up over 18 percent of the total population.

Although the foreign white stock will become a dwindling part of the population in the decades which lie ahead, the proportion of nonwhites, mainly Negroes, is likely to increase. In 1960, there were 20.7 million nonwhites in the U.S., or 11.4 percent of the total. By 1990 it is estimated by the U.S. Bureau of the Census that nonwhites will double, increasing to 41.5 million. By 1990, nonwhites may, therefore, make up some 14.5 percent of the American people.

By reason of the "Negro Revolt," the most acute present manifestation of chaos in the United States, a closer examination of Negro population trends is required. In 1790, as recorded in the first census of the United States, there were fewer than 800,000 Negroes in the nation, but they made up about 20 percent of the total population. By that date they had already been resident in the colonies for 175 years, mainly as the property or indentured servants of their white masters.

Negro Americans remained about one-fifth of the total population until 1810. From then to 1930 they were an ever declining proportion of the total, as slave traffic ceased and white immigration continued. By 1930 the proportion of Negroes had diminished to less than one-tenth of the total. Since 1940, however, the Negro growth rate has been greater than that of the white population, and their proportion had risen to 11 percent by 1967.

In 1790, 91 percent of all Negroes lived in the South. The first large migratory flow of Negroes out of the South began during World War I, prompted by the need for wartime labor and the freeing of the Negro from the soil, with the diversification of agriculture and the onset of the delayed industrial revolution in the South. This migration of Negroes from the South was greatly increased during and after World War II. As a result, the proportion of total Negroes located in the North and West almost quadrupled between 1910 and 1960, increasing from 11 to 40 percent.

The migratory movement of Negroes from the South to the North and West effected not only a regional redistribution but also, significantly, an urban-rural redistribution. In 1910, before the out-migration of the Negro from the South began, 73 percent lived in rural areas. By 1960, within fifty years, the Negro had been transformed from 73 percent rural to 73 percent urban, and had become more urbanized than the white population.

The great urban concentration of Negro Americans is also revealed by their location in metropolitan areas. By 1910, only 29 percent of Negroes lived in the Standard Metropolitan Statistical Areas. By 1960, this concentration had increased to 65 percent. By 1960, 51 percent of all Negroes lived in the central cities of the SMSA's. Moreover, the 24 SMSA's with one million or more inhabitants contained 38 percent, and their central cities 31 percent, of all Negro Americans.

Again I draw on my recent projections estimating nonwhite population in metropolitan areas (SMSA's) by residence in central city and ring (Hodge and Hauser, 1968). They show that present trends may well take the nation farther down the road toward a *de facto* "apartheid society." By 1985 the concentration of nonwhites in central cities (as defined in 1960) would increase to 58 percent from the level of 51 percent in 1960, while the concentration of white population in central cities would diminish by almost a third to 21 percent in 1985 from 30 percent in 1960. In consequence, by 1985, 75 percent of all nonwhites within metropolitan areas would be resident in central cities and only 25 percent in the suburbs. In contrast, by 1985, 70 percent of the whites would inhabit the suburbs and only 30 percent live in central cities. Thus, of the total population in SMSA's, the proportion of nonwhite would increase from 11.7 percent in 1960 to 15.1 percent by 1985. But the proportion of population in central cities which would be nonwhite would increase by about 73 percent, rising from 17.8 percent in 1960 to 30.7 percent in 1985.

Negro population changes, past and in prospect, have resulted in greatly increased sharing with whites of the same geographical local areas, accompanied by increased pressure for social contact and social interaction. The acute tensions which characterize white-black relationships in the United States today represent a compounding of the impact of the social morphological revolution. For within the framework of the general population explosion and implosion in the entire nation, there have occurred even more dramatic population explosion and implosion among Afro-Americans. These developments have greatly exacerbated the problems of inter-group relations. The large increase in the population of Afro-Americans in urban and metropolitan areas over a relatively short period of time, and the contrast in background and life-styles between blacks and whites by reason of the disadvantaged position of blacks over the years, have combined to produce tensions that may well constitute the most serious domestic problem in the United States for some time to come (Hauser, 1966; Hauser, 1967a; Hauser, 1968a).

CONSEQUENCES OF THE SOCIAL MORPHOLOGICAL REVOLUTION

The combined effects of the population explosion, the population implosion, and population diversification have produced in the realm of the social the equivalent of a mutation in the realm of the genetic. The social morphological revolution has profoundly altered human nature and the social order. In broad overview the social morphological revolution has modified the human aggregation as a physical construct and as an economic mechanism; it has transformed human behavior and social organization, including the nature of government; it has generated and aggravated a host of problems—physical, personal, social, institutional, and governmental.

Examples of the physical problems are given by the problems relating to housing supply and quality, circulation of persons and goods, solid and human waste removal, air and water pollution, recreational facilities, urban design, and the management of natural resources.

Examples of personal, social and organizational problems are given by the incidence of delinquency and crime, alcoholism, drug addiction, and mental disorder. It is evident in the current revolt of youth, which at the extremes include the "hippie," who resolves his problems by retreat, and the "activist," who resolves his problems by beating his head against the doors of the Pentagon, or police clubs at the University of California at Berkeley and at other universities. It is revealed also in unemployment, poverty, racism, bigotry, inter-group conflict, family disorganization, differential morbidity and mortality, labor-management conflict, the conservative-liberal debate, the maladministration of criminal justice; and in corruption, malapportionment and inertia in government, and the fragmentation and paralysis of local government. It is further revealed by continuing resort to physical force as a means for the resolution of conflicts of interest. No matter how laudable the goals, when force is employed by labor and management, by students, by advocates of peace, by minority groups, or in most extreme form by nations at war, it is a mechanism incompatible with the continued viability of contemporary society. In fact, if society is to remain viable, when there is disorder, it has no alternative to the use of overwhelming collective force for restoration of order. Of course, upon the restoration of order, the causes of disorder must be investigated and removed, or tensions may mount and produce even greater disorder. The point is that contemporary society, by reason of unprecedented interdependence, is highly vulnerable and easily disrupted—a fact which is increasingly perceived and exploited by dissident persons and groups.

These types of problems may be viewed sociologically as consequences of the social morphological revolution which generated secondary group, as distinguished from primary group, association; inter-personal relations based on utility from emotion and sentiment; the conjugal or nuclear, from the extended family; formal from informal social control; rational from traditional behavior; enacted from crescive institutions; and bureaucracy from small-scale and informal organization. Especially significant have been the changes in the elements and processes of the socialization of the child—the transformation of the helpless biological specimen, the infant, into a human being or member of society. In brief, the social morphological revolution transformed the "little community" (Redfield, 1955), which has characterized predecessor societies, into the "mass society" (Mannheim, 1940:61).

It is my contention that the confusion and disorder of contemporary life may be better understood and dealt with as frictions in the transition still under way from the little community to the mass society; and that the chaos of contemporary society, in large part, is the product of dissonance and conflict among the strata of culture which make up our social heritage. The problems or frictions are often visible manifestations of what my former teacher and colleague, William Fielding Ogburn, termed "cultural lag" (Ogburn, 1922:200ff).

Permit me to provide a few concrete examples of cultural lag in contemporary society—examples of special significance and impact. I do so, as a sociologist, to illustrate the use of the analytical framework provided by the social morphological revolution in the consideration of specific social problems.

Governance

Focusing on the United States, consider the example of cultural lag in our system of governance. Needless to say, confusion and disorder in government have a multiplier impact on other realms of chaos.

Consider some of the elements involved in the raging "conservative-liberal" debate. In the ongoing political context, the polemic centers on the role of government in the social and economic order. It is evident in the attitudes toward "big government," and, in general, in anachronistic political ideology (Hauser, 1967c). Three illustrations of "cultural lag" in ideology help to explain the paralysis which afflicts this nation in efforts to deal with the acute problems which beset us.

One is the inherited shibboleth that "that government is best which governs least." The doctrine made considerable sense when our first census was taken in 1790. At that time, 95 percent of the American people lived on farms or in towns having fewer than 2,500 persons. What was there for government to do, compared with the situation in 1960, in which 70 percent of the American people lived in urban places and about 63 percent were residents of metropolitan areas? Can you visualize a United States today without a Social Security System, without a Public Health Service, without a Federal Reserve Board, without the Interstate Commerce Commission, and without the Civil Aeronautics Administration? The slogan "that government is best which governs least" is a good example of a cultural survival which has persisted beyond its time.

Or contemplate next the shibboleth [that] each man in pursuing his own interest, "as if guided by an invisible hand," promotes the interest of the entire society. This also made sense in the United States in 1790. Each person pursuing his own interest and supporting his family on a farm or in a small town was, to be sure, automatically acting in the interest of society. But can you imagine a United States today without a Food and Drug Administration, a Securities and Exchange Commission, a Federal Trade Commission, and a Federal Communications Commission? The recent Federal intervention into automobile safety is a timely reminder of the fact that what is in the best interest of the Detroit automotive manufacturer is not necessarily in the best interest of the American people. The chasm between reality in economic behavior and extreme forms of classical and neo-classical economics grows broader and deeper with each passing year as the social morphological revolution continues in its inexorable course.

Consider, also, the shibboleths that taxes are what governments take away from the people and that government expenditures must be kept to a minimum. The Ways and Means Committee of the 90th House of Representatives and the majority in both Houses afford an excellent example of cultural lag and its consequences in their vestigial behavior in respect to the income tax surcharge. The critical question that the Congress should have asked is, "What are the essential needs of the United States to maintain this nation as a viable society?" And the next step should have been to arrange to finance the necessary programs. Taxes in a mass society are not what the government takes away from people, but rather what the people pay for essential services required for collective living in an interdependent society which, among other things, generates needs which cannot be met by the free market. Congress, exemplifying cultural lag, cut deeply into essential programs already pathetically inadequate to provide desperately needed services to many millions of Americans. Perhaps the highlight in the insensitivity and anachronistic character of the 90th House of Representatives was given by its Marie Antoinette type of performance which, in respect to the Afro-American urban slum residents, in effect said, "Let them have rats."

Furthermore, apart from these examples of ideological atavisms, consider the irony in the national political situation, in which by reason of seniority provisions for committee memberships and chairmanships in the Congress and the one-party system in the post-bellum South, this most underdeveloped region of the United States, which is still in the early stages of the social morphological revolution, maintains a vise-like grip on the national legislative process—a grip bolstered by the filibuster which permits tyranny by a minority.

There are many other evidences of cultural lag in the Federal government and on the state and local levels of government. The rapidity with which this nation has become urbanized has produced serious malapportionment in the House of Representatives in the Congress, in state assemblies, and in municipal councils. For example, in 1960, there were 39 states with an urban population majority, but not a single state in the Union where the urban population controlled the state legislature (David and Eisenberg, 1961). This condition accelerated Federal interventionism. For it was the insensitivity to urban problems, the problems of the mass society, by the malapportioned rural-dominated legislatures that drew the Federal government into such realms as public housing, urban renewal, highways and expressways, civil rights, mass transportation, and education. To the addicts of the outmoded slogans discussed above, these programs are viewed as the violation of "states' rights." But it is an ironic thing that the most vociferous advocates of states' rights have played a major role, by their ignoring of twentieth-century mass society needs, in bringing about the increased centralization of governmental functions.

A final example of cultural lag in the American system of governance is given by the chaos in local government (Hauser, 1961). The framework for the structure of local government in the United States is the local governmental structure of 18th-century England. The Constitutional fathers did not, and could not have been expected to, anticipate the emergence of population agglomerations of great size, density, and heterogeneity, which transcended not only municipal and township lines but also county and state boundaries. In consequence, our metropolitan clumpings of people and economic activities are characterized by governmental fragmentation which paralyzes local efforts to deal with metropolitan area-wide problems, such as those relating to air and water pollution, traffic congestion, crime, employment, housing, and education.

By reason of its implications for the socialization of the child, the consequences of governmental fragmentation for public education at the primary and secondary levels are especially worthy of attention. It may be argued that public school education is today converting this nation into a caste society, stratified by race and by economic status. I illustrate this with another neologism for which I apologize. I refer to the "pre-conception IQ," the IQ of the child before he is conceived (Hauser, 1968a). The child with a very high pre-conception IQ, high enough to select white-skinned parents who live in the suburbs, has by this astute act guaranteed unto himself an input for public school education two to ten times that of the child with a miserably low pre-conception IQ, stupid enough to select black-skinned parents in the inner-city slums. The child with an intermediate pre-conception IQ, bright enough to select white-skinned parents but too stupid to pick parents living in the suburbs, gets an intermediate education. This is a way of saying that the child in the suburbs gets a first-class education, the white child living toward the periphery gets a second-class education, and the child in the inner city, black or white, gets a third- or fourth-rate education. As a result, education is no longer performing its historic mission in this nation in contributing to national unity and to the maintenance of an open society. On the contrary, the kind of education we now have in our slums and ghettos is recycling the present chaotic situation into perpetuity. Our metropolitan areas today have blacks who were born in the city, reared in the city, educated in the city, and who have not acquired the basic, the salable or the citizenship skills prerequisite to their assuming the responsibilities and obligations as well as the rights of American citizenship. Quite apart from other factors operating, it is clear that the failure of local governmental structure to keep up with the social morphological revolution is a major element in this disastrous situation.

Racism

Without question, the most serious domestic problem which haunts the United States today is the Negro Revolt. There are only three considerations necessary to understand the "why" of this situation. First, the Afro-American has been on this continent for three and a half centuries. He involuntarily spent two and a half centuries in slavery; he spent a half century in the rural slum South under the unfulfilled promises of the Emancipation Proclamation; and he has spent an additional half century in the slum ghettos of metropolitan America, in the North and South.

Second, since World War II the entire world has been swept by what has felicitously been called "the revolution of rising expectations." This is the first generation in the history of man in which no peoples are left on the face of this earth who are willing to settle for second place in level of living and who do not insist on freedom and independence if not already achieved. This revolution of rising expectations has not bypassed Afro-Americans. In a fundamental sense the Negro Revolt is simply America's local manifestation of the revolution of rising expectations.

Third, there is a shorter-run and a more immediate consideration. With the Johnson Administration and the success of previous Congresses in the passage of civil rights legislation, new vistas of opportunity and new expectations were aroused in the black community. It is an ironic thing that the Negro Revolt and the riots are not in spite of these advances but in a sense because of them. Blacks were led to believe that they were finally achieving full equality in the American scene. But what happened in reality? There was little to match the Federal leadership on the state front in terms of gubernatorial leadership, or on the local front in terms of mayoral leadership, or in leadership in the private sector. Nothing substantial happened to change the reality of living in rat-infested slums and of unemployment rates two to three times that of whites. Little was done to change the character of the segregated communities in which the Negro lived, and little was done to change the character of the woefully deficient educational opportunities for the black child. As the gap between expectation and reality increased, so did frustration, alienation, and bitterness which have led to violence.

Underlying all three of these factors which account for the present restiveness, hostility, and violence of Afro-Americans is "white racism," the major cause of the present crisis, the term appropriately designated as such by the Kerner Commission (National Advisory Commission on Civil Disorders, 1968:91). Although immigrant newcomers to the United States have, on the whole, also been greeted with prejudice and discriminatory practices, the Negro, since his involuntary importation as a slave, has been the victim of a much more widespread, persistent, and virulent racist theory and practice.

Racist doctrine may be understood as a negative and extreme form of ethnocentrism, the product of the isolated little community of relatively small size [and] density, and cultural homogeneity. The persistence of racist attitudes and behavior constitutes another example of cultural lag —the survival of a little community into the mass society. A prejudicial attitude towards other human beings, whether in the positive form of ethnocentrism or its negative counterpart as hostility towards others on a categoric basis, is a cultural atavism—an anachronistic set of attitudes incompatible with the requirements of cooperative association in a mass society. In the context of large, dense and heterogeneous population agglomerations, racism necessarily spells trouble and conflict. It should not be too surprising that white racism is now breeding or exacerbating black racism, and, therefore, intensifying hostility and conflict. Furthermore, the paralysis of government in the United States, as described above, further compounds the crisis and offers little hope of any short-run resolution of tension and conflict. This nation, on its present course, may well be in for an indefinite period of guerrilla warfare on the domestic as well as on the international front (Hauser, 1968a:4–10).

Other Examples of Cultural Lag

There are many other examples of cultural lag in American society ranging from the trivial to the significant. In the trivial category is the persistence of the string, designed before the advent of the pin and the button to keep collars closed against inclement weather. This string has become the necktie, a relatively harmless, if not always aesthetic, vestige which has acquired a new function, i.e. decoration. But other vestiges are not as harmless. They include the constitutional right to bear arms —admittedly necessary in eighteenth-century America but a dangerous anachronism in the last third of twentieth-century America. They include also the inalienable rights of labor to strike and of management to shut down and employ the lockout, often through trial by ordeal of the public. In twentieth-century mass society, labor's right to strike and management's right to lockout may be described as the rights of labor and management to revert to the laws of the jungle—to resolve their conflicts of interest by means of brute force. The same can be said of the so-called right of the students to impose their views through the employment of force, or of any person or group who fails to resolve conflicts of interest in a mass society by an adjudicative or democratic procedure.

Cultural atavisms are replete, also, in the administration of criminal justice, for many of the governing codes and procedures are of pre-social morphological revolution origin and constitute a menace to mass society.

Finally, and by no means to exhaust the universe of cultural lags, mention should be made of organized religion as a living museum of cultural atavisms adding to the confusion and disorder of contemporary life. Sunday morning Christians have learned to honor and revere the messenger, his mother and his colleagues; they have learned to observe the ritual and practices of their churches which have endured for two millennia; but they have not received, or certainly they have not heeded, the message. For the message of the Judeo-Christian tradition is found in the concept of the Fatherhood of God—which implies the brotherhood of man. And comparable things can be said of the adherents of the other religions, the Jews, the Moslems, the Hindus, the Buddhists, etc.

Interestingly enough, the concept of the brotherhood of man, apart from its supernatural context, is an excellent example of an ancient ethical principle which has great applicability to contemporary as well as to previous societies. Although I have pointed to cultural survivals which create confusion and disorder, this is not to be interpreted to mean that all that is the product of the past is incompatible with the present. In fact, it may be argued that the increased interdependence and vulnerability of the mass society place a greater premium on this moral principle than any earlier society ever did. This is an example of a principle of mass living that has not yet taken hold despite its longevity, yet the adoption of which in deed, as well as in word, may be prerequisite to the continued existence of mankind.

Before departing from the subject of religion, I cannot, as a demographer, refrain from calling attention to the cultural dissonance represented by Pope Paul VI's recent encyclical "Of Human Life," which ignores the findings of empirical demography (*New York Times*, 1968: 20–21). This example of cultural lag closely parallels that afforded by the Roman Catholic Church during the reign of Pope Paul V, which, some three centuries ago, similarly ignored the findings of empirical astronomy and produced the Galileo incident.

Among the most serious consequences of the failure of contemporary American society to keep pace with the social morphological revolution [are] the deficiencies in the process of socialization. Bronfenbrenner (1968) illuminates this problem in his comparative study of education in the United States and the Soviet Union. In the U.S.S.R. the child is so inbred with a sense of belonging and obligation to the society of which he is an infinitesimal part that he tends to lack initiative and creativity. In the United States, in contrast, the child is so little the recipient of a sense of membership in, and responsibility to, the social order that, although he develops great initiative and creativity, his attitude is essentially one of concern with how he gets his and unconcern with others. We have yet to achieve the golden mean in order to produce a harmonious mass society consisting of people with a balance of initiative, creativity and social responsibility.

On the international front, there is similar evidence of cultural lag. Most grave in its consequences, obviously, is the failure to achieve the resolution of national conflicts of interest by means other than physical force. Vietnam, the Middle East, and Nigeria are but a few timely reminders of this fact. The social morphological revolution has generated a highly interdependent, vulnerable and shrunken world, increasing the probability and intensifying the nature of conflicts of interest. But the traditional means of resolving international tensions and hostilities, namely, war, in a society which possesses the hydrogen bomb, carries with it the threat of the ultimate disaster, even the extinction of mankind. Nevertheless, contemporary diplomatic policies and contemporary military postures are more the product of societies of the past than of the present.

To be sure, some progress has been made in the evolving of machinery for the peaceful resolution of international disputes as exemplified by the League of Nations, the World Court, the United Nations and the Specialized Agencies. But it is not yet certain that the United Nations will not follow the League of Nations into oblivion as is actually desired by some of our most anachronistic organizations, such as the Daughters of the American Revolution and the John Birch Society. If the plague of deleterious cultural survivals which afflicts contemporary society cannot be effectively dealt with, it may well be that nuclear holocaust will be the means to undo both the process and the products of the social morphological revolution.

Finally, again on the international front, mention must be made of the cleavages between the have and have-not nations, between the socialist and communist nations, and between the factions within these blocs. The great disparities in levels of living among the nations of the world and the great international ideological differences, in part products of the differential impact of the social morphological revolution, constitute the most serious threats to peace and are harbingers of potential disaster. It remains to be seen whether contemporary society can muster the will to utilize available knowledge in a manner to override ideological, structural and procedural atavisms to cope with these problems. In this year, officially proclaimed by the United Nations as the International Human Rights Year, it is a sad commentary on the role of this nation that the Congress has reduced foreign aid appropriations to an all-time low. And it is an even sadder commentary on the state of international affairs that the world spends well over 100 billion dollars annually for the military, while the developing nations, after a disastrous "Development Decade," still starve for capital and other resources to achieve their economic development goals.

THE ROLE OF THE SOCIAL SCIENCES INCLUDING SOCIOLOGY

In contemporary society the approach to the solution of our problems, whether on the international or on the national front, is characteristically bifurcated, reflecting deep ideological cleavage. The approach to problem solution tends to be "conservative" or "liberal," or variations from "reactionary" to "revolutionary." It is my contention, again utilizing the social morphological framework, that the conservative and the liberal reflect the ideology of the social morphological conditions in which they were reared or to which they were exposed. It is not an accident, for example, that Barry Goldwater comes from a state which as recently as 1940 had a population density about the same as that of the United States in 1790—4.4 persons per square mile, and only 6.6 in 1950 and 11.5 in 1960. Nor is it a mere coincidence that Senator Jacob Javits, in contrast, comes from a state with population densities of 281.2 in 1940, 309.3 in 1950, and 350.1 in 1960 (Hauser, 1967c).

Needless to say, in a society such as that of the United States, in which the State of Alabama and the State of New York are simultaneously present, there is an extreme range in social morphological conditions. Furthermore, "urbanism as a way of life" is neither confined to the boundaries of a city nor ubiquitous and pervasive within it. That is, rural residents in a complex mass society may, by reason of their own life paths, take on urban patterns of thought and action and *vice versa*.

The conservative, including the reactionary, is the person socialized in a milieu which, although contemporary by the calendar, is essentially that of eighteenth and nineteenth century America. The liberal, including the revolutionary, in contrast, is the person who has been reared in a milieu more the product of the social morphological revolution. The conservative is essentially the representative of the past in the present; the liberal is more clearly the representative of the present.

This does not necessarily mean that the liberal has the answers for the solution of contemporary problems. The liberal, who is sure that he has the right answers because they are non-traditional or different from that of the conservative, is subject to the same basic blindness as is the conservative. The basic point is that the "right" answer is neither to be found in the "old," as old, nor the "new," as new. It is to be found rather in the specific analysis of a specific problem situation to which the application of knowledge and wisdom finds possible solutions quite independently of whether they are "old" or "new," or "conservative" or "liberal," or any variation of these postures.

Both the conservative and liberal approaches *per se* are as inconsistent with the contemporary urban and metropolitan order as the horse and buggy or any other outmoded artifact. The unprecedented problems arising as frictions of social change can be resolved by neither the conservative nor the liberal approach.

If the approach to the resolution of contemporary social problems is neither to be conservative nor liberal, what is it to be? The answer is the "social engineering" approach. The social engineering position, as distinguished from the conservative or liberal one, represents an utterly new approach to contemporary problems. It is an approach born of the social morphological revolution to cope with the problems engendered by it.

It is not possible here fully to trace the emergence of the social engineering approach. It may be briefly stated that it is a recent product of the whole series of developments which distinguishes the post-Newtonian from the pre-Newtonian world. The more recent of these developments has led to the application of the method of science to social, as well as to physical and biological phenomena; and to the emergence of social-engineering activities to parallel the engineering activities based on the physical and biological sciences. That is, the social engineer, as yet represented by a pathetically few professions—e.g., the public administrator, the city manager, the social worker, the educator, the criminologist, the planner, the professional businessman—is emerging to apply the knowledge of social science to the solution of social problems, in the same manner as the electronics engineer applies the knowledge of physics to electronics problems, or the biological engineer, the physician, applies the knowledge of the life sciences to problems of ill health.

Only by the adoption of the social-engineering approach can we get beyond the conservative-liberal approach. Only in this manner can we avoid the blindness of both the conservative and the liberal—the one convinced that the past contains the answers to the present; the other, that the past does not. That both the conservative and liberal approaches are blind may be argued on the basis of two generalizations, validated by the evidence produced by social science. The first is that if you find what is right and stick to it, you are bound to be wrong. For the world does not stay put; it changes. The second is that no degree of disillusionment with the past, no level of good intentions, and no amount of zeal by themselves necessarily provide an appropriate answer to anything.

The social-engineering approach is an approach as independent as possible of existent stereotyped postures or attitudes. It is neither conservative nor liberal. Republican nor Democratic, any more than is an electronic engineer's approach, or the approach of any expert confronted with a problem which requires an effective and efficient solution. It is a twentieth-century approach consonant with twentieth-century metropolitan life and adapted to the resolution of twentieth-century problems.

The social-engineering approach is dependent on knowledge, drawn from social science, and wisdom, based on experience in problem solving. It is the role of the social sciences, in general, as well as sociology in particular, to provide the necessary knowledge. That is the object of research, data collection, data processing and analysis.

The practical purpose of social data is to permit social accounting

(Hauser, 1967b). Accounting first was a set of principles and practices for collecting, collating, and reporting information relating to the activities of an organization, so that they could be evaluated in relation to the organization's objectives. In contemporary language, accounting is an information-control system, designed to serve the needs of administrators of an organization or a program.

Accounting procedures evolved in the development of private business and have only relatively recently been applied to the evaluation and control of an entire economy. The Employment Act of 1946 in the United States, which created the President's Council of Economic Advisers and requires an annual Economic Report to the nation, represents a major institutional invention to cope with the economic problems of the twentieth-century American economy.

A hopeful indication that the social morphological revolution is producing mechanisms for the resolution of the social problems it has precipitated lies in the bill introduced in the 90th Congress calling for the establishment of a parallel Council of Social Advisers and an annual Social Report to the nation (Subcommittee on Government Research, 1968). Furthermore, the Department of Health, Education, and Welfare, through its Advisory Panel on Social Indicators, and upon instruction from the President of the United States, has been engaged in the preparation of a prototype Social Report.

The unprecedented period of high level economic activity, uninterrupted by depression or recession, that this nation has recently experienced is certainly related to the existence and activities of the Council of Economic Advisers. We are now experiencing a costly inflation, and we are now threatened by a possible recession mainly because the Congress, a repository of cultural lag, has not heeded, or tardily heeded, the recommendations of the Administration based on the findings of the Council of Economic Advisers.

It is my judgment that had this nation possessed a Council of Social Advisers since 1947, along with the Council of Economic Advisers, and had the recommendations of such a Council been heeded by the Administration and the Congress, the "urban crisis" which sorely affects us would not have reached its present acute stage.

It is the role of the social sciences, including sociology, to generate the knowledge on the basis of which social policy and social action may be directed to the solution of our problems. The primary function of the social scientist is research, the production of knowledge. It is not the function of the social scientist, *qua* scientist, to be a social engineer (Hauser, 1949). To be sure, many of us social scientists have been called upon to perform both roles in the early stage of the development of the social sciences, but there can be no question about the fact that the two roles are distinct and that each, in the long run, will be better performed as separate and specialized activities.

More specifically, it is the role of the social scientist, including the sociologist, to develop and produce the "social indicators" which will permit effective social accounting. Fortunately, the social morphological revolution has generated much in the way of social statistics and other types of knowledge, which are already quite impressive even if still deficient and in relatively early stages of evolution (Raymond M. Bauer, 1967; Hauser, 1967b; Hauser, 1963).

Social accounting will become possible only after consensus is achieved on social goals. The development of social goals is neither a scientific function nor a social engineering function. It is a function that must be performed by society as a whole, acting through its political and other leaders. In a democratic society it presumably reflects the desires of the majority of the people.

Although a majority of the people must fix the goals of a society, the social scientist and the social engineer are in a strategic position to participate in goal formation. They must work closely with political and other leaders to help develop a broad spectrum of choices, which will reflect, insofar as possible, the requirements and consequences of specific goals. I have elsewhere proposed one set of social goals for consideration—published in a . . . report of the Joint Economic Committee of the Congress (Hauser, 1968b).

Concluding Observations

Man is the only significant culture-building animal on earth. He not only adapts to environment, he creates it as well. He has created a world in which mankind itself is the crucial environment—a mankind characterized by large numbers, high densities and great heterogeneity. He is still learning how to live in this new world he has created. The product of the chief components of the social morphological revolution —the population explosion, the population implosion and population diversification—together with rapid technological and social change— is contemporary society, a chaotic society, an anachronistic society. It is a society characterized by dissonant cultural strata—by confusion and disorder. It is also a society which for the first time in human history possesses the capacity to destroy itself—globally as well as nation by nation.

In addition to the acceleration in the rate of technological and social change, and partly in response to it, society has acquired a greater capacity for social change. Virtually instantaneous world-wide social interaction is possible with modern means of communication;

and the mass media, bolstered by communication satellites and new educational hardware, create new opportunities for the modification and creation of attitudes and behaviorisms consistent with the realities of the contemporary world. But, although the capability for social change has undoubtedly increased, adequate and effective mechanisms for the control of social change, for accommodation [of] and adaptation to the changing social milieu, as well as to the changing material world, have yet to be evolved. Planning as a mechanism for rational decision-making is still in its infancy and has yet to develop an integrated approach with apposite administrative, economic and social planning, along with physical planning. Progress is being made in this respect, however. In this nation, for example, planning has become a respectable word now if modified by the term "city"; but when modified by such terms as "metropolitan," "regional," or "national," it is still considered a dangerous thought in some quarters. But planning, in ever broader contexts, will undoubtedly be a first step in the dissipation of confusion and the restoration of order.

That we live in a chaotic world should not be too surprising in view of the perspective provided by calendar considerations. Only twelve human generations have elapsed since the "modern era" began. Only seven human generations have elapsed since this nation was founded. Only six generations have elapsed since mankind acquired the means to permit the proliferation of cities of a million or more inhabitants. Only two generations have elapsed since the onset of significant internal migratory flows of Afro-Americans. Fewer than two generations have elapsed since the United States became an urban nation. Less than one generation has elapsed since the advent of the explosive power of the atom. Little more than a decade has elapsed since the Supreme Court decision outlawing *de jure* segregation in schools—and a clear-cut judicial decision on *de facto* segregation is yet to come.

Furthermore, only two human generations have elapsed since Durkheim and Weber and, to confine my attention to my own teachers and colleagues, less than one since Burgess, Ogburn, Redfield, and Wirth. The social sciences, in general, and sociology in particular, are still emergent sciences. It was only during the century roughly from about 1750 to 1850 that the physical sciences achieved the respectability and acceptance that paved the way, through engineering, for the transformation of the physical and material world. It was only during the century roughly from 1850 to 1950 that the bio-medical sciences achieved a similar status that paved the way, by means of bio-medical engineering, for the remarkable increase in longevity and health. It is to be hoped that the century from 1950 to 2050 will be the period during which the social sciences, including sociology, will achieve a level of respectability and acceptance that will pave the way for social engineering to eliminate the chaos that characterizes contemporary society. The question is whether mankind can muddle through without collective suicide before rational decision-making overtakes the confusion and disorder of our tottering transitional society.

It is to be emphasized that a modern Armageddon is not mankind's only alternative to continuing national or international chaos. For the social morphological revolution has also produced a material world, a social milieu, and an emancipated and reflective man who has the capacity to dissipate confusion and restore order. The social morphological revolution has initiated and nurtured the social sciences, including sociology; it has required the collection and funding of social knowledge in various forms, including social statistics; it has evolved a number of social engineering professions which are still proliferating, including planning; and it has opened up the new vistas of social accounting.

With the stress I have placed on the need for the restoration of order, I should make it clear that I recognize that disorder cannot, and should not, be entirely eliminated. For disorder betokens the need for change, often desirable, as well as necessary. Order as such is not by itself a discrete goal of high priority. Hitler, for example, achieved a high degree of order in his Third Reich; and Stalin, in his version of a communist society. The task is rather to welcome disorder, both in Durkheim's sense of helping to define the limits of order and as a symptom of needed change, but to control the levels of disorder, while effecting change, so that it does not threaten the viability of society.

In the United States, at the present time, "law and order" has become a political slogan with many overtones. But the disorder which afflicts American society by reason of the Negro Revolt and that of other minority groups, including the poor, points to the inadequacies of the slogan. The slogan is but a half-truth; and as Oliver Wendell Holmes once observed, "A half-truth is like a half-brick—it can be thrown a lot farther." The entire slogan, to meet the needs of our society, should be "law, justice, and order." For until justice is achieved by our minorities, we will not have order, unless we choose to make ourselves over into a repressive society.

I am aware that I have treaded perilously on the border between social science and social engineering. I may be accused of polluting the science of sociology with the stigmata of social policy and implied, if not explicit, proposals for social action. I am sensitive, as well as open, to such criticism because I firmly believe in maintaining a sharp boundary between science and engineering, as I have indicated above. . . .

In March, 1946, after the shock of the first atomic bomb and the first radar contact with the moon, I delivered a paper entitled, "Are the Social Sciences Ready?" It was a question raised by the then only prospect for the creation of the National Science Foundation, which might include provisions for the support of the social sciences as well as the natural sciences.

I stated at that time (Hauser, 1946):

Much has been said or written by social scientists, philosophers of science and others to explain the disparities in the roles of the natural and the social sciences in human affairs. Whatever the reasons may be, we might well at this juncture be impressed with two outstanding facts: first, that the social sciences have provided more knowledge and understanding about our social, political and economic life than society has actually used; second, that the social sciences have not produced enough.

My purpose in dealing with policy matters as social facts in this paper is now, as it was [then], not to persuade sociologists or other social scientists to enter the realm of policy formation and social action *qua* scientists. It is rather my twofold purpose to stress: . . . one, that sociology has accumulated more knowledge than is yet being utilized by society; and two, that there is a great and increasing need for more knowledge—and for more solid knowledge of the type outlined in my 1946 paper.

I conclude with a variation on my major theme. The chaotic society when understood as an anachronistic society can be transformed into a coeval or synchronous society. The first step in this direction lies, necessarily, in the comprehension of the nature and consequences of the social morphological revolution—which will be the product of research. More knowledge than we now possess is needed. But we have sufficient knowledge, even now, to state that the remediation of our chaotic society can be accomplished by bridging the gap between the social sciences, including sociology, and social policy and action.

REFERENCES

Annals of the American Academy of Political and Social Science.
  1967 *Social Goals and Indicators for American Society.* Volume I, May 1967 and Volume II, September 1967.
Bauer, Raymond M. (ed.)
  1967 *Social Indicators.* Cambridge: M.I.T. Press.
Braidwood, Robert J. and Gordon R. Willey (eds.)
  1962 *Courses Toward Urban Life.* Chicago: Aldine.
Breese, Gerald.
  1966 *Urbanization in Newly Developing Countries.* Englewood Cliffs: Prentice-Hall.
Bronfenbrenner, Urie.
  1968 *On the Making of New Men,* unpublished.

Childe, V. Gordon.
1941 *Man Makes Himself.* London: Watts.
1946 *What Happened in History.* London: Penguin Books.
David, Paul T., and Ralph Eisenberg.
1961 *Devaluation of the Urban and Suburban Vote,* Volume I. Charlotteville, Virginia: University of Virginia Press.
Davis, Kingsley.
1955 "The origin and growth of urbanization in the world." *American Journal of Sociology,* 60(March):433.
Durkheim, Emile.
1897–98 *L'annee Sociologique.* Volume II.
1933 *On the Division of Labor in Sociology.* New York: Macmillan.
1938 *The Rules of Sociological Method.* Glencoe: The Free Press.
Galbraith, John Kenneth.
1958 *The Affluent Society.* Boston: Houghton Mifflin.
Gras, N. S. B.
1922 *An Introduction to Economic History.* New York: Harper & Row.
Hauser, Philip M.
1946 "Are the social sciences ready?" *American Sociological Review,* 11(August):379–384.
1949 "Social science and social engineering." *Philosophy of Science,* 16(July).
1961 *On the Impact of Population and Community Changes on Local Government.* (Seventh Annual Wherrett Lecture on Local Government) Pittsburgh: Institute of Local Government, University of Pittsburgh.
1963 "Statistics and Society." *Journal of the American Statistical Association,* 58(March):1–12.
1965 and Leo F. Schnore (eds). *The Study of Urbanization.* New York: Wiley, Chapter 1.
1966 "Demographic factors in the integration of the Negro." Pp. 71–101 in Talcott Parsons and Kenneth B. Clark (eds.), *The Negro American.* Boston: Houghton Mifflin.
1967a "Environmental forces shaping our cities." Pp. 31–45 in The National Conference on Social Welfare (ed.), *The Social Welfare Forum.* New York: Columbia University Press.
1967b "Social accounting." Pp. 839–876 in Paul F. Lazarsfeld, William H. Sewell and Harold L. Wilensky (eds.), *The Uses of Sociology.* New York: Basic Books.
1967c "Lao-Tze, Confucius and the conservative-liberal debate." *Proceedings of the American Philosophical Society,* 3(October): 259–267.
1968a "After the riots, what?" *The University of Chicago Magazine,* 60(May):4–10.
1968b "Twentieth century national goals in the development of human resources." Pp. 38–51 in *Federal Programs for the Development*

of Human Resources (90th Congress, 2nd Session, Joint Committee Print, Subcommittee on Economic Progress, Joint Economic Committee, Congress of the United States). Washington, D.C.: U.S. Government Printing Office.

Hodge, Patricia Leavey, and Philip M. Hauser.
1968 The Challenge of America's Metropolitan Population Outlook—1960 to 1985, Chapter I (Research Report Number 3). Washington, D.C.: The National Commission on Urban Problems.

Mannheim, Karl.
1940 Man and Society in an Age of Reconstruction: Studies in Modern Social Structure (trans. Edward Shils). London: K. Paul, Trench, Trubner, Ltd.

Mumford, Lewis.
1961 The City in History. New York: Harcourt, Brace & World.

National Advisory Commission on Civil Disorders.
1968 Report of the National Advisory Commission on Civil Disorders. Washington, D.C.: U.S. Government Printing Office.

The New York Times.
1968 July 30:20–21.

Ogburn, William F.
1922 Social Change. New York: The Viking Press, Inc.

Redfield, Robert.
1955 The Little Community: Viewpoints for the Study of a Human Whole. Chicago: University of Chicago Press.

Subcommittee on Government Research of the Committee on Government Operations.
1968 "Full Opportunity and Social Accounting Act," (S843). Introduced by Senator Walter F. Mondale and ten other Senators. See Hearings Before the Subcommittee on Government Research of the Committee on Government Operations, First Session on S843, Parts I, II, III, Washington, D.C.: U.S. Government Printing Office.

Tawney, Richard Henry.
1920 The Acquisitive Society. New York: Harcourt, Brace & Howe.

Turner, Ralph.
1941 The Great Cultural Traditions, Volume I, The Ancient Cities. New York: McGraw-Hill.

United Nations.
1953 The Determinants and Consequences of Population Trends. New York: United Nations.
1966 World Population Prospects. New York: United Nations.

U.S. Bureau of the Census.
1960 Historical Statistics of the United States, Colonial Times to 1967, Washington, D.C.: U.S. Government Printing Office.
1962 Historical Statistics of the United States, Colonial Times to 1957: Continuation to 1962 and Revisions, Washington, D.C.: U.S. Government Printing Office.

1967 *Statistical Abstract of the United States, 1967,* Washington, D.C.: U.S. Government Printing Office (annual).

Wallas, Graham.

1916 *The Great Society: A Psychological Analysis.* New York: Macmillan (latest edition in 1967 by the University of Nebraska Press, Lincoln, Nebraska).

Wellemeyer, Fletcher, and Frank Lorimer.

1962 "How many people have ever lived on earth." *Population Bulletin,* 18(February).

Wirth, Louis.

1956 *Community Life and Social Policy.* Chicago: University of Chicago Press.

CHAPTER 2

CONSCIOUSNESS III:
THE NEW GENERATION

CHARLES A. REICH

The word "consciousness" generally implies a *state of awareness*. This awareness can be either of what is happening to oneself—to the emotions or to the body—or what may be happening outside the self—in the physical or social world in which a person lives. As such, this consciousness is more than a set of attitudes or values, more than information or opinions. It is the way people are able to "make sense" of their world; it is their entire perception of reality, what some writers have called *Weltanschauung* or world view. We might say, then, that each period in history, and people in different places, can be characterized by a unique consciousness. Charles Reich's book *The Greening of America* is about consciousness.

Reich believes that in its 200-year history the United States has witnessed three separate "consciousnesses" among its people. The first, Consciousness I, was that of the pioneer, farmer, small businessman, or anyone else striving to "carve out" a place for himself. Consciousness II represents the values and styles of life in the "Corporate State." It sees a structured, well-ordered world of large organizations—both public and private—that the individual is supposed to function in and uphold. Consciousness III represents a drastic departure from either of the other two; it is the consciousness of the new generation.

Every form of consciousness is both a reaction to what has happened in the past and an adaptation to the present reality. In the case of Consciousness I, the American pioneers were liberated from the constraints imposed by the status system and village life in the Old World. They had come to the new land in search of freedom and opportunity. When they had arrived they had discovered that the individual could actually have an impact. With strength, intelligence, and endurance a man could make his way in the world; there was a frontier to be tamed, and this could only be accomplished by strong, fiercely independent, resourceful men. Nature—that is, the environment—was seen as an enemy: something that had to be beaten and brought to heel under the strong hand of man. The Consciousness I man worked for himself and not for society. He was willing to cut himself off from the larger community of man in this way. Human nature was seen as fundamentally evil, and a constant struggle against one's fellow men as well as the environment was believed to be the most natural condition.

While industrialization progressed in the nation, the mighty industrialists of the late nineteenth and early twentieth centuries were embodiments of Consciousness I. Building an industrial empire was, after all, little different from taming a savage frontier. And today, there are still many who believe fully in the American Dream, believing that the only limits upon their achievement come from within themselves.

Consciousness II was created by and for the Corporate State. The "rugged individualists" who characterized the period of Consciousness I were replaced by the organization men and functionaries of Consciousness II. The world is seen in organizational terms: The individual must make his way through a world directed by unseen others. Consciousness II supports a mediocracy where individuals are judged on the basis of tests, credentials, or achievements. One is told, early in life, to find what he is best suited for so that he may begin achieving.

It is a world that believes in gradual change through reform—not revolution. It is the well-ordered, smoothly functioning world of big business and big government. The state is a corporate entity containing *both* government and business; so much so that often the boundaries separating them are indistinct. The people of Consciousness II are willing to accept a compartmentalized, alienated existence. For many, work is, at best, something to be endured. It is not something from which any satisfaction or enjoyment can be derived. The individual reconciles himself to a series of separate lives. In each he has an accepted role to play; at work he may be the public relations officer for an industrial concern that is polluting the environment; at home he claims to be concerned and interested in the problems of ecology, thinking himself an "outdoorsman" because he takes his annual three-week vacation in a mobile home. Most tragic of all, perhaps, is the fact that he sees such a schizophrenic existence as perfectly natural. These are the functionaries who ask no longer if what they are doing is right or wrong, good or evil, but if it is the most economic, expedient, and efficient way to get the job done.

Critics have charged that the corporate world of Consciousness II is an artificial and plastic one. The values and goals of the people are essentially identical to those of the organization for which they work. People do things not because they really enjoy doing them but because they are *supposed* to enjoy doing them. Pastimes, places, and even people are interchangeable to the Consciousness II person and his family.

The roots of Consciousness III are set deeply in post–World War II America. The "baby boom" immediately following the war ensured that in approximately two decades youth, almost by dint of number alone, would exert a considerable force on the structure and character of the country. As these young people matured they found the promise of the American Dream elusive, at best. They had all that America could offer in the way of material wealth, yet their lives were somehow empty; they felt spiritually unfulfilled. This was the first generation of Americans that really had come to grips with the problems posed by the technological revolution. On the positive side, possibilities never even considered before were now readily available, and on the negative was the omnipresent threat of universal destruction through nuclear holocaust.

This new generation, however, was set apart from those preceding it by one other very significant factor: It preserved a sense of identity, a feeling of "we-ness." It hoped to discover what its parents seemed to have lost—a meaning to life, excitement in existence, uncomplicated acceptance of one's fellows, and a sense of community.

"Consciousness III: The New Generation" is about this search and some of the things that have been discovered. Where the process will lead, whether those now actively searching for new meanings and life-styles will be co-opted and "sell out" to the system, and whether some even more radical form of change will occur can only be guessed at now. *The Greening of America* suggests a number of fascinating possibilities.

Charles A. Reich teaches law at Yale University Law School. His writings have been published widely in scholarly and popular journals, and his lectures are among the most widely attended on the Yale campus.

Beginning with a few individuals in the mid-nineteen-sixties, and gathering numbers ever more rapidly thereafter, Consciousness III has sprouted up, astonishingly and miraculously, out of the stony soil of the American Corporate State. So spontaneous was its appearance that no one, not the most astute or the most radical, foresaw what was coming

"Consciousness III: The New Generation," by Charles A. Reich, pp. 233–85 in *The Greening of America*, 1970, is reprinted by permission of the publisher, Random House, Inc.

or recognized it when it began. It is not surprising that many people think it a conspiracy, for it was spread, here and abroad, by means invisible. Hardly anybody of the older generation, even the FBI or the sociologists, knows much about it, for its language and thought are so different from Consciousness II as to make it virtually an undecipherable secret code. Consciousness III is, as of this writing, the greatest secret in America although its members have shouted as loudly as they could to be heard.

We must pause over the origins of Consciousness III, lest it seem too improbable and too transitory to be deemed as fundamental as Consciousness I and Consciousness II. One element in its origin [is] the impoverishment of life, the irrationality, violence, and claustrophobia of the American Corporate State. But how did this corporate machine, seemingly designed to keep its inhabitants perpetually on a treadmill, suddenly begin producing something altogether new and unintended? The new consciousness is the product of two interacting forces: the promise of life that is made to young Americans by all of our affluence, technology, liberation, and ideals, and the threat to that promise posed by everything from neon ugliness and boring jobs to the Vietnam War and the shadow of nuclear holocaust. Neither the promise nor the threat is the cause by itself; but the two together have done it.

The promise comes first. We have all heard the promise: affluence, security, technology make possible a new life, a new permissiveness, a new freedom, a new expansion of human possibility. We have all heard it, but to persons born after World War II it means something very different. Older people learned how to live in a different world; it is really beyond them to imagine themselves living according to the new promises. The most basic limitations of life—the job, the working day, the part one can play in life, the limits of sex, love and relationships, the limits of knowledge and experience—all vanish, leaving open a life that can be lived without the guideposts of the past. In the world that now exists, a life of surfing *is* possible, not as an escape from work, a recreation or a phase, but as a *life*—if one chooses. The fact that this choice is actually available is the truth that the younger generation knows and the older generation cannot know.

The promise is made real to members of the younger generation by a sense of acceptance about themselves. To older generations, particularly Consciousness II people, great issues were presented by striving to reach some external standard of personal attractiveness, popularity, ability at sports, acceptance by the group. Many lives, including some outstanding careers, were lived under the shadow of such personal issues; even late in life, people are still profoundly influenced by them. Of course the new generation is not free of such concerns. But to an astonishing degree, whether it is due to new parental attitudes, a less tense, less inhibited childhood, or a different experience during school years, these are not the issues which plague the younger generation. If the hero of *Portnoy's Complaint* is the final and most complete example of the man dissatisfied with the self that he is, the new generation says, "Whatever I am, I am." He may have hang-ups of all sorts, insecurities, inadequacies, but he does not reject himself on that account. There may be as many difficulties about work, ability, relationships, and sex as in any other generation, but there is less guilt, less anxiety, less self-hatred. Consciousness III says, "I'm glad I'm me."

The new generation has also learned lessons from technology, by being born with it, that the older generation does not know, even though it invented technology. It is one thing to know intellectually that there is a Xerox machine that can copy anything, a pill that can make sexual intercourse safe, or a light motorcycle that can take two people off camping with ten minutes' preparation, but it is quite another thing to live with these facts, make use of them, and thus learn to live *by* them.

These experiences and promises are shared to some extent by the youth of every industrial nation, and the new consciousness is, as we know, not limited to the United States. But Consciousness III, the specifically American form, is not based on promise alone. A key word in understanding its origin is *betrayal*.

Older people are inclined to think of work, injustice and war, and of the bitter frustrations of life, as the human condition. Their capacity for outrage is consequently duller. But to those who have glimpsed the real possibilities of life, who have tasted liberation and love, who have seen the promised land, the prospect of a dreary corporate job, a ranch-house life, or a miserable death in war is utterly intolerable. Moreover, the human condition, if that is what it is, has been getting steadily worse in the Corporate State; more and more life-denying just as life should be opening up. And hovering over everything is the threat of annihilation, more real and more terrifying to the young than to anyone else. To them, the discrepancy between what could be and what is, is overwhelming; perhaps it is the greatest single fact of their existence. The promise of America, land of beauty and abundance, land of the free, somehow has been betrayed.

They feel the betrayal in excruciatingly personal terms. Between them and the rich possibilities of life there intervenes a piercing insecurity—not the personal insecurity their parents knew, but a cosmic insecurity. Will the nation be torn apart by riots or war? Will their lives be cut short by death or injury in Vietnam? Will the impersonal machinery of the state—schools, careers, institutions—overwhelm them? Above all, will they escape an atomic holocaust (they were, as many people have pointed out, the generation of the bomb)? Insecurity sharpens their consciousness and draws them together.

Parents have unintentionally contributed to their children's condemnation of existing society. Not by their words, but by their actions, attitudes, and manner of living, they have conveyed to their children the message "Don't live the way we have, don't settle for the emptiness of our lives, don't be lured by the things we valued, don't neglect life and love as we have." With the unerring perceptiveness of the child, their children have read these messages from the lifeless lives of their "successful" parents, have seen marriages break up because there was nothing to hold them, have felt cynicism, alienation, and despair in the best-kept homes of America. And will have none of it.

Kenneth Keniston, in *Young Radicals,* found that one of the most telling forces in producing the political ideals of the new generation is the contrast between their parents' ideals (which they accept) and their parents' failure to live these same ideals. Keniston found that young radicals show a *continuity* of ideals from childhood on; they simply stayed with them while their parents failed to.

We might add to this that our society, with its dogmatic insistence on one way of seeing everything, its dominating false consciousness, and its ever-widening gap between fact and rhetoric, invites a sudden moment when the credibility gap becomes too much, and invites cataclysmic consequences to the consciousness of a young person when that occurs. For so vehemently does the society insist that its "truth" be accepted wholly and undeviatingly down the line, and so drastic are the discrepancies once seen, that a single breach in the dike may bring a young person's entire conversion. All that is needed is to participate in one peace demonstration and find *The New York Times* report of it inexcusably false, and the whole edifice of "truth" collapses. Such "conversions" are constantly seen on campuses today; a freshman arrives, his political views are hometown-Consciousness I, and suddenly he is radicalized. The fabric of manufactured "truth," spread taut and thin, breaches, and one breach leaves it irrevocably in tatters.

If a history of Consciousness III were to be written, it would show a fascinating progression. The earliest sources were among those exceptional individuals who are found at any time in any society: the artistic, the highly sensitive, the tormented. Thoreau, James Joyce, and Wallace Stevens all speak directly to Consciousness III. Salinger's Holden Caulfield was a fictional version of the first young precursors of Consciousness III. Perhaps there was always a bit of Consciousness III in every teen-ager, but normally it quickly vanished. Holden sees through the established world: they are "phonies" and he is merciless in his honesty. But what was someone like Holden to do? A subculture of "beats" grew up, and a "beatnik" world flourished briefly, but for most people it represented only another dead end. Other Holdens might reject the legal profession and try teaching literature or writing instead, letting their hair grow a bit longer as well. But they remained separated individuals, usually ones from affluent but unhappy, tortured family backgrounds, and their differences with society were paid for by isolation.

Unquestionably the blacks made a substantial contribution to the origins of the new consciousness. They were left out of the Corporate State, and thus they had to have a culture and life-style in opposition to the State. Their music, with its "guts," contrasted with the insipid white music. Their way of life seemed more earthy, more sensual than that of whites. They were the first openly to scorn the Establishment and its values; as Eldridge Cleaver shows in *Soul on Ice,* and Malcolm X shows in his autobiography, they were radicalized by the realities of their situation. When their music began to be heard by white teen-agers through the medium of rock 'n' roll, and when their view of America became visible through the civil rights movement, it gave new impetus to the subterranean awareness of the beat generation and the Holden Caulfields.

The great change took place when Consciousness III began to appear among young people who had endured no special emotional conditions, but were simply bright, sensitive children of the affluent middle class. It is hard to be precise about the time when this happened. One chronology is based on the college class of 1969, which entered as freshmen in the fall of 1965. Another important date is the summer of 1967, when the full force of the cultural revolution was first visible. But even in the fall of 1967 the numbers involved were still very small. The new group drew heavily from those who had been exposed to the very best of liberal arts education—poetry, art, theatre, literature, philosophy, good conversation. Later, the group began to include "ordinary" middle-class students. In time there were college athletes as well as college intellectuals, and lovers of motorcycles and skiing as well as lovers of art and literature. But the core group was always white, well educated, and middle class.

Among today's youth, the phenomenon of "conversions" is increasingly common. It is surprising that so little has been written about these conversions, for they are a striking aspect of contemporary life. What happens is simply this: in a brief span of months, a student, seemingly conventional in every way, changes his haircut, his clothes, his habits, his interests, his political attitudes, his way of relating to other people, in short, his whole way of life. He has "converted" to a new consciousness. The contrast between well-groomed freshmen pictures and the same individuals in person a year later tells the tale. The clean-cut, hardworking, model young man who despises radicals and hippies can become one himself with breathtaking suddenness. Over and over again, an individual for whom a conversion seemed impossible—a star athlete, an honor student, the small-town high school boy with the American Legion scholarship—transforms himself into a drug-using, long-haired, peace-loving "freak." Only when he puts on a headband and plays unexpectedly skillful touch football or basketball, or when a visitor to his old room back home catches sight of his honor society certificate, is his earlier life revealed.

As the new consciousness made youth more distinct, the younger generation began discovering itself as a generation. Always before, young people felt themselves tied more to their families, to their schools, and to their immediate situations than to "a generation." But now an entire culture, including music, clothes, and drugs, began to distinguish youth. As it did, the message of consciousness went with it. And the more the older generation rejected the culture, the more a fraternity of the young grew up, so that they recognized each other as brothers and sisters from coast to coast. That is its history up to this writing; let us now try to describe the content of Consciousness III.

A few warnings are needed. First, in attempting to describe Consciousness III systematically and analytically, we are engaging in an intellectual process which Consciousness III rejects; they have a deep skepticism of both "linear" and analytic thought. Second, we shall be talking about an idealized consciousness, and not about something that is to be seen in all aspects in any one person. The members of the new generation have their doubts, hang-ups and failings too, and Consciousness III may coexist with earlier patterns and values. Third, Consciousness III itself is just in an early stage of development, and probably the elements of it would have to be described differently in one or two years.

The foundation of Consciousness III is liberation. It comes into being the moment the individual frees himself from automatic acceptance of the imperatives of society and the false consciousness which society imposes. For example, the individual no longer accepts unthinkingly the personal goals proposed by society; a change of personal goals is one of the first and most basic elements of Consciousness III. The meaning of liberation is that the individual is free to build his own philosophy and values, his own life-style, and his own culture from a new beginning.

Consciousness III starts with self. In contrast to Consciousness II, which accepts society, the public interest, and institutions as the primary reality, III declares that the individual self is the only true reality. Thus it returns to the earlier America: "Myself I Sing." The first commandment is: thou shalt not do violence to thyself. It is a crime to allow oneself to become an instrumental being, a projectile designed to accomplish some extrinsic end, a part of an organization or a machine.

It is a crime to be alienated from oneself, to be a divided or schizo-phrenic being, to defer meaning to the future. One must live completely at each moment, not with the frenzied "nowness" of advertising, but with the utter *wholeness* that Heidegger expresses. The commandment is: be true to oneself.

To start from self does not mean to be selfish. It means to start from premises based on human life and the rest of nature, rather than prem-ises that are the artificial products of the Corporate State, such as power or status. It is not an "ego trip" but a radical subjectivity de-signed to find genuine values in a world whose official values are false and distorted. It is not egocentricity, but honesty, wholeness, genuine-ness in all things. It starts from self because human life is found as individual units, not as corporations and institutions; its intent is to start from life.

Consciousness III postulates the absolute worth of every human being —every self. Consciousness III does not believe in the antagonistic or competitive doctrine of life. Competition, within the limits of a sport like tennis or swimming, is accepted for its own pleasure, although even as athletes III's are far less competitive (and sometimes, but not always, poorer athletes as a result). But III's do not compete "in real life." They do not measure others, they do not see others as something to struggle against. People are brothers, the world is ample for all. In consequence, one never hears the disparagements, the snickers, the judgments that are so common among I's and II's. A boy who was odd in some way used to suffer derision all through his school days. Today there would be no persecution; one might even hear one boy speak, with affection, of "my freaky friend." Instead of insisting that everyone be measured by given standards, the new generation values what is unique and different in each self; there is no pressure that any-one be an athlete unless he wants to; a harpsichord player is accepted on equal terms. No one judges anyone else. This is a second com-mandment.

Consciousness III rejects the whole concept of excellence and com-parative merit that is so central to Consciousness II. III refuses to evaluate people by general standards, it refuses to classify people, or analyze them. Each person has his own individuality, not to be com-pared to that of anyone else. Someone may be a brilliant thinker, but he is not "better" at thinking than anyone else, he simply possesses his own excellence. A person who thinks very poorly is still excellent in his own way. Therefore people are in no hurry to find out another person's background, schools, achievements, as a means of knowing him; they regard all of that as secondary, preferring to know him un-adorned. Because there are no governing standards, no one is rejected. Everyone is entitled to pride in himself, and no one should act in a way that is servile, or feel inferior, or allow himself to be treated as if he were inferior.

It is upon these premises that the Consciousness III idea of community and of personal relationships rests. In place of the world seen as a jungle, with every man for himself (Consciousness I) or the world seen as a meritocracy leading to a great corporate hierarchy of rigidly drawn relations and manoeuvers for position (Consciousness II), the world is a community. People all belong to the same family, whether they have met each other or not. It is as simple as that. There are no "tough guys" among the youth of Consciousness III. Hitchhikers smile at approaching cars, people smile at each other on the street, the human race rediscovers its need for each other. "I felt lonesome, so I came looking for some people," a III will say. Something in the makeup and pride of a I or II will keep him from "confessing" that "weakness" in quite such an open way. But III does not want to stand head and shoulders above the crowd. III values, more than a judgeship or executive title, the warmth of the "circle of affection" in which men join hands. In personal relations, the keynote is honesty, and the absence of socially imposed duty. To be dishonest in love, to "use" another person, is a major crime. A third commandment is: be wholly honest with others, use no other person as a means. It is equally wrong to alter oneself for someone else's sake; by being one's true self one offers others the most; one offers them something honest, genuine, and, more important, something for them to respond to, to be evoked by. A work of art is not valued because it changes itself for each person who views it, it retains its own integrity and thus means something unique and marvelous to those who see it. Being true to oneself is, so Consciousness III says, the best and only way to relate to others. Consciousness III rejects most of what happens between people in our world: manipulation of others, forcing anyone to do anything against his wish, using others for one's own purposes, irony and sarcasm, defensive standoffishness. III also rejects relationships of authority and subservience. It will neither give commands nor follow them; coercive relations between people are wholly unacceptable. And III also rejects any relationships based wholly on role, relationships limited along strictly impersonal and functional lines. There is no situation in which one is entitled to act impersonally, in a stereotyped fashion, with another human being; the relationship of businessman to clerk, passenger to conductor, student to janitor must not be impersonal.

But to observe duties toward others, after the feelings are gone, is no virtue and may even be a crime. Loyalty is valued but not artificial duty. Thus the new generation looks with suspicion on "obligations" and contractual relations between people, but it believes that honesty can produce far more genuine relationships than the sterile ones it observes among the older generation. To most people, there is something frightening about the notion that no oath, no law, no promise, no indebtedness holds people together when the feeling is gone. But for the new generation that is merely recognition of the truth about human beings. Moreover, getting rid of what is artificial is essential to make way for what is real, and Consciousness III considers genuine relationships with others, friendship, companionship, love, the human community, to be among the highest values of life.

The premise of self and of values based on human life leads directly to a radical critique of society. Many people are puzzled by the radicalism of Consciousness III—have they been infiltrated by communists, are they influenced by a "few left-wing agitators," have they been reading Marx? It does indeed seem astonishing that naïve young people, without political experience, should come up with a critique of society that seems to have escaped the most scholarly as well as the most astute and experienced of their elders. But there is no mystery, no conspiracy, and very little reading of Marx. Older people begin by assuming that much of the structure of the Corporate State is necessary and valid; starting there they never get very far. The young people start with entirely different premises, and all is revealed to them.

What Consciousness III sees, with an astounding clarity that no ideology could provide, is a society that is unjust to its poor and its minorities, is run for the benefit of a privileged few, is lacking in its proclaimed democracy and liberty, is ugly and artificial, . . . destroys environment and self, and is, like the wars it spawns, "unhealthy for children and other living things." It sees a society that is deeply untruthful and hypocritical; one of the gifts of the young is to see through phoniness and cant, and Consciousness III sees through the Establishment verities of our society with corrosive ease.

Consciousness III sees not merely a set of political and public wrongs, such as a liberal New Dealer might have seen, but also the deeper ills that Kafka or the German expressionists or Dickens would have seen: old people shunted into institutional homes, streets made hideous with neon and commercialism, servile conformity, the competitiveness and sterility of suburban living, the loneliness and anomie of cities, the ruin of nature by bulldozers and pollution, the stupid mindlessness of most high school education, the coarse materialism of most values, the lovelessness of many marriages, and, above all, the plastic, artificial quality of everything; plastic lives in plastic homes.

All of Consciousness III's criticisms of society were brought into sharpest focus by the Vietnam War. For the war seemed to sum up the evils of our society: destruction of people, destruction of environment, depersonalized use of technology, war by the rich and powerful against the poor and helpless, justification based on abstract rationality, hypocrisy and lies, and a demand that the individual, regardless of his conscience, values, or self, make himself into a part of the war machine, an impersonal projectile bringing death to other people. Those who said they could not go believed that compulsory service in a war they hated would be so total a destruction of their genuine values that even if they did return to the United States, they could never return to the ranks of the genuinely living.

The initial premise of self leads not only to a critique of society, it also leads, in many representatives of Consciousness III, to a deep personal commitment to the welfare of the community. This may sound contradictory to those who wrongly equate the premise of self with selfishness, and it may seem to contradict the premise that the individual, not society, is the reality. But there is no contradiction. It is quite true that the individual does not accept the goals or standards set by society. But of course he recognizes that society has a vast influence on the welfare of people everywhere, including his own desire to be an independent being. Mostly he sees this influence as bad, but he also sees how much better things could be. And therefore, for the sake of the welfare of individuals, he is committed to the improvement of society. It is the manner of commitment that differs from II.

There is one essential qualification to what we have said: dedication to the community is not to include means that do violence to the self. A Consciousness III person will not study law to help society, if law is not what he wants to do with his life, nor will he do harm to others in order to promote some good, nor will he deny himself the experiences of life for any cause. The political radical of Consciousness III is thus very different from the radical of the Old Left, the communist, socialist, or civil libertarian ready to dedicate himself and his life to the cause, puritanical, sour, righteous. To the new consciousness, to make himself an object to serve the cause would be to subvert the cause.

Subject to this qualification, the key to the Consciousness III commitment lies in the concept of full personal responsibility. In the case of Consciousness II, commitment to society means commitment to reform in the general direction already established by society (equality, better education), the notion of "reform" merely meaning that the "liberal" is somewhat ahead of where society is at. And the commitment has limits; the liberal enjoys his high status, his elegant house, his security, and comfort, and fights his battle from that position. Consciousness III feels that, if he is to be true to himself, he must respond *with* himself. He may take a job, such as teaching in a ghetto school, which offers neither prestige nor comfort, but offers the satisfaction of personal contact with ghetto children. He must live on a modest scale to retain the freedom that his commitment demands. He must take risks. And at the same time, he must be wholly himself in what he does.

He knows that he is an agent of change, whether he plays music or works in a ghetto, so long as he affirms himself in his work, and so long as his work expresses the full responsibility of his feelings.

It is this notion of personal responsibility which makes the new generation, when it finds itself excluded from the decision-making process, demand a part in that process. For the liberal, it is sufficient to say, "I oppose air pollution, but in my job I have nothing to do with it, no responsibility in that direction, all I can do is try to influence those who do." That, to Consciousness III, is not being responsible; if one is not part of the decision-making process, responsibility requires that one gain such power.

It is this same personal responsibility that makes the young student feel himself to be an adult, not a person getting ready for life. By attempting to be fully alive *now,* young people grow more serious, more thoughtful, more concerned with what is happening in the world. Many adults of the older generation have smooth baby faces, the faces of men interested only in the Sunday ball game, the nearest skirt, or the bowling league, as if they were permanent juveniles, as if they never, not once in their lives, faced their world and took its concerns on themselves, or accepted the responsibilities of full consciousness. The faces of Consciousness III seem to have lived more, even in their short years. A look at a college classbook of today, compared with one of fifteen years ago, tells the difference. That is one reason why the people of Consciousness III have a sense of each other as a generation with something in common.

During the Columbia confrontation, a group of Columbia varsity athletes were invited to an alumni meeting to receive awards, then disinvited when they asked to make statements on the campus situation. The alumni didn't want to think of athletes having political views. The athletes, fencers who had won a national championship and basketball players who had won the Ivy League championship, then picketed the alumni meeting in a driving rain in their varsity C blazers, until the alumni finally let them in and let them speak (*The New York Times,* May 25, 1968). It wasn't the athletes' "job" to picket in the rain; they could have signed a letter if they wanted to express themselves.

At the Heptagonal Track Meet held at Yale in May of 1970, the athletes of eight of the participating schools insisted that, before the meet could begin, a statement of their views on public issues be read over the loudspeakers by a spokesman who was a member of one of the teams. The statement, expressing profound concern over the invasion of Cambodia, the persecution of Black Panthers, and other issues, also took the position, in explicit language, that athletics should not serve as an escape from public responsibility for the athletes themselves or for the fans; as an additional reminder, many of the athletes wore red or black ribbons on their sleeves or shorts during competition. No doubt many alumni and others in the stands were less than pleased with this intrusion of reality onto Yale's playing fields. When members of the Annapolis and West Point teams expressed dissatisfaction with the statement, they were offered an opportunity to express their own views; instead, they left without competing. But coaches, officials, and fans were forced to realize that the athletes who did compete were not the smooth-faced, ever-juvenile jocks of American expectations. They were serious adults. And they thought it essential, if they were to be *whole* as selves, to make a *personal* response, and thereby, as Sartre's Orestes did in *The Flies,* assume responsibility that "was not theirs," and thus achieve a full existence.

Because it accepts no imposed system, the basic stance of Consciousness III is one of openness to any and all experience. It is always in a state of becoming. It is just the opposite of Consciousness II, which tries to force all new experience into a pre-existing system, and to assimilate all new knowledge to principles already established. Although we can attempt to describe the specific content of Consciousness III at a given moment, its lasting essence is constant change, and constant growth of each individual.

These are the premises of Consciousness III and some of its resulting relationships with existing society. This is how it defines itself against the prevailing truths and values. But to see the affirmative scope of Consciousness III we must survey the life-style and culture it is in the process of creating. The culture is so expansive and varied that we must be selective; we shall deal with several major elements in some detail: clothes, career, music, community and consciousness. There are other elements, and it is all in a process of rapid change and development, but these will suggest the nature of what is being sought.

One quality unites all aspects of the Consciousness III way of life: energy. It is the energy of enthusiasm, of happiness, of hope. Some people assume that what they are seeing is merely the energy of youth, but it is greater than this; other generations never had such energy even in their youth. Consciousness III draws energy from new sources: from the group, the community, from eros, from the freedom of technology, from the uninhibited self.

A good place to begin is clothes, for the dress of the new generation expresses a number of the major themes of Consciousness III in a very vivid and immediate way. The first impression the clothes give is of uniformity and conformity—as if everyone felt obliged to adopt the same style. We shall try to show that this is an erroneous impression —that there is agreement on certain principles, but great individuality within those principles. Another first impression is of drabness—browns, greens, blue jeans. This is an accurate observation and for a reason.

They are a deliberate rejection of the neon colors and plastic, artificial look of the affluent society. They are inexpensive to buy, inexpensive to maintain. They suggest that neither individuality nor distinction can be bought in a clothing store; clothes are primarily functional. The clothes are earthy and sensual. They express an affinity with nature; the browns, greens, and blues are nature's colors, earth's colors, not the colors of the machine, and the materials are rough and tactile. The clothes are like architecture that does not clash with its natural sur-roundings but blends in. And the clothes have a functional affinity with nature too; they don't show dirt, they are good for lying on the ground.

These clothes express freedom. Expensive clothes enforce social con-straints; a grease spot on an expensive suit is a social error, so is a rip in a tailored ladies' coat, or a missing button. A man in an expen-sive suit must be careful of every move he makes, where he sits, what he leans against. A well-dressed woman is hardly able to walk or move. The new clothes give the wearer freedom to do anything he wants. He can work in them, read in them, roll down a hill in them, ride a bike in them, play touch football, dance, sit on the floor, go on a camping trip, sleep in them. Above all, they are comfortable.

The freedom of new clothes expresses a second principle as well: a wholeness of self, as against the schizophrenia of Consciousness II. There is not one set of clothes for the office; another for social life, a third for play. The same clothes can be used for every imaginable activity, and so they say: it is the same person doing each of these things, not a set of different masks or dolls, but one many-sided, *whole* individual. We do not have another, secret life outside the office; as we are here, we are always. At the same time, these clothes say: a single individual may do many different things in the course of a day, he is not limited to a single role or a role-plus-recreation; each individual is truly protean, with unlimited possibilities including the possibility of whatever new and spontaneous thing may come along. Consciousness III is extremely reluctant to go to a restaurant or hotel where it is necessary to "dress up"—this would require a loss of wholeness and self; a dishonest constraint.

One reason the clothes are not "uniform," as people think, is that they are extremely expressive of the human body, and each body is different and unique. Men's suits really *are* uniform; they look the same on a man as they do on the rack in the clothing store; they hide the fact that one man may be muscular, another flabby, one soft, one bony, one hairy, another smooth. The pants give no hint of a man's legs, and when they wrinkle along body lines, they are quickly taken to the dry cleaners to be pressed back into straight lines. Jeans express the shape of legs, heavy or thin, straight or bowed. As jeans get more wrinkled, they adapt even more to the particular legs that are wearing them. Sitting across from a man in a business suit, it is as if he did not have a body at all, just a face and a voice. Jeans make one conscious of the body, not as something separate from the face but as part of the whole individual; Consciousness III believes that a person's body is one of the essential parts of his self, not something to be ignored while one carries on a conversation with his face and mind. Also the new clothes make the wearer conscious of his own body; a man's suit is at odds with his body all day long. The new clothes are a declaration of sensuality, not sensuality-for-display as in Madison Avenue style, but sensuality as a part of the natural in man. There is no masculinity or femininity hang-up. A boy does not feel he has to dress in a certain way or "he will not be a man"; he is not that anxious or concerned about his own masculinity.

If the individual wishes, he can add touches to his clothes that make them a costume, expressing whatever he feels at the moment. With the magic deftness of stage sorcery, a headband can produce an Indian, a black hat a cowboy badman. When a high fashion woman wears a costume, say a "matador" suit, it seems to have been imposed on her, mask-like, by her designer. She is an object that has been decorated. But the costumes of the young are not masks, they are expressions of an inner, perhaps momentary state of mind. The individual is free to be inventive, playful, humorous. A boy can wear a military dress jacket, all buttons and brass, and both mock the military establishment and at the same time express his small-boy's love of uniforms and parade-ground pomp. Likewise with a Mexican peasant's blanket-shawl, or a David Copperfield hat, boots of all descriptions, gangster suits, phantom-of-the-opera cloaks. These costumes do not hide the real person as role-dress does, they show a state of mind and thus reveal him to us, and they add to the gaiety and humor of the world. Costumes raise existential questions for the person wearing them. For they confront a person, whenever he dresses, with questions that are never posed in our society —questions of identity and self. They allow experimentation and changes of mood that are characteristic of, and essential to, youth. But they nudge the wearer with deep questions, because their very freedom reminds him that he does have choice.

Bell bottoms have to be worn to be understood. They express the body, as jeans do, but they say much more. They give the ankles a special freedom as if to invite dancing right on the street. They bring dance back into our sober lives. A touch football game, if the players are wearing bell bottoms, is like a folk dance or a ballet. Bell bottoms, on girls or boys, are happy and comic, rollicking. No one can take himself entirely seriously in bell bottoms. Imagine a Consciousness II university professor, or even a college athlete, in bell bottoms, and all of his pretensions become funny; he has to laugh at himself.

The new clothes demonstrate a significant new relationship between man and technology. Basically they are machine-made and there is no attempt to hide that fact, no shame attached to mass-produced goods, no social points lost for wearing something that sells at $4.99 from coast to coast and has its measurements printed on the outside for all to read. That is the freedom and economy of mass production, a thing to be valued, not despised or evaded, as seekers after "quality" do. Touches of the handmade, of the personal—beads, a hand-tooled belt, decorations sewed onto jeans—are then added to the mass-produced base. Imagine a Consciousness II intellectual buying a cheap unstylish suit and then adding a handmade tie! Consciousness II has to have a non-mass-produced, tailor-made suit from England. He is ashamed of, or "above," the mass production that is the foundation of his own society. Consciousness III starts from the machine, but is not imprisoned by it; he wears his own individuality on top of it.

The new clothes express profoundly democratic values. There are no distinctions of wealth or status, no elitism; people confront one another shorn of these distinctions. In places where status or money is important, clothes tell the story. On Wall Street, one can tell the banker or lawyer from the mere employee by the expensive, tasteful suit. On the campus, the faculty member is set off from the graduate student by tweed jacket and tie; law professors are distinguished from the unworldly humanities teachers by businesslike suits. And in former times, the prep school undergraduate could be recognized and distinguished from the public school boy. All of these differences spoke of competition, advantage, and disadvantage. The new clothes deny the importance of hierarchy, status, authority, position, and they reject competition.

In these many different ways, the new clothes make it possible for people to be as direct, honest, and natural with each other as possible, given other barriers. To the extent that clothes can do it, people have the opportunity to meet one another as real, total persons, mind, face, and body, not defended or walled off by any barriers or certifications. There is no automatic respect or deference, such as the executive expects when he walks into his club and receives obsequious bows from the steward, but people are more clearly visible to each other, and they can be respected just as people.

Finally, in a threatening time, the new clothes express a shared set of attitudes and values. They express the new unity of youth, and the reality of the new consciousness. It is not an exclusive society; the smiles are for anyone who will smile back. But the new generation feels beleaguered, and it finds strength in recognizing brothers and sisters. Two people who do not know each other at all, passing on a highway, might shoot V-signals at each other, and thus affirm the new and growing brotherhood.

To understand the Consciousness III attitude toward career, we must deal not so much with the style they have adopted (for it is still very preliminary and experimental), but with the style and values they reject. Here the change of goals that is so basic to Consciousness III assumes its full significance. The central point is easy to say but very hard for an older person really to grasp, so deeply does it go against the grain of Consciousness I and II. It is that the goals of status, a position in the hierarchy, security, money, possessions, power, respect, and honor are not merely wrong, they are *unreal*. A person whose life is one long ego trip or power trip has not merely chosen one kind of satisfaction in preference to others; he has chosen goals that have no real relationship to personal growth, satisfaction, or happiness.

When a Consciousness II person meets a federal judge, or the head of a giant corporation, or the holder of a distinguished professorship, he takes notice. The position itself makes the man worth meeting and the occasion memorable. A member of the new generation, on the other hand, might be completely, blankly unaware of the titles, positions, and reputations of persons he has met. Students a few years ago were keenly aware of whether they were being taught by an assistant professor or an associate professor. Students today have no idea at all of their teachers' rank. They do not see it because it is not there. It is a curious thing: the professor has put the best part of his life into acquiring a regalia of titles, degrees, publications, professional reputation, and the student *does not even see it.*

In terms of their own lives, Consciousness III people simply do not imagine a career along the old vertical, escalator lines. It is not especially important to get into a particular university, or to make a good record when there, or to get a good job afterwards. They are not planning to get anything "settled." They conceive of life as a whole series of goals and choices, and a career as something that will be constantly changing. Whether a young man goes to one college or another, or into one occupation or another, is not the all-important decision his parents think it is; all choices are the "right" choice (for all lead outward) and a career comprises the many different experiences, some planned, some fortuitous, that one might have. Instead of intense, ambitious concentration, one can relax and see what happens. The world is the way Arlo Guthrie described it in "Alice's Restaurant": illogical and improbable.

This world demands a different personality than the old world, which asked for aggressive, disciplined, competitive pursuit of definite goals. One prime attribute is that it is anti-competitive. The tough high school athlete, measuring and one-upping his opponents, catches a whiff of the elixir of Consciousness III and he plays varsity basketball with a happier sense of enjoyment, or he quits altogether in order to play his guitar. A young hiker of five years ago would tell you how many peaks he had climbed and how fast; the same hiker, touched by the elixir, would say, "I just go along and dig."

There are several different patterns by which these attitudes have been translated into life-styles. The closest to a "straight" career would be to pursue an ordinary career, such as teaching or law or medicine, but substituting for the usual goals the objective of having some worthwhile experiences and serving the community to the best of one's ability. A second choice combines the first with "going underground"—the individual is secretly at war with society, and aims to get the better of society whenever he can, like the Henry Miller of *Tropic of Capricorn,* who ran riot with his job at the Cosmodemonic Telegraph Company of North America. The third is a new line of work—as a rock musician or light show artist—that combines a remunerative "career" with a new life-style. The fourth is an "ordinary" job—such as working for the post office—combined with a new life-style the rest of the time. The fifth option is the drop-out—usually someone who quits school and lives on the border of things (the Berkeley street people are mostly this sort of drop-out). Finally, there is the full hippie life, an attempt to live as if the Corporate State did not exist and some new form of community were already here. Other choices are now being tried.

Unsympathetic observers of the new generation frequently say that one of its prime characteristics is an aversion to work. The observers are prevented, by their disapproving, puritanical outlook, from understanding the real significance of what they see. The attitude of Consciousness III toward career is indeed based on the belief that most work available in our society is meaningless, degrading, and inconsistent with self-realization. The new generation is not "lazy," and it is glad enough to put great effort into any work that is worthwhile, whether it is hours of practice on a musical instrument, or working on a communal farm, or helping to create People's Park in Berkeley. But they see industrialized work as one of the chief means by which the minds and feelings of people are dominated in the Corporate State. It is work, unrelenting, driven, consuming, that comes between the professor and his students, the lawyer and his family, the bank employee and the beauty of nature. Consciousness III regards freedom from such work, making possible the development of an individual's true potential as a human being, to be among the greatest and most vital forms of liberation.

When we turn to the music of Consciousness III, we come to the chief medium of expression, the chief means by which inner feelings are communicated. Consciousness III has not yet developed a widely accepted written poetry, literature, or theatre; the functions of all of these have so far been assumed by music and the lyrics that go with it. Music has become the deepest means of communication and expression for an entire culture. When someone puts a dime in the jukebox of a restaurant frequented by young people there is a moment of community. As the music starts, the people in the restaurant begin to *move*. Some nod heads, some drum fingers, others tap feet, others move their whole bodies. They glance with smiles of agreement toward the person who made the selection. If it is a song from the established canon, like Bob Dylan's "Mr. Tambourine Man," everyone knows the words, and many sing along to themselves. Even those just entering the restaurant join in.

The dominant means of communication in our society—words—has been so abused, distorted and pre-empted that at present it does not seem adequate for people of the new consciousness. Music, on the other hand, says all the things they want to say or feel. It tells of the discovery of soul by whites—a depth of feeling long denied to most Americans. It expresses raunchy, sweaty sex. It is a repository of fantastic energy—as anyone who has watched a rock band knows. It can tell of a tranquil and fresh closeness to nature—sea, mountains, wind, and clouds. It can express the staccato experience of modern American life. What other music than rock, played on the car radio, comes anywhere near being appropriate to the wonders and anxieties, the beauty and the tension and the excitement, of driving across one of the great bridges of San Francisco Bay? In another mood, the music tells of loneliness, the solitary self. It is a poetry of the wonder of being young and all aware ("I Am a Child," by Neil Young) and of love and heartbreak between the generations ("Teach Your Children," by Graham Nash). It can express the feelings of youth toward the good things of an older America ("Rockin' Chair" and "King Harvest," by J. R. Robertson), or the violence, fervor, and fury of revolution in the streets ("We Can Be Together," by Paul Kantner). It can express the terrors and transiency of youth in an alien society ("Four Days Gone," by Stephen Stills), the strangeness and mystery of the unpredictable new patterns of life ("St. Stephen," by the Grateful Dead), the happiness of discovering companions in the journey ("Stand," by Sylvester Stewart; "Look at You Look at Me," by Dave Mason and J. Capaldi); and yearnings that are profoundly spiritual and religious ("I Shall Be Released," by Bob Dylan). It brings out a poetry in people who, if confined to words, would be awkward and prosaic. It expresses, as the rock bands also show, a total way of life. In its supreme moments, it carries the listener into a new world ("Dark Star," by the Grateful Dead). Most of all, perhaps, it expresses freedom, not the technical state of freedom that we all possess by virtue of the law, but the living of freedom. For the new consciousness, this music is not a pastime, but a necessity, on a par with food and water.

Indeed, the new music has achieved a degree of integration of art into everyday life that is probably unique in modern societies; to find anything comparable one would have to look to the Middle Ages or primitive men. Like a medieval cathedral or the carvings in a tribal village, the art of rock is constantly present as a part of everyday life, not something to be admired in a museum or listened to over coffee, after dinner and the day's work are done. It is significant that nearly everyone who deeply feels the music also makes an attempt at playing an instrument and even at composing. For the lover of rock, as for men in earlier times, art is a daily companion to share, interpret, and transfigure every experience and emotion.

The new music was built out of materials already in existence: blues, rock 'n' roll, folk music. But although the forms remained, something wholly new and original was made out of these older elements—more original, perhaps, than even the new musicians themselves yet realize. The transformation took place in 1966–67. Up to that time, the blues had been an essentially black medium. Rock 'n' roll, a blues derivative, was rhythmic, raunchy, teen-age dance music. Folk music, old and modern, was popular among college students. The three forms remained musically and culturally distinct, and even as late as 1965, none of them were expressing any radically new states of consciousness. Blues expressed black soul; rock, as made famous by Elvis Presley, was the beat of youthful sensuality; and folk music, with such singers as Joan Baez, expressed antiwar sentiments as well as the universal themes of love and disillusionment.

In 1966–1967 there was a spontaneous transformation. In the United States, it originated with youthful rock groups playing in San Francisco. In England, it was led by the Beatles, who were already established as an extremely fine and highly individual rock group. What happened, as well as it can be put into words, was this. First, the separate musical traditions were brought together. Bob Dylan and the Jefferson Airplane played folk rock, folk ideas with a rock beat. White rock groups began experimenting with the blues. Of course, white musicians had always played the blues, but essentially as imitators of the Negro style; now it began to be the white bands' own music. And all of the groups moved toward a broader eclecticism and synthesis. They freely took over elements from Indian ragas, from jazz, from American country music, and as time went on from even more diverse sources (one group seems . . . to have been trying out Gregorian chants). What developed was a protean music, capable of an almost limitless range of expression.

The second thing that happened was that all the musical groups began using the full range of electric instruments and the technology of electronic amplifiers. The twangy electric guitar was an old country-western standby, but the new electronic effects were altogether different—so different that a new listener in 1967 might well feel that there had never been any sounds like that in the world before. The high, piercing, unearthly sounds of the guitar seemed to come from other realms. Electronics did, in fact, make possible sounds that no instrument up to that time could produce. And in studio recordings, multiple tracking, feedback, and other devices made possible effects that not even an electronic band could produce live. Electronic amplification also made possible a fantastic increase in volume, the music becoming as loud and penetrating as the human ear could stand, and thereby achieving a "total" effect, so that instead of an audience of passive listeners, there were now audiences of total participants, feeling the music in all of their senses and all of their bones.

Third, the music became a multimedia experience, a part of a total environment. In the Bay Area ballrooms, the Fillmore, the Avalon, or Pauley Ballroom at the University of California, the walls were covered with fantastic changing patterns of light, the beginning of the new art of the light show. And the audience did not sit, it danced. With records at home, listeners imitated these lighting effects as best they could, and heightened the whole experience by using drugs. Often music was played out of doors, where nature—the sea or tall redwoods—provided the environment.

Fourth, each band began to develop a personality; often they lived together as a commune, and their music expressed their group life. The names of the groups, while often chosen rather casually and for public effect, nevertheless expressed the anti-Establishment, "outsider" identity of the groups. One way to gauge this is to imagine congressmen from the House Internal Security Committee (formerly HUAC) trying to grasp the derivations and nuances of such names as Notes From Underground, Loading Zone, Steppenwolf, the Cleanliness and Godliness Skiffle Band. A name such as the Grateful Dead, with its implications of atomic holocaust, Hiroshima, bitter alienation from society, and playful, joking don't-give-a-damnness, would baffle the security investigators for a long time. The name may have been chosen for the band's own esoteric reasons. But it suggests the idea that in our society the living are really dead, and only the "dead" are really alive; this idea would probably escape the investigators altogether. In short, the bands, by achieving a high degree of individual identity, and being clearly "outsiders," members of the youth culture themselves, became groups with which young audiences could feel a great closeness and rapport. By contrast, Consciousness II people have little identification with band members or the musicians in a symphony orchestra.

Fifth, musician-listener rapport has been heightened by two other kinds of participation: an enormous number of the young listeners had instruments or even bands and played the new music themselves, and both bands and listeners considered drugs to be an integral part of the musical experience. Consciousness II people may love Mozart, or jazz, but comparatively few of them spend much time playing an instrument. The use of drugs, especially because they are illegal, establishes a blood-brotherhood before the musicians even begin to play. And drugs, as we shall point out later, add a whole new dimension to creativity and to experience.

Sixth, a pulsing new energy entered into all the forms of music. Not even the turbulent fury of Beethoven's Ninth Symphony can compete for sheer energy with the Rolling Stones. Earlier popular songs, jazz, and classical music all have their own greatness, but the driving, screaming, crying, bitter-happy-sad heights and depths and motion of the new music add a dimension unknown in any earlier Western music. The older music was essentially intellectual; it was located in the mind and in the feelings known to the mind; the new music rocks the whole body, and penetrates the soul.

Seventh, the new music, despite its apparently simple form and beat, gradually evolved a remarkably complex texture. It has a complexity unknown to classical music, even to symphonies written for full orchestra. Beethoven seems like a series of parallel lines, sometimes vertical, sometimes diagonal; Mozart a flow of rounded forms, but as few as three rock musicians, such as Cream, or Crosby, Sills & Nash, can set up a texture of rhythms, timbres, kinds of sounds, emotions that create a world by contrast to which the classical composers seem to have lived in a world of simple verities, straightforward emotions, and established, reassuring conventions. It is no criticism of the eighteenth- or nineteenth-century geniuses to say that today's music has found a world they never knew.

Eighth, not only did many young people play the new music in one form or another, a great many, amateur and professional alike, began composing it. Nearly all of the successful rock groups of today write most of their own words and music. The distinction between composer and performer as professions has virtually disappeared. Thus songs are highly personal to the singer, not a mere "interpretation" of someone else's thought. Also, what is undeniably a mass culture is at the same time a genuine folk culture, because it is not imposed upon the people but written by them. And the writing is not limited to professional musicians; amateur and casual groups also compose some of their own material. And when one group does play another person's song, the group freely adds to it. There is no such thing, then, as the musician who tries in all things to be faithful to some remote composer, reserving for himself a display of skill and subtlety, spirit and nuance. The new music is a music of unrestrained creativity and self-expression.

Ninth, the new music has achieved a height of knowledge, understanding, insight, and truth concerning the world, and people's feelings, that is incredibly greater than what other media have been able to express. Journalists, writers for opinion journals, social scientists, novelists have all tried their hand at discussing the issues of the day. But almost without exception, they have been far more superficial than writers of rock poetry, and what is even more striking, several years behind the musicians. Compare a writer for *The New York Times,* or for *The New Republic,* talking about contemporary political and social ills, with Dylan's "It's All Right Ma (I'm Only Bleeding)" or "Subterranean Homesick Blues." Compare a sociologist talking about alienation with the Beatles' "Eleanor Rigby" or "Strawberry Fields Forever." But more important than comparisons is the fact that rock music has been able to give critiques of society at a profound level ("Draft Morning," by the Byrds, "Tommy," by The Who) and at the same time express the longings and aspirations of the new generation ("Get Together," by Chet Powers, "Comin' Back to Me," by Marty Balin). The music has achieved a relevance, an ability to penetrate to the essence of what is wrong with society, a power to speak to man "in his condition" that is perhaps the deepest source of its power.

If we combine all of these aspects of the transformation we can begin to see how vastly different the new music is from the older forms that it seems superficially to resemble. The blues offers an example. The essence of blues is radical subjectivity; the singer follows a form, but he cannot help but express his own personality, his own life experiences, his own encounters with his world. When Janis Joplin, a white girl, sang "Ball and Chain" to a pulsing, communal audience of middle-class young white people, it was not the same as a black singer in the classic blues tradition. It was contemporary American white "soul," and it spoke of the bomb, and the war, drugs, and the cops as well as the intense sexuality of the blues and the yearnings and mysteries of black soul. A similar transformation takes place when the new groups play jazz, early rock, folk songs, or even classical music. Procol Harum's "Salty Dog" sounds like an ordinary folk song about a sea voyage when it is first heard. But when one listens more closely there is much more: classical music is blended into a folk style; the song has an almost unbearable tension; drums build up powerful climaxes; gulls' cries and a bosun's pipe give an eerie feeling; the words do not quite make sense; the captain is apparently mad; death is in the air; the ship goes to places unknown to man; the simple sea song has become an awesome, mysterious and frightening "trip" to some place beyond man's experience. Happy, sad, or spiritual, the new music transforms older forms into "trips" that enter a dimension which the original forms never reached.

What the new music has become is the first true example of a contemporary American culture that is originated by the people themselves, not by an elite or by the false consciousness machinery of corporate producers. Instead of an alienating false culture designed to rob us of self-knowledge, the new music has been, from the beginning, a source of that truth that is greater than mere facts, the kind of truth Ken Kesey meant when he said, "But it's the truth even if it didn't happen." Thus it is that America, the land of mass-produced ugliness, has finally created a music that is, beyond anything else, unbelievably *beautiful*. It is stirring, it is deeply moving, it is, like the greatest art, profoundly warming to the spirit and the soul. And so it touches and transforms each area of the new generation's experiences and feelings. The complex, frantic, disjointed machinelike experiences of modern urban existence were presented, with piercing notes of pain, and dark notes of anger, by Cream. The mystical transcendence of ordinary experience achieved by the hippies, the drug world, and the spiritual realm, soaring fantasy and brilliant patterns of rhythm and sound, are the domain of the San Francisco acid rock of the Jefferson Airplane, and the psychedelic meditations of the early music of Country Joe and the Fish. Irony, satire, mockery of the Establishment and of rational thought were the specialty of the Mothers of Invention. The open road is the realm of James Taylor in songs like "Fire and Rain" and "Country Road." A uniquely personal but universal view of the world has been achieved by the Beatles, gentle, unearthly, the world transformed. They are the supreme music makers of our time, and from "I Want to Hold Your Hand" to "With a Little Help from My Friends" to "Here Comes the Sun" they have been with us through the "long, cold, lonely winter," offering their help, inviting us to their magical land, reminding us, when we needed it most, that "it's alright." Another highly personal view of the world, but one close to the experiences of young listeners, is that of Bob Dylan. Dylan has gone through a whole cycle of experience, from folk music to social protest and commentary, next to folk rock, then to the extraordinary personal world of the ballad "Sad-Eyed Lady of the Lowlands," and finally to the serene, but achieved, innocence of the country music of the album "Nashville Skyline." Perhaps more than any other individual in the field of music, Dylan has been, from the very beginning, a true prophet of the new consciousness.

Among the most important forms of the new music is the blues, for it expresses what is common to all the individual types of music we have discussed—experience coming from the self, coming deeply, honestly, and searchingly from the self, expressing thoughts and feelings that most people conceal from their own view and from others. For the black man in the South, the blues expressed his identity, an identity oppressed, forbidden, and denied in other ways. So long as whites in America did not realize that their own identity was also oppressed and denied, so long as whites failed to search for their own selves, there could be no white "soul," no white blues to sing. The white man could be sentimental or romantic, but he had no knowledge of himself, and therefore no words of his own for the blues. The new generation, in its discovery of self, in its discovery of oppression, also discovered white "soul," and that is what its music is starting to tell about. The new music is uniquely and deeply personal, allowing individuals and groups to express their special vision of the world to all their brothers and sisters; it deals with the entire world as seen and felt by the new consciousness, and it takes listeners to places they have never been before.

But no single form of music can really claim pre-eminence. It is the richness and variety and continually changing quality of the new music that is its essence. It defies analysis and explication by critics because it never stands still to be analyzed; it ranges from the mystic expressiveness of Procol Harum, the emotional intensity of Jimi Hendrix, the heavy sounds of Led Zeppelin, to anywhere else the heads of the new generation have been. Its essence is the total scene: a huge and happy noontime crowd in Lower Sproul Plaza at Berkeley, some standing, some sitting, some dancing; every variety of clothes and costume, knapsacks and rolled-up sleeping bags; piled-up Afro hair and shoulder-length golden-blond hair; a sense of everyone's sharing the values and experience that the scene represents, music by the Crabs, a local group, mostly soaring, ecstatic, earthy rock that shakes the crowd, the buildings, and the heavens themselves with joy; and above the scene, presiding over it, those benevolent deities, the sungod, the ocean breeze, the brown-green Berkeley hills.

The Consciousness III idea of community among people is another basic aspect of the new culture. It rests on two integrated concepts: respect for the uniqueness of each individual, and the idea expressed by the word "together." We have already described the recognition of each individual as one of the initial premises of Consciousness III. Now we must attempt to explain the idea of "together." It does not mean what the suburbs speak of as "togetherness," an external conformity gained by doing things as a family unit, looking alike, adapting to one another. At the same time, "together" does not necessarily mean a relationship such as love, mutual dependence, or friendship, although it could accompany any of these. "Together" expresses the relationship among people who feel themselves to be members of the same species, who are related to each other and to all of nature by the underlying order of being. People are "together" when they experience the same thing in the same way. They need not be in love, they need not even be friends, and they need not give one another anything, materially or emotionally, to be together. A great throng can be together in a peace march or a rock festival; a small group can feel an intense sense of "together" listening to a record or watching a sunset or a storm. Many aspects of the new culture help produce this feeling, music perhaps most universally. The individuals preserve every bit of their individuality. They simply come together to share a feeling, a moment, or an experience, and thus feel united in a community based on having their heads in the same place at the same time.

Consciousness III is beginning to experiment with small communities of different sorts. Many of the communes that have sprung up in various parts of the country are based primarily on shared values, such as love of desert sunsets and use of drugs; the members get along with each other, but did not come together on the basis of personal affinity, as is the case with lifelong friendships. They are sharing a "trip." These "trip communities" are one aspect of the so-called hippie communes, with their unusual mixture of casual uncommittedness and intense communal feeling.

Consciousness III people are engaged in a constant search to discover forms and ways to be "together." They experiment with traveling together, with inventing games, with sensitivity groups, with political confrontations, building occupations, and demonstrations. Many of them believe that sharing creative work, such as playing in a band, composing music, making a film, writing a play, or studying poetry, will ultimately prove to be the most satisfying way to be "together"; they believe that where people are really "together," their motivation will be higher and their creativity multiplied far beyond the sum total of what they could produce as individuals.

Some students now in college are making plans to live with a group of friends as a community after graduation, pursuing different occupations but doing as much as possible as a community, perhaps including growing some of their own food. Such a commune might include married couples and children as well as single people. It would not be the more casual "trip commune" but a permanent living arrangement, an "extended family," perhaps with a number of different homes. In form it remains amorphous, but the idea clearly reflects the belief of many students that once one has experienced being "together" with people, conventional social relationships seem pointless and boring, and the prospect of life separated from one's friends seems too barren to be accepted any longer.

What the new generation has already achieved is a way of being with other people that is closer, warmer, more open, more sensitive, more capable of sharing, than prior generations have known. It is as if some unseen divider, a glass partition, a plastic coating, a separating curtain of conversation, had been removed, leaving people effortlessly closer. People of an earlier generation tried to get to know each other by asking questions that were searching or personal, by learning about each other's past lives, interests, and experiences, by striving for some almost psychoanalytic "truth." The new generation's knowledge of each other is more like the total perception of an artist. It is less intellectual, less translatable into words. They are all the closer to each other because their being together is not mediated or separated by words.

Of all of the characteristics man possesses, surely the one he must prize most highly is consciousness. We do not mean the special kinds of consciousness we have discussed in this book, but consciousness with a small "c," consciousness in the Henry James sense—awareness of all the phenomena of one's world. It is this consciousness that distinguishes the poet, the artist, the human being who is sensitive to others. Dostoevsky's underground man, in *Notes From Underground,* says, "Though I stated at the beginning that consciousness, in my opinion, is the greatest misfortune for man, yet I know man loves it and would not give it up for any satisfaction." Man shares many of his qualities with other forms of life; consciousness is what makes him distinctively human.

Of all the qualities of human beings that are injured, narrowed, or repressed in the Corporate State, it is consciousness, the most precious and the most fragile, that suffers the most. There is, as we have seen, a vast apparatus, working unceasingly to create a false consciousness in people. One aspect of this force seeks to manipulate our political consciousness, another to change our awareness of our own needs. But consciousness is also profoundly affected simply by the din and over-stimulation of our society. It is pounded, battered, strained, exhausted, and inevitably, dulled. A traffic jam, buying a ticket at an airport, or a day in a busy office gives consciousness such a merciless beating that it must develop an insensitive coating to survive. Encounters with people are so many, so brutish and impersonal, so fleeting and so harrowing that consciousness must be desensitized to reduce the pain. Television commercials, canned music in elevators, threatening notices in monthly bills assault us, and the only defense is to become less sensitive and less aware.

The terrible thing that happens to a person living in the Corporate State is that he suffers a substantial, and eventually permanent, impairment of consciousness. If the State impaired our eyesight, or our hearing, it would be bad enough, but permanent damage to consciousness is a worse loss. We lose all of our senses; we are unable to be adequately aware of people, or of the rest of the phenomena of the world. Man ought naturally to see his life as a steady growth of consciousness, which he cultivates with all his efforts; instead he must see it diminished, so that childhood and youth are the only times of life when man still has his consciousness. The faces in the subway are the faces of impaired consciousness, unmoving and unmoved.

One final aspect of the culture of Consciousness III is an effort to restore, protect, and foster human consciousness. It is most important because its aim is nothing less than to restore man's awareness of himself, of other people, of nature, of his own life. It seeks to make man, in everything that he does or experiences, more alive. To "blow one's mind" means to become more aware.

The aspects of culture we have already discussed, clothes, the non-directed career, music, and community, are all major components of the effort to increase consciousness. Here we shall mention several more. They divide themselves naturally into two categories: the effort to resist imposed consciousness and the effort to counteract dulling and blunting.

The search for consciousness begins with an effort to shake off the "false consciousness" imposed by society. One must counteract the influence of mass media, mass education, advertising, and all the other pressures on the mind. The devices for doing this are just in the experimental stage: underground newspapers, including high school underground newspapers, "free university" classes, and all kinds of discussion groups; personal participation in events, such as demonstrations, personal experience with law enforcement, personal work in areas such as ghettos, mental hospitals, or in the Peace Corps; extensive reading. One device is particularly important: an individual cannot hope to achieve an independent consciousness unless he cultivates, by whatever means are available, including clothes, speech mannerisms, illegal activities, and so forth, the feeling of being an *outsider*. Only the person who feels -himself to be an outsider is genuinely free of the lures and temptations of the Corporate State. Only he can work in a bank or go to a cocktail party in "safety" because he will not be taken in. So the new generation struggles to feel itself as outsiders, and it identifies with the blacks, with the poor, with Bonnie and Clyde, and with the losers of this world, celebrated in folk songs such as Bob Dylan's album "John Wesley Harding." These suggest that only by an antisocial posture can people really be "alive" in a society that is essentially dead. Of course, every time the Establishment commits violence against the new generation, this increases their sense of being outsiders. But even more important is the creation of group identity among the outsiders. In one sense the whole "youth world" is an effort to achieve an independent consciousness.

Freedom from imposed consciousness requires freedom from the domination of technology. The new culture is built on the technology of the Corporate State, but not in the same way as the State's own culture is built: in the new culture, it is the technology that is dominated, not the people. The new generation's music makes use of modern electronics; its art (e.g., films) is technically sophisticated; its habits (reading) require affluence; its sexual mores require the pill. But the new generation does not use technology the way the older one does. Consciousness III does not use it for status or conspicuous consumption, nor for power over people, or competitive "success." They do not use it to further rationalize society, to make life less challenging, more passive; they do not use it as a substitute for experience. They do not ignore its aesthetic, environmental, and human consequences. In short, instead of letting the technology dictate to them, instead of being the frenetic, driven victims of its demands, they use it as intelligent men and women might, to further their own lives. A key illustration of this is the fact that technology is not allowed to rob them of experience.

Another effort is directed against the imposition of a role, and its ways of thinking. Escape from a role is painfully difficult for most people, which shows how important an effort it is. The high school athlete-leader, cool, competent, straight, finds it a tremendous effort to free himself from this role; he must learn to approach people instead of waiting to be sought after, make himself emotionally vulnerable, wear absurd clothes, spend time with people who are definitely not part of the accepted crowd. Fighting off a role makes for conflict with parents, school authorities, coaches; it is a prime source of misunderstanding, but it is essential to get rid of the imposed response.

One last aspect of trying to escape imposed consciousness is concerned with so-called rational thought. Consciousness III is deeply suspicious of logic, rationality, analysis, and of principles. Nothing so outrages the Consciousness II intellectual as this seeming rejection of reason itself. But Consciousness III has been exposed to some rather bad examples of reason, including the intellectual justifications of the Cold War and the Vietnam War. At any rate, Consciousness III believes it essential to get free of what is now accepted as rational thought. It believes that "reason" tends to leave out too many factors and values—especially those which cannot readily be put into words and categories. It believes that undue faith is put on "principle" when there are always other principles that have been neglected; if "free self-determination" is the principle behind the Vietnam War, what about that other principle, "Thou shalt not kill"? It believes that thought can be "non-linear," spontaneous, disconnected. It thinks rational conversation has been overdone as a means of communication between people, and it has invented a new term, "rapping," for communication when it does take the form of words. Above all, it wants new dimensions.

In its desire to escape any imposed system, Consciousness III declares experience to be the most precious of all commodities. All experience has value, all of it has something to teach, none of it is rejected because it fails to accord with some pre-existing scheme of things. Of course this does not mean that the Consciousness III person will engage in actions that violate his basic values; he will never kill or rape to try the experience. But subject to these limits, he is open to trying new things; he does not judge or reject them in advance.

All of these are examples of means that are being used to escape patterns of thought imposed by the Corporate State—to liberate the mind.

But what about the dulling of the mind? This is the problem of the man who has worked in a chemical plant so long that he has lost the sense of smell, or a man whose eyesight has dimmed. The most direct way to restore sensitivity is, of course, to begin a series of exposures to forgotten sensations. The Consciousness III person does a great deal of this. He burns incense in his home to restore the sense of smell. He attends a T-group or sensitivity group to restore awareness of other people; the experiments may range from telling personal feelings and experiences to touching other people's bodies (a necessary antidote, perhaps, to the desensitizing that inevitably takes place when people are forced to bump up against each other but "not feel it" in subways and buses). He takes "trips" out into nature; he might lie for two hours and simply stare up at the arching branches of a tree. He finds that motorcycling restores a sense of free motion. He might cultivate visual sensitivity, and the ability to meditate, by staring for hours at a globe lamp. He discovers Bach and Mozart. He seeks out art, literature, drama, for their value in raising consciousness.

One of the most important means for restoring dulled consciousness is psychedelic drugs. They combine with all the other means we have mentioned (for example, marijuana might be smoked while looking at the sea, or while listening to music) but they are important in themselves. Many people confuse the psychedelic drugs with the narcotic drugs and with liquor, and assume that oblivion, or a lowered awareness, or hallucinations, are the consequence of psychedelic drugs. The term "getting stoned" is confusing; it implies losing consciousness, rather than a higher awareness. But getting dulled has nothing to do with the psychedelic experience; using marijuana is more like what happens when a person with fuzzy vision puts on glasses. Listening to a familiar piece of music, such as a Bach orchestral suite, the mind is newly conscious of the bass line; listening to a conversation, the mind is more aware of the nuances of each voice. Music assumes shapes and comes out into the room, it is so vivid and so tangible. Grass is a subtle and delicate experience, an educated experience (one that has to be learned), and it is not too different from the heightened awareness that an unusually sensitive or artistic person has. Significantly, it is a sensitivity too delicate for the hassles of today's world; a truly sensitive person just could not stand to ride to New York on the Penn Central railroad. The other psychedelic drugs, such as mescaline and LSD, are much more powerful than marijuana, and may well be dangerous to some individuals. They make possible a higher range of experience, extending outward to deep self-knowledge, to the religious, and to vision. But the principle of increased awareness is the same.

Marijuana causes a concentration on what is immediately present: color, smells, sensory experiences, "nowness." The self is isolated, turns inward, feels loose, detached, soft, gentle. The hold of uptightness is relaxed, allowing all sorts of "illogical" relationships to seem perfectly natural; there are visual juxtapositions of sights that have no "rational" relationship, such as a huge box of Corn Flakes between two buildings on a city street, and the logic of the outside world is suspended; why not nuzzle the furry carpet of a formal, wall-to-wall living room, if one feels like nuzzling? In some less uptight society, marijuana would be just a toy, a harmless "high." But in a society that keeps its citizens within a closed system of thought, that depends so much on systematic indoctrination, and an imposed consciousness, marijuana is a maker of revolution, a truth-serum. Because it concentrates on "nowness" as reality, it takes people outside the enclosed system, releases them from domination of their thought, and makes *unreal* what society takes most seriously: time, schedules, rational connections, competition, anger, excellence, authority, private property, law, status, the primacy of the state, the standards imposed by other people and by society. It is a truth-serum that repeals false consciousness.

Used continually and to excess, drugs become a factor that dulls consciousness. They diminish awareness, cut off reality, and separate people from human contacts. Perhaps their greatest affirmative significance is to provide an initial breakthrough, a shattering of the euphoria and mythology of the Corporate State, a beginning of a new way of thinking. In the long run, they are not enough to support a new consciousness, and they may eventually become yet another bar to reality.

The effect of psychedelic drugs does not end when the drug itself wears off; it is lasting in the sense that the user finds his awareness and sensitivity have increased, whether he is using drugs at the time or not. In other words, something has been learned. In fact, there may come a time when a drug user feels that drugs are no longer necessary to him, or at least that they have become of lesser importance; he has achieved the increased awareness he wanted and it is part of him now.

All of the various efforts of the new generation to increase awareness combine to produce a remarkable phenomenon: the Consciousness III person, no matter how young and inexperienced he may be, seems to possess an extraordinary "new knowledge." Governor Rockefeller goes on an official trip to Latin America and returns "heartened" by his reception; the ordinary citizen, if he is not particularly sophisticated, may actually believe that the Governor was well received; the person with "new knowledge" sees right through the pretense and knows, without reading the newspapers carefully, that the Governor was practically run out of each country and survived only by virtue of forceful repression of protest by each regime. He does not "know" the facts, but he still "knows" the truth that seems hidden from others. The explanation for this political sophistication is primarily the repeal of pretense and absurdity. It is absurd to think that someone named Rockefeller, representing the United States from a limousine, will be "warmly" welcomed by a populace, just as it is absurd to think that high school students revere their principal or believe what is patriotically said at school assemblies. In a country as burdened as ours is with hypocrisy and myth, the mere repeal of untruth becomes a profound insight.

One of the ways to describe this "new knowledge" is to say that it is capable of ignoring categories. We are all limited in our thinking by artificially drawn lines; we cannot get beyond the idea that a university is "private property" or that prose is different from poetry. When the category-barriers are removed, "new" relationships are seen. But the "new knowledge" is more than this; it is as if everything, from political affairs to aesthetics, were seen with new eyes; the young people of Consciousness III see effortlessly what is phony or dishonest in politics, or what is ugly and meretricious in architecture and city planning, whereas an older person has to go through years of education to make himself equally aware. It might take a Consciousness II person twenty years of reading radical literature to "know" that law is a tool of oppression; the young drug user just plain "knows" it. Nothing is more difficult for an older person to believe in than this "new knowledge," but it is such a striking phenomenon, extending even to long-haired California teen-agers hitchhiking their way to the beach, whose experience with political thinking or newspaper reading is limited, that it must be taken seriously.

Much of what we have said is summed up by the phrase "where his head is at." The implication of the phrase is that we are dealing with some dimension utterly outside of the way most people in America have become accustomed to the world. One has only to look at the "Comix" of R. Crumb to realize what it means to have a head that is in some extraordinary place; the world of R. Crumb is not merely brilliant or satiric or grotesque, it is *in another place* than most people have been. It is a common observation among today's college students that freshmen, and even more so, high school students, have heads that are amazing even to the college students.

Perhaps the deepest source of consciousness is nature. Members of the new generation seek out the beach, the woods, and the mountains. They do not litter these places with beer cans, they do not shatter the silences with power boats or motorcycle noises. They do not go to nature as a holiday from what is real. They go to nature as a source. The salt water of the sea is the salt in their blood; the freedom of the sea is their freedom. The forest is where they came from, it is the place where they feel closest to themselves, it is renewal. They do not pay much attention to hiking equipment, or picnic gear for the beach, or swimming attire;

they are likely to wade into the salt water with blue jeans still on. Nature is not some foreign element that requires equipment. Nature is them.

All of this search for increased consciousness culminates in an attitude that is the very antithesis of Consciousness II: a desire for innocence, for the ability to be in a state of wonder or awe. It is of the essence of the thinking of the new generation that man should be constantly open to new experience, constantly ready to have his old way of thinking changed, constantly hoping that he will be sensitive enough and receptive enough to let the wonders of nature and mankind come to him. Consciousness II regards it as a sign of weakness to be surprised or awed; III cultivates the experience. Consciousness III says "the full moon blew my mind" and is proud of it; II has seen the moon before and takes it in stride. For Consciousness III, camping, surfing, watching sunsets and stars, lying in the grass, humor and play, new forms of community, art, literature, knowledge and mystery are all freshly created. In *Why Are We in Vietnam?* Norman Mailer's hero, D.J., rids himself of the machine consciousness and, in the vastness of Alaska's remote Brooks Range, rediscovers a childlike, breathless sense of wonder; this is the quality that Consciousness III supremely treasures, to which it gives its ultimate sign of reverence, vulnerability, and innocence, "Oh wow!"

CHAPTER 3

TECHNOCRACY'S CHILDREN

THEODORE ROSZAK

One of the consequences of the division of labor, which has been discussed in an earlier selection, has been the emergence of the highly specialized expert. Often in the public eye, the expert not only solves problems but readily advances plans for averting future difficulties. In recent years, essentially every area of our lives has become the legitimate purview of one or more experts. Invariably the expert is, or claims to be, a man or woman of science. In the name of efficiency the force of the scientific method is brought to bear on either the personal or societal problem. As a result of searching rational scrutiny, a workable solution is quickly brought forth. The position of the expert is reaffirmed, and the public is comforted by knowing that help is so readily available.

No matter what the problem may be, we are confident that some expert proficient in a natural or social science can provide a solution. Society and the psyche are viewed in a mechanistic fashion: Inputs can be controlled and altered to modify output behavior. The method is appealing in its simplicity. For example, one need simply consult the well-known sexual therapists, follow their regimen, and then look forward to a trouble-free, fulfilling love life. For the less ambitious or, more likely, less affluent, there are expertly prepared sex manuals. One need only follow the detailed directions provided by these experts to realize his (or her) full potential. One gets the impression, after perusing several of the most popular books, that sex is, after all, little more than a kind of physical activity. One simply needs to change his manipulative practices (control of inputs) to achieve greater satisfaction and fulfillment (output behavior). The difficulty, of course, rests in the fact that human beings are qualitatively more than a body and a nervous system; the whole is greater than the sum of its parts.

The same difficulty impedes the application of "expert technology" to societal-level problems. Despite the efforts of an expert Council of Economic Advisers the national economy often appears, at best, shaky. Exclusive reliance on technological rationality may cause, and probably already has caused, as many new problems as it solves. His obsession with measurement and cataloguing compels the expert to exclude or disregard what is not immediately apparent. Unfortunately though, it appears that much of what man needs to sustain himself is not readily amenable to empirical measurement. Theodore Roszak, in "Technocracy's Children," has commented with insight on a system that seemingly supplies its members with all their material wants but is incapable of addressing their spiritual needs.

The starting point for Roszak's analysis is the conflict between youth and the existent social order. In Europe this conflict has occurred along rather traditional lines: The youth protesters identify with the traditional symbols, philosophies, and figures of the political left. In America, however, the conflict is against an opponent more pervasive and formidable than an existent political regime. The struggle is against what Roszak has labeled the "technocracy."

"Technocracy" is a "social form in which an industrial society reaches the peak of its organizational integration." It represents the aspiration to achieve a new level of social organization of which every part has been fully rationalized. This quality ensures that each part is now open to scrutiny and adjustment by those charged with organizational upkeep. At the heart of this organization is the highly trained expert—or those who employ the expert. In the technocracy nothing remains small or simple. The experts quickly evolve a complex technical language that seems to place even the most basic ideas beyond the layman's grasp. Elaborate information systems are devised so that the work of the technocracy may be even more rationalized. The process feeds upon itself. The extension of the system to an area with which heretofore it had no contact will almost certainly result in the replacement of the old with the new.

The technocracy confounds those who attempt to place a conventional political label upon it. This quality of ideological elusiveness makes it difficult to perceive it as a political phenomenon. As it is, we define it as worthwhile, as a "cultural imperative which is beyond question, beyond discussion." In support and encouragement of the technocratic order we have convinced ourselves (and continue to do so) of the inherent "rightness" of the technocratic conception of the world. In this view all of man's vital needs are entirely technical in character. These needs can be analyzed, quantified, and, ultimately, satisfied through the application of a rational technology. "If a problem does *not* seem to have such a technical solution it must not be a real problem," the technicians of the new order argue. Another important view is "that this formal analysis of our needs has now achieved 99 percent completion." Social friction, it is held, is just a minor breakdown in communication that can be easily remedied by collective reason. Lastly, only the experts really know what we want and need. It is they alone who can ensure our well-being. And, not at all surprising, these experts are on government or corporate payrolls.

The technocracy requires that we surrender our autonomy for a life of comfort and security. Without saying so, it asks us to be satisfied with fulfillment of only a portion of our human needs. Rewards are predictable and bland; life's rhythm seems easy to follow; and little real protest is ever mounted.

Today there are those, such as minority-group members, who are denied access to material wealth. From their perspective there is little wrong with the offered life-style; uninterested in change, they clamor for their share. Once it is granted to them, their acceptance of the system becomes absolute. The system has learned that external threats are efficiently and permanently dealt with by co-opting the troublesome elements. Repression is seldom entirely effective, because it often necessitates the use of force in the future.

As we have seen, since the late 1960s, youth have risen in protest against the expansion of technocracy. The insidious repression of the spirit and the ennui engendered by life in a society that refused to feel any excitement encouraged their search for forms of behavior that could provide more satisfaction. Put off by the refusal of their parents to act, and encouraged by "permissive" child-rearing practices that stressed expression rather than repression, protesters emanating from the higher educational institutions did not at all seem unreasonable. Academia represented the soft underbelly of the technocracy, the place where dissent would be most clearly felt.

The dissent, Roszak suggests, brought forth a curious coalition. Students, of course, were involved. Much of the direction and organizational expertise was provided by graduate students and older people present in the university setting. Perhaps most surprising was the presence of adult radicals in the ranks of the youthful dissidents. Rejected by and, in turn, rejecting the working class—which has been the traditional target of radical activists—the adult radical turned to the youth of the middle classes, believing, as Roszak does, that "the young have become one of the very few social levers dissent has to work with."

Whether the coalition will endure and ultimately encourage new political forms can only be guessed at now. What is clear, though, is that the technocratic order has not been able to meet adequately the needs of all its subjects. By leaving people discontented and unfulfilled, the technocratic order virtually ensures an endless supply of new dissidents. What supporters of the system have failed to realize is that human wants, needs, and problems cannot be understood by means of the same processes that can be used to build a nuclear bomb or send a man to the moon.

Theodore Roszak was born in Chicago in 1933 and received his Ph. D. degree from Princeton University in 1954. A member of the History Department of California State College at Hayward, he was editor of, and a contributor to, *The Dissenting Academy* (1968). His articles and reviews have appeared in several of the most popular radical and intellectual journals.

The struggle of the generations is one of the obvious constants of human affairs. One stands in peril of some presumption, therefore, to suggest that the rivalry between young and adult in Western society during the current decade is uniquely critical. And yet it is necessary to risk such presumption if one is not to lose sight of our most important contemporary source of radical dissent and cultural innovation. For better or worse, most of what is presently happening that is new, provocative, and engaging in politics, education, the arts, social relations (love, courtship, family, community) is the creation either of youth who are profoundly, even fanatically, alienated from the parental generation or of those who address themselves primarily to the young. It is at the level of youth that significant social criticism now looks for a responsive hearing as, more and more, it grows to be the common expectation that the young should be those who act, who make things happen, who take the risks, who generally provide the ginger. It would be of interest in its own right that the age-old process of generational disaffiliation should now be transformed from a peripheral experience in the life of the individual and the family into a major lever of radical social change. But if one believes, as I do, that the alienated young are giving shape to something that looks like the saving vision our endangered civilization requires, then there is no avoiding the need to understand and to educate them in what they are about.

The reference . . . is primarily to America, but it is headline news that generational antagonism has achieved international dimensions. Throughout the West (as well as in Japan and parts of Latin America) it is the young who find themselves cast as the only effective radical opposition within their societies. Not all the young, of course: perhaps only a minority of the university campus population. Yet no analysis seems to make sense of the major political upheavals of the decade other than that which pits a militant minority of dissenting youth against the sluggish consensus-and-coalition politics of their middle-class elders. This generational dichotomy is a new fact of political life, one which the European young have been more reluctant to accept than their American counterparts. The heirs of an institutionalized left-wing legacy, the young radicals of Europe still tend to see themselves as the champions of "the people" (meaning the working class) against the oppression of the bourgeoisie (meaning, in most cases, their own parents). Accordingly, they try valiantly to adapt themselves to the familiar patterns of the past. They reach out automatically along time-honored ideological lines to find allies—to the workers, the trade unions, the parties of the left—only to discover that these expected alliances strangely fail to materialize and that they stand alone and isolated, a vanguard without a following.

In Germany and Italy the major parties of the left opposition have allowed themselves to be co-opted into the mainstream of respectable politicking—perhaps even to the point of joining governing coalitions. Despite the fact that German students (less than 5 per cent of whom come from working-class families) risk the wrath of the police to crusade beneath banners bearing the names of Rosa Luxemburg and Karl Liebknecht, the backlash their street politics produces is as sharp among the workers as the bourgeoisie. When Berlin students demonstrate against the war in Vietnam, the trade unions respond (as in February, 1968) with counterdemonstrations supporting Washington's version of "peace and freedom" in Southeast Asia.

In Britain, the Aldermaston generation and its disillusioned successors have long since had to admit that the Labour Party, angling always for the now decisive middle-class vote, is little more than Tweedledum to the Tories' Tweedledee. As for the British working class, the only cause that has inspired a show of fighting spirit on its part during the sixties (other than the standard run of wages and demarcation grievances) is the bloody-minded cry to drive the colored immigrants from the land.

In France, the battle-scarred students of the May, 1968, Rebellion have had to watch the much-mellowed CGT and PC conniving to function as President de Gaulle's labor lieutenants in the maintenance of responsible, orderly government against the menace of "anarchy" in the streets. If the students march by rebellious thousands to the barricades, their cautious parents march in behalf of the status quo by the tens of thousands and vote by the millions for the General and the managerial elite he has recruited from the *Ecole polytechnique* for the purpose of masterminding the new French affluence. Even the factory workers who swelled the students' ranks from thousands to millions during the early stages of the May, 1968, General Strike seem to have decided that the essence of revolution is a bulkier pay envelope.

Over and again it is the same story throughout Western Europe; the students may rock their societies; but without the support of adult social forces, they cannot overturn the established order. And that support would seem to be nowhere in sight. On the contrary, the adult social forces—including those of the traditional left—are the lead-bottomed ballast of the status quo. The students march to the Internationale, they run up the red flag, they plaster the barricades with pictures of Marxist heroes old and new—but the situation they confront stubbornly refuses to yield to a conventional left-right analysis. Is it any wonder that, in despair, some French students begin to chalk up the disgruntled slogan *"Je suis marxiste, tendance Groucho"* ("I'm a Marxist of the Groucho variety")? At last they are forced to admit that the entrenched consensus which repels their dissent is the generational phenomenon which the French and German young have begun to call "daddy's politics."

If the experience of the American young has anything to contribute to our understanding of this dilemma, it stems precisely from the fact that the left-wing of our political spectrum has always been so pathetically foreshortened. Our young are therefore far less adept at wielding the vintage rhetoric of radicalism than their European counterparts. But where the old categories of social analysis have so little to tell us (or so I will argue here), it becomes a positive advantage to confront the novelty of daddy's politics free of outmoded ideological preconceptions. The result may then be a more flexible, more experimental, though perhaps also a more seemingly bizarre approach to our situation. Ironically, it is the American young, with their underdeveloped radical background, who seem to have grasped most clearly the fact that, while such immediate emergencies as the Vietnam war, racial injustice, and hardcore poverty demand a deal of old-style politicking, the paramount struggle of our day is against a far more formidable, because far less obvious, opponent, to which I will give the name "the technocracy"— a social form more highly developed in America than in any other society. The American young have been somewhat quicker to sense that in the struggle against *this* enemy, the conventional tactics of political resistance have only a marginal place, largely limited to meeting immediate life-and-death crises. Beyond such front-line issues, however, there lies the greater task of altering the total cultural context within which our daily politics takes place.[1]

---

[1] For a comparison of American and European student radicalism along the lines drawn here, see Gianfranco Corsini, "A Generation Up in Arms," *The Nation*, June 10, 1968.

Daniel Cohn-Bendit and his spontaneous revolutionaries in France are something of an exception to what I say here about the young European radicals. Cohn-Bendit's anarchist instincts (which greatly riled the old-line leftist student groups during the May, 1968, troubles) provide him with a healthy awareness of "the bureaucratic phenomenon" in modern industrial society and of the way in which it has subtly eroded the revolutionary potential of the working class and

By the technocracy, I mean that social form in which an industrial society reaches the peak of its organizational integration. It is the ideal men usually have in mind when they speak of modernizing, up-dating, rationalizing, planning. Drawing upon such unquestionable imperatives as the demand for efficiency, for social security, for large-scale co-ordination of men and resources, for ever higher levels of affluence and ever more impressive manifestations of collective human power, the technocracy works to knit together the anachronistic gaps and fissures of the industrial society. The meticulous systematization Adam Smith once celebrated in his well-known pin factory now extends to all areas of life, giving us human organization that matches the precision of our mechanistic organization. So we arrive at the era of social engineering in which entrepreneurial talent broadens its province to orchestrate the total human context which surrounds the industrial complex. Politics, education, leisure, entertainment, culture as a whole, the unconscious drives, and even, as we shall see, protest against the technocracy itself: all these become the subjects of purely technical scrutiny and of purely technical manipulation. The effort is to create a new social organism whose health depends upon its capacity to keep the technological heart beating regularly. In the words of Jacques Ellul:

> Technique requires predictability and, no less, exactness of prediction. It is necessary, then, that technique prevail over the human being. For technique, this is a matter of life and death. Technique must reduce man to a technical animal, the king of the slaves of technique. Human caprice crumbles before this necessity; there can be no human autonomy in the face of technical autonomy. The individual must be fashioned by techniques, either negatively (by the techniques of understanding man) or positively (by the adaptation of man to the technical framework), in order to wipe out the blots his personal determination introduces into the perfect design of the organization.[2]

In the technocracy, nothing is any longer small or simple or readily

of its official left-wing leadership. He therefore warns strongly against "hero-worshiping" the workers. But even so, he continues to conceive of "the people" as the workers, and of the workers as the decisive revolutionary element, the students functioning only as their allies and sparkplugs. This leads him to the conclusion that the subversion of the status quo need not await a total cultural transformation, but can be pulled off by "insurrectional cells" and "nuclei of confrontation" whose purpose is to set an example for the working class. See Daniel and Gabriel Cohn-Bendit, *Obsolete Communism: The Left-Wing Alternative* (New York: McGraw-Hill, 1969), especially the keen analysis of the working partnership between "empiricist-positivist" sociology and technocratic manipulation, pp. 35–40.

[2] Jacques Ellul, *The Technological Society,* trans. John Wilkinson (New York: A. A. Knopf, 1964), p. 138. This outrageously pessimistic book is thus far the most global effort to depict the technocracy in full operation.

apparent to the non-technical man. Instead, the scale and intricacy of all human activities—political, economic, cultural—transcend the competence of the amateurish citizen and inexorably demand the attention of specially trained experts. Further, around this central core of experts who deal with large-scale public necessities, there grows up a circle of subsidiary experts who, battening on the general social prestige of technical skill in the technocracy, assume authoritative influence over even the most seemingly personal aspects of life: sexual behavior, child-rearing, mental health, recreation, etc. In the technocracy everything aspires to become purely technical, the subject of professional attention. The technocracy is therefore the regime of experts—or of those who can employ the experts. Among its key institutions we find the "think-tank," in which is housed a multi-billion-dollar brainstorming industry that seeks to anticipate and integrate into the social planning quite simply everything on the scene. Thus, even before the general public has become fully aware of new developments, the technocracy has doped them out and laid its plans for adopting or rejecting, promoting or disparaging.[3]

Within such a society, the citizen, confronted by bewildering bigness and complexity, finds it necessary to defer on all matters to those who know better. Indeed, it would be a violation of reason to do otherwise, since it is universally agreed that the prime goal of the society is to keep the productive apparatus turning over efficiently. In the absence of expertise, the great mechanism would surely bog down, leaving us in the midst of chaos and poverty. . . . The roots of the technocracy reach deep into our cultural past and are ultimately entangled in the scientific world-view of the Western tradition. . . . For our purposes here it will be enough to define the technocracy as that society in which those who govern justify themselves by appeal to technical experts who, in turn, justify themselves by appeal to scientific forms of knowledge. And beyond the authority of science, there is no appeal.

Understood in these terms, as the mature product of technological progress and the scientific ethos, the technocracy easily eludes all traditional political categories. Indeed, it is characteristic of the technocracy to render itself ideologically invisible. Its assumptions about reality and its values become as unobtrusively pervasive as the air we breathe. While daily political argument continues within and between the capitalist and collectivist societies of the world, the technocracy increases and consolidates its power in both as a trans-political phenomenon following

[3] For a report on the activities of a typical technocratic brain trust, Herman Kahn's Hudson Institute, see Bowen Northrup's "They Think For Pay," in *The Wall Street Journal*, September 20, 1967. Currently, the Institute is developing strategies to integrate hippies and to exploit the new possibilities of programmed dreams.

the dictates of industrial efficiency, rationality, and necessity. In all these arguments, the technocracy assumes a position similar to that of the purely neutral umpire in an athletic contest. The umpire is normally the least obtrusive person on the scene. Why? Because we give our attention and passionate allegiance to the teams, who compete within the rules; we tend to ignore the man who stands above the contest and who simply interprets and enforces the rules. Yet, in a sense, the umpire is the most significant figure in the game, since he alone sets the limits and goals of the competition and judges the contenders.

The technocracy grows without resistance, even despite its most appalling failures and criminalities, primarily because its potential critics continue trying to cope with these breakdowns in terms of antiquated categories. This or that disaster is blamed by Republicans on Democrats (or vice versa), by Tories on Labourites (or vice versa), by French Communists on Gaullists (or vice versa), by socialists on capitalists (or vice versa), by Maoists on Revisionists (or vice versa). But left, right, and center, these are quarrels between technocrats or between factions who subscribe to technocratic values from first to last. The angry debates of conservative and liberal, radical and reactionary touch everything except the technocracy, because the technocracy is not generally perceived as a political phenomenon in our advanced industrial societies. It holds the place, rather, of a grand cultural imperative which is beyond question, beyond discussion.

When any system of politics devours the surrounding culture, we have totalitarianism, the attempt to bring the whole of life under authoritarian control. We are bitterly familiar with totalitarian politics in the form of brutal regimes which achieve their integration by bludgeon and bayonet. But in the case of the technocracy, totalitarianism is perfected because its techniques become progressively more subliminal. The distinctive feature of the regime of experts lies in the fact that, while possessing ample power to coerce, it prefers to charm conformity from us by exploiting our deep-seated commitment to the scientific world-view and by manipulating the securities and creature comforts of the industrial affluence which science has given us.

So subtle and so well rationalized have the arts of technocratic domination become in our advanced industrial societies that even those in the state and/or corporate structure who dominate our lives must find it impossible to conceive of themselves as the agents of a totalitarian control. Rather, they easily see themselves as the conscientious managers of a munificent social system which is, by the very fact of its broadcast affluence, incompatible with any form of exploitation. At worst, the system may contain some distributive inefficiencies. But these are bound to be repaired—in time. And no doubt they will be. Those who gamble that either capitalism or collectivism is, by its very nature, incompatible with a totally efficient technocracy, one which will finally eliminate material poverty and gross physical exploitation, are making a risky wager. It is certainly one of the oldest, but one of the weakest, radical arguments which insists stubbornly that capitalism is *inherently* incapable of laying golden eggs for everyone.

The great secret of the technocracy lies, then, in its capacity to convince us of three interlocking premises. They are:

1. That the vital needs of man are (contrary to everything the great souls of history have told us) purely technical in character. Meaning: the requirements of our humanity yield wholly to some manner of formal analysis which can be carried out by specialists possessing certain impenetrable skills and which can then be translated by them directly into a congeries of social and economic programs, personnel management procedures, merchandise, and mechanical gadgetry. If a problem does not have such a technical solution, it must not be a *real* problem. It is but an illusion—a figment born of some regressive cultural tendency.

2. That this formal (and highly esoteric) analysis of our needs has now achieved 99 per cent completion. Thus, with minor hitches and snags on the part of irrational elements in our midst, the prerequisites of human fulfillment have all but been satisfied. It is this assumption which leads to the conclusion that wherever social friction appears in the technocracy, it must be due to what is called a "breakdown in communication." For where human happiness has been so precisely calibrated and where the powers that be are so utterly well intentioned, controversy could not possibly derive from a substantive issue, but only from misunderstanding. Thus we need only sit down and reason together and all will be well.

3. That the experts who have fathomed our heart's desires and who alone can continue providing for our needs, the experts who *really* know what they're talking about, all happen to be on the official payroll of the state and/or corporate structure. The experts who count are the certified experts. And the certified experts belong to headquarters.

One need not strain to hear the voice of the technocrat in our society. It speaks strong and clear, and from high places. For example:

Today these old sweeping issues have largely disappeared. The central domestic problems of our time are more subtle and less simple. They relate not to basic clashes of philosophy or ideology, but to ways and means of reaching common goals—to research for sophisticated solutions to complex and obstinate issues. . . .

What is at stake in our economic decisions today is not some grand warfare of rival ideologies which will sweep the country with passion, but the practical management of a modern economy. What we need are not labels and clichés but more basic discussion of the sophisticated and technical questions involved in keeping a great economic machinery moving ahead. . . .

I am suggesting that the problems of fiscal and monetary policy in the Sixties as opposed to the kinds of problems we faced in the Thirties demand subtle challenges for which technical answers—not political answers—must be provided.[4]

Or, to offer one more example, which neatly identifies elitist managerialism with reason itself:

Some critics today worry that our democratic, free societies are becoming overmanaged. I would argue that the opposite is true. As paradoxical as it may sound, the real threat to democracy comes, not from overmanagement, but from undermanagement. To undermanage reality is not to keep free. It is simply to let some force other than reason shape reality. That force may be unbridled emotion; it may be greed; it may be aggressiveness; it may be anything other than reason. But whatever it is, if it is not reason that rules man, then man falls short of his potential.

Vital decision-making, particularly in policy matters, must remain at the top. This is partly, though not completely, what the top is for. But rational decision-making depends on having a full range of rational options from which to choose, and successful management organizes the enterprise so that process can best take place. It is a mechanism whereby free men can most efficiently exercise their reason, initiative, creativity and personal responsibility. The adventurous and immensely satisfying task of an efficient organization is to formulate and analyze these options.[5]

Such statements, uttered by obviously competent, obviously enlightened leadership, make abundantly clear the prime strategy of the tech-

[4] John F. Kennedy, "Yale University Commencement Speech," *New York Times,* June 12, 1962, p. 20.

[5] From Robert S. McNamara's recent book *The Essence of Security* (New York: Harper & Row, 1968), pp. 109–10. In the present generation, it is second- and third-level figures like McNamara who are apt to be the technocrats par excellence: the men who stand behind the official façade of leadership and who continue their work despite all superficial changes of government. McNamara's career is almost a paradigm of our new elitist managerialism: from head of Ford to head of Defense Department to head of the World Bank. The final step will surely be the presidency of one of our larger universities or foundations. Clearly it no longer matters *what* a manager manages; it is all a matter of juggling vast magnitudes of things: money, missiles, students . . .

nocracy. It is to level life down to a standard of so-called living that technical expertise can cope with—and then, on that false and exclusive basis, to claim an intimidating omnicompetence over us by its monopoly of the experts. Such is the politics of our mature industrial societies, our truly *modern* societies, where two centuries of aggressive secular skepticism, after ruthlessly eroding the traditionally transcendent ends of life, have concomitantly given us a proficiency of technical means that now oscillates absurdly between the production of frivolous abundance and the production of genocidal munitions. Under the technocracy we become the most scientific of societies; yet, like Kafka's K., men throughout the "developed world" become more and more the bewildered dependents of inaccessible castles wherein inscrutable technicians conjure with their fate. True, the foolproof system again and again bogs down in riot or apathetic rot or the miscalculations of overextended centralization; true, the chronic obscenity of thermonuclear war hovers over it like a gargantuan bird of prey feeding off the bulk of our affluence and intelligence. But the members of the parental generation, storm-tossed by depression, war, and protracted warscare, cling fast to the technocracy for the myopic sense of prosperous security it allows. By what right would they complain against those who intend only the best, who purport to be the agents of democratic consensus, and who invoke the high rhetorical sanction of the scientific world view, our most unimpeachable mythology? How does one take issue with the paternal beneficence of such technocratic Grand Inquisitors? Not only do they provide bread aplenty, but the bread is soft as floss: it takes no effort to chew, and yet is vitamin-enriched.

To be sure, there are those who have not yet been cut in on the material advantages, such as the "other Americans" of our own country. Where this is the case, the result is, inevitably and justifiably, a forceful, indignant campaign fixated on the issue of integrating the excluded into the general affluence. Perhaps there is an exhausting struggle, in the course of which all other values are lost sight of. But, at last (why should we doubt it?), all the disadvantaged minorities are accommodated. And so the base of the technocracy is broadened as it assimilates its wearied challengers. It might almost be a trick, the way such politics works. It is rather like the ruse of inveigling someone you wish to capture to lean all his weight on a door you hold closed—and then, all of a sudden, throwing it open. He not only winds up inside, where you want him, but he comes crashing in full tilt.

In his analysis of this "new authoritarianism," Herbert Marcuse calls our attention especially to the technocracy's "absorbent power": its capacity to provide "satisfaction in a way which generates submission and weakens the rationality of protest." As it approaches maturity, the technocracy does indeed seem capable of anabolizing every form of discontent into its system.

Let us take the time to consider one significant example of such "repressive desublimation" (as Marcuse calls it). The problem is sexuality, traditionally one of the most potent sources of civilized man's discontent. To liberate sexuality would be to create a society in which technocratic discipline would be impossible. But to thwart sexuality outright would create a widespread, explosive resentment that required constant policing; and, besides, this would associate the technocracy with various puritanical traditions that enlightened men cannot but regard as superstitious. The strategy chosen, therefore, is not harsh repression, but rather the *Playboy* version of total permissiveness which now imposes its image upon us in every slick movie and posh magazine that comes along. In the affluent society, we have sex and sex galore—or so we are to believe. But when we look more closely we see that this sybaritic promiscuity wears a special social coloring. It has been assimilated to an income level and social status available only to our well-heeled junior executives and the jet set. After all, what does it cost to rent these yachts full of nymphomaniacal young things in which our playboys sail off for orgiastic swimming parties in the Bahamas? *Real* sex, we are led to believe, is something that goes with the best scotch, twenty-seven-dollar sunglasses, and platinum-tipped shoelaces. Anything less is a shabby substitute. Yes, there is permissiveness in the technocratic society; but it is only for the swingers and the big spenders. It is the reward that goes to reliable, politically safe henchmen of the status quo. Before our would-be playboy can be an assembly-line seducer, he must be a loyal employee.

Moreover, *Playboy* sexuality is, ideally, casual, frolicsome, and vastly promiscuous. It is the anonymous sex of the harem. It creates no binding loyalties, no personal attachments, no distractions from one's primary responsibilities—which are to the company, to one's career and social position, and to the system generally. The perfect playboy practices a career enveloped by noncommittal trivialities: there is no home, no family, no romance that divides the heart painfully. Life off the job exhausts itself in a constant run of imbecile affluence and impersonal orgasms.

Finally, as a neat little dividend, the ideal of the swinging life we find in *Playboy* gives us a conception of femininity which is indistinguishable from social idiocy. The woman becomes a mere playmate, a submissive bunny, a mindless decoration. At a stroke, half the population is reduced to being the inconsequential entertainment of the technocracy's pampered elite.

As with sexuality, so with every other aspect of life. The business of inventing and flourishing treacherous parodies of freedom, joy, and fulfillment becomes an indispensable form of social control under the technocracy. In all walks of life, image makers and public relations specialists assume greater and greater prominence. The regime of experts relies on a lieutenancy of counterfeiters who seek to integrate the discontent born of thwarted aspiration by way of clever falsification.

Thus:

We call it "education," the "life of the mind," the "pursuit of the truth." But it is a matter of machine-tooling the young to the needs of our various baroque bureaucracies: corporate, governmental, military, trade union, educational.

We call it "free enterprise." But it is a vastly restrictive system of oligopolistic market manipulation, tied by institutionalized corruption to the greatest munitions boondoggle in history and dedicated to infantilizing the public by turning it into a herd of compulsive consumers.

We call it "creative leisure": finger painting and ceramics in the university extension, tropic holidays, grand athletic excursions to the far mountains and the sunny beaches of the earth. But it is, like our sexual longings, an expensive adjunct of careerist high-achievement: the prize that goes to the dependable hireling.

We call it "pluralism." But it is a matter of the public authorities solemnly affirming everybody's right to his own opinion as an excuse for ignoring anybody's troubling challenge. In such a pluralism, critical viewpoints become mere private prayers offered at the altar of an inconsequential conception of free speech.

We call it "democracy." But it is a matter of public opinion polling in which a "random sample" is asked to nod or wag the head in response to a set of prefabricated alternatives, usually related to the *faits accompli* of decision makers, who can always construe the polls to serve their own ends. Thus, if 80 per cent think it is a "mistake" that we ever "went into" Vietnam, but 51 per cent think we would "lose prestige" if we "pulled out now," then the "people" have been "consulted" and the war goes on with their "approval."

We call it "debate." But it is a matter of arranging staged encounters between equally noncommittal candidates neatly tailored to fit thirty minutes of prime network time, the object of the exercise being to establish an "image" of competence. If there are interrogators present, they have been hand-picked and their questions rehearsed.

We call it "government by the consent of the governed." But even now, somewhere in the labyrinth of the paramilitary agencies an "area specialist" neither you nor I elected is dispatching "special advisers" to a distant "trouble spot" which will be the next Vietnam. And somewhere in the depths of the oceans a submarine commander neither you nor I elected is piloting a craft equipped with firepower capable of cataclysmic devastation and perhaps trying to decide if—for reasons neither you or I know—the time has come to push the button.

It is all called being "free," being "happy," being the "Great Society."

From the standpoint of the traditional left, the vices of contemporary America we mention here are easily explained—and indeed too easily. The evils stem simply from the unrestricted pursuit of profit. Behind the manipulative deceptions there are capitalist desperados holding up the society for all the loot they can lay hands on.

To be sure, the desperados are there, and they are a plague of the society. For a capitalist technocracy, profiteering will always be a central incentive and major corrupting influence. Yet even in our society, profit taking no longer holds its primacy as an evidence of organizational success, as one might suspect if for no other reason than that our largest industrial enterprises can now safely count on an uninterrupted stream of comfortably high earnings. At this point, considerations of an entirely different order come into play among the managers, as Seymour Melman reminds us when he observes:

> The "fixed" nature of industrial investment represented by machinery and structures means that large parts of the costs of any accounting period must be assigned in an arbitrary way. Hence, the magnitude of profits shown in any accounting period varies entirely according to the regulations made by the management itself for assigning its "fixed" charges. Hence, profit has ceased to be the economists' independent measure of success or failure of the enterprise. We can define the systematic quality in the behavior and management of large industrial enterprises not in terms of profits, but in terms of their acting to maintain or to extend the production decision power they wield. Production decision power can be gauged by the number of people employed, or whose work is directed, by the proportion of given markets that a management dominates, by the size of the capital investment that is controlled, by the number of other managements whose decisions are controlled. Toward these ends profits are an instrumental device—subordinated in given accounting periods to the extension of decision power.[6]

Which is to say that capitalist enterprise now enters the stage at which large-scale social integration and control become paramount interests in and of themselves: the corporations begin to behave like public authorities concerned with rationalizing the total economy. If profit remains an important lubricant of the system, we should recognize that other systems may very well use different lubricants to achieve the same

---

[6] Seymour Melman, "Priorities and the State Machine," *New University Thought*, Winter 1966–67, pp. 17–18.

end of perfected, centralized organization. But in so doing they still constitute *technocratic* systems drawing upon their own inducements.

In the example given above of *Playboy* permissiveness, the instruments used to integrate sexuality into industrial rationality have to do with high income and extravagant merchandizing. Under the Nazis, however, youth camps and party courtesans were used for the same integrative purpose—as were the concentration camps, where the kinkier members of the elite were rewarded by being allowed free exercise of their tastes. In this case, sexual freedom was not assimilated to income level or prestige consumption, but to party privilege. If the communist regimes of the world have not yet found ways to institutionalize sexual permissiveness, it is because the party organizations are still under the control of grim old men whose puritanism dates back to the days of primitive accumulation. But can we doubt that once these dismal characters pass from the scene—say, when we have a Soviet version of Kennedy-generation leadership—we shall hear of topless bathing parties at the Black Sea resorts and of orgiastic goings-on in the *dachas?* By then, the good apparatchiks and industrial commissars will also acquire the perquisite of admission to the swinging life.

It is essential to realize that the technocracy is not the exclusive product of that old devil capitalism. Rather, it is the product of a mature and accelerating industrialism. The profiteering could be eliminated; the technocracy would remain in force. The key problem we have to deal with is the paternalism of expertise within a socioeconomic system which is so organized that it is inextricably beholden to expertise. And, moreover, to an expertise which has learned a thousand ways to manipulate our acquiescence with an imperceptible subtlety.

Perhaps the clearest way to illustrate the point, before we finish with this brief characterization of the technocracy, is to take an example of such technician-paternalism from a non-capitalist institution of impeccable idealism: the British National Health Service. Whatever its shortcomings, the NHS is one of the most highly principled achievements of British socialism, a brave effort to make medical science the efficient servant of its society. But of course, as time goes on, the NHS will have to grow and adapt to the needs of a maturing industrial order. In June, 1968, the BBC (TV) produced a documentary study of the NHS which gave special emphasis to some of the "forward thinking" that now transpires among the experts who contemplate the future responsibilities of the service. Among them, the feeling was unmistakably marked that the NHS is presently burdened with too much lay interference, and that the service will never achieve its full potential until it is placed in the hands of professionally competent administrators.

What might one expect from these professionals, then? For one thing, better designed and equipped—notably, more automated—hospitals.

Sensible enough, one might think. But beyond this point, the brainstorming surveyed by the documentary became really ambitious—and, mind, what follows are perfectly straight, perfectly serious proposals set forth by respected specialists in their fields. No put-ons and no dire warnings these, but hard-nosed attempts to be practical about the future on the part of men who talked in terms of "realities" and "necessities."

The NHS, it was suggested, would have to look forward to the day when its psychiatric facilities would take on the job of certifying "normal" behavior and of adjusting the "abnormal"—meaning those who were "unhappy and ineffectual"—to the exacting demands of modern society. Thus the NHS would become a "Ministry of Well-Being," and psychiatric manipulation would probably become its largest single duty.

Further: the NHS would have to take greater responsibility for population planning—which would include administration of a program of "voluntary euthanasia" for the unproductive and incompetent elderly. The NHS might have to enforce a program of compulsory contraception upon all adolescents, who would, in later life, have to apply to the Service for permission to produce children. It would then be the job of the NHS to evaluate the genetic qualities of prospective parents before granting clearance to beget.[7]

How are we to describe thinking of this kind? Is it "left-wing" or "right-wing"? Is it liberal or reactionary? Is it a vice of capitalism or socialism? The answer is: it is none of these. The experts who think this way are no longer part of such political dichotomies. Their stance is that of men who have risen above ideology—and so they have, insofar as the traditional ideologies are concerned. They are simply—the experts. They talk of facts and probabilities and practical solutions. Their politics *is* the technocracy: the relentless quest for efficiency, for order, for ever more extensive rational control. Parties and governments may come and go, but the experts stay on forever. Because without them, the system does not work. The machine stops. And *then* where are we?

How do the traditional left-wing ideologies equip us to protest against such well-intentioned use of up-to-date technical expertise for the purpose of making our lives more comfortable and secure? The answer is: they don't. After all, locked into this leviathan industrial apparatus as we are, where shall we turn for solutions to our dilemmas if not to the experts? Or are we, at this late stage of the game, to relinquish our trust

[7] The program referred to is the documentary "Something for Nothing," produced for BBC-1 by James Burke and shown in London on June 27, 1968. In a 1968 symposium on euthanasia, Dr. Eliot Slater, editor of the *British Journal of Psychiatry,* was of the opinion that even if the elderly retain their vigor, they suffer from the defect of an innate conservatism. "Just as in the mechanical world, advances occur most rapidly where new models are being constantly produced, with consequent rapid obsolescence of the old, so too it is in the world of nature." Quoted in "Times Diary," *The Times* (London), July 5, 1968, p. 10.

in science? in reason? in the technical intelligence that built the system in the first place?

It is precisely to questions of this order that the dissenting young address themselves in manifestoes like this one pinned to the main entrance of the embattled Sorbonne in May, 1968:

> The revolution which is beginning will call in question not only capitalist society but industrial society. The consumer's society must perish of a violent death. The society of alienation must disappear from history. We are inventing a new and original world. Imagination is seizing power.[8]

Why should it be the young who rise most noticeably in protest against the expansion of the technocracy?

There is no way around the most obvious answer of all: the young stand forth so prominently because they act against a background of nearly pathological passivity on the part of the adult generation. It would only be by reducing our conception of citizenship to absolute zero that we could get our senior generation off the hook for its astonishing default. The adults of the World War II period, trapped as they have been in the frozen posture of befuddled docility—the condition Paul Goodman has called "the nothing can be done disease"—have in effect divested themselves of their adulthood, if that term means anything more than being tall and debt-worried and capable of buying liquor without having to show one's driver's license. Which is to say: they have surrendered their responsibility for making morally demanding decisions, for generating ideals, for controlling public authority, for safeguarding the society against its despoilers.

Why and how this generation lost control of the institutions that hold sway over its life is more than we can go into here. The remembered background of economic collapse in the thirties, the grand distraction and fatigue of the war, the pathetic if understandable search for security and relaxation afterwards, the bedazzlement of the new prosperity, a sheer defensive numbness in the face of thermonuclear terror and the protracted state of international emergency during the late forties and fifties, the red-baiting and witch-hunting and out-and-out barbarism of the McCarthy years—no doubt all these played their part. And there is also the rapidity and momentum with which technocratic totalitarianism came rolling out of the war years and the early cold war era, drawing on heavy wartime industrial investments, the emergency centralization of decision making, and the awe-stricken public reverence for science. The situation descended swiftly and ponderously. Perhaps no society

[8] From *The Times* (London), May 17, 1968: Edward Mortimer's report from Paris.

could have kept its presence of mind; certainly ours didn't. And the failure was not only American. Nicola Chiaromonte, seeking to explain the restiveness of Italian youth, observes,

> . . . the young—those born after 1940—find themselves living in a society that neither commands nor deserves respect. . . . For has modern man, in his collective existence, laid claim to any god or ideal but the god of possession and enjoyment and the limitless satisfaction of material needs? Has he put forward any reason for working but the reward of pleasure and prosperity? Has he, in fact, evolved anything but this "consumer society" that is so easily and falsely repudiated? [9]

On the American scene, this was the parental generation whose god Allen Ginsberg identified back in the mid-fifties as the sterile and omnivorous "Moloch." It is the generation whose premature senility Dwight Eisenhower so marvelously incarnated and the disease of whose soul shone so lugubriously through the public obscenities that men like John Foster Dulles and Herman Kahn and Edward Teller were prepared to call "policy." There are never many clear landmarks in affairs of the spirit, but Ginsberg's *Howl* may serve as the most public report announcing the war of the generations. It can be coupled with a few other significant phenomena. One of them would be the appearance of *MAD* magazine, which has since become standard reading material for the junior high school population. True, the dissent of *MAD* often sticks at about the Katzenjammer Kids level: but nevertheless the nasty cynicism *MAD* began applying to the American way of life—politics, advertising, mass media, education—has had its effect. *MAD* brought into the malt shops the same angry abuse of middle-class America which comics like Mort Sahl and Lenny Bruce were to begin bringing into the night clubs of the mid-fifties. The kids who were twelve when *MAD* first appeared are in their early twenties now—and they have had a decade's experience in treating the stuff of their parents' lives as contemptible laughing stock.

At a more significant intellectual level, Ginsberg and the beatniks can be associated chronologically with the aggressively activist sociology of C. Wright Mills—let us say with the publication of Mills' *Causes of World War III* (1957), which is about the point at which Mills' writing

[9] The "falsely" in this quotation relates to Chiaromonte's very astute analysis of a doctrinaire blind spot in the outlook of Italian youth—namely their tendency to identify the technocracy with capitalism, which, as I have suggested, is a general failing of European youth movements. This very shrewd article appears in *Encounter,* July, 1968, pp. 25–27. Chiaromonte does not mention the factor of fascism in Italy, but certainly in Germany the cleavage between young and old has been driven deeper than anything we know in America by the older generation's complicity with Nazism.

turned from scholarship to first-class pamphleteering. Mills was by no means the first postwar figure who sought to tell it like it is about the state of American public life and culture; the valiant groups that maintained radical journals like *Liberation* and *Dissent* had been filling the wilderness with their cries for quite as long. And as far back as the end of the war, Paul Goodman and Dwight Macdonald were doing an even shrewder job of analyzing technocratic America than Mills was ever to do—and without relinquishing their humanitarian tone. But it was Mills who caught on. His tone was more blatant; his rhetoric, catchier. He was the successful academic who suddenly began to cry for action in a lethargic profession, in a lethargic society. He was prepared to step forth and brazenly pin his indictment like a target to the enemy's chest. And by the time he finished playing Emile Zola he had marked out just about everybody in sight for accusation.

Most important, Mills was lucky enough to discover ears that would hear: his indignation found an audience. But the New Left he was looking for when he died in 1961 did not appear among his peers. It appeared among the students—and just about nowhere else. If Mills were alive today, his following would still be among the under thirties. . . .

Admittedly, the dissent that began to simmer in the mid-fifties was not confined to the young. The year 1957 saw the creation at the adult level of resistance efforts like SANE and, a bit later, Turn Toward Peace. But precisely what do groups like SANE and TTP tell us about adult America, even where we are dealing with politically conscious elements? Looking back, one is struck by their absurd shallowness and conformism, their total unwillingness to raise fundamental issues about the quality of American life, their fastidious anticommunism, and above all their incapacity to sustain any significant initiative on the political landscape. Even the Committee of Correspondence, a promising effort on the part of senior academics (formed around 1961) quickly settled for publishing a new journal. Currently the diminishing remnants of SANE and TTP seem to have been reduced to the role of carping (often with a deal of justice) at the impetuous extremes and leftist flirtations of far more dynamic youth groups like the Students for a Democratic Society, or the Berkeley Vietnam Day Committee, or the 1967 Spring Mobilization. But avuncular carping is not initiative. And it is a bore, even if a well-intentioned bore, when it becomes a major preoccupation. Similarly, it is the younger Negro groups that have begun to steal the fire from adult organizations—but in this case with results that I feel are apt to be disastrous.

The fact is, it is the young who have in their own amateurish, even grotesque way, gotten dissent off the adult drawing board. They have torn it out of the books and journals an older generation of radicals authored, and they have fashioned it into a style of life. They have turned the hypotheses of disgruntled elders into experiments, though often without the willingness to admit that one may have to concede failure at the end of any true experiment.

When all is said and done, however, one cannot help being ambivalent toward this compensatory dynamism of the young. For it is, at last, symptomatic of a thoroughly diseased state of affairs. It is not ideal, it is probably not even good that the young should bear so great a responsibility for inventing or initiating for their society as a whole. It is too big a job for them to do successfully. It is indeed tragic that in a crisis that demands the tact and wisdom of maturity, everything that looks most hopeful in our culture should be building from scratch—as must be the case when the builders are absolute beginners.

Beyond the parental default, there are a number of social and psychic facts of life that help explain the prominence of the dissenting young in our culture. In a number of ways, this new generation happens to be particularly well placed and primed for action.

Most obviously, the society is getting younger—to the extent that in America, as in a number of European countries, a bit more than 50 per cent of the population is under twenty-five years of age. Even if one grants that people in their mid-twenties have no business claiming, or letting themselves be claimed for, the status of "youth," there still remains among the authentically young in the thirteen to nineteen bracket a small nation of twenty-five million people. (As we shall see below, however, there is good reason to group the mid-twenties with their adolescent juniors.)

But numbers alone do not account for the aggressive prominence of contemporary youth. More important, the young seem to *feel* the potential power of their numbers as never before. No doubt to a great extent this is because the market apparatus of our consumer society has devoted a deal of wit to cultivating the age-consciousness of old and young alike. Teen-agers alone control a stupendous amount of money and enjoy much leisure; so, inevitably, they have been turned into a self-conscious market. They have been pampered, exploited, idolized, and made almost nauseatingly much of. With the result that whatever the young have fashioned for themselves has rapidly been rendered grist for the commercial mill and cynically merchandised by assorted hucksters—*including* the new ethos of dissent, a fact that creates an agonizing disorientation for the dissenting young (and their critics) and to which we will return presently.

The force of the market has not been the only factor in intensifying age-consciousness, however. The expansion of higher education has done even more in this direction. In the United States we have a college population of nearly six million, an increase of more than double over 1950. And the expansion continues as college falls more and more into the standard educational pattern of the middle-class young.[10] Just as the dark satanic mills of early industrialism concentrated labor and helped create the class-consciousness of the proletariat, so the university campus, where up to thirty thousand students may be gathered, has served to crystallize the group identity of the young—with the important effect of mingling freshmen of seventeen and eighteen with graduate students well away in their twenties. On the major campuses, it is often enough the graduates who assume positions of leadership, contributing to student movements a degree of competence that the younger students could not muster. When one includes in this alliance that significant new entity, the non-student—the campus roustabout who may be in his late twenties—one sees why "youth" has become such a long-term career these days. The grads and the non-students easily come to identify their interests and allegiance with a distinctly younger age group. In previous generations, they would long since have left these youngsters behind. But now they and the freshmen just out of high school find themselves all together in one campus community.

The role of these campus elders is crucial, for they tend to be those who have the most vivid realization of the new economic role of the university. Being closer to the technocratic careers for which higher education is supposed to be grooming them in the Great Society, they have a delicate sensitivity to the social regimentation that imminently confronts them, and a stronger sense of the potential power with which the society's need for trained personnel endows them. In some cases their restiveness springs from a bread-and-butter awareness of the basic facts of educational life these days, for in England, Germany, and France the most troublesome students are those who have swelled the numbers in the humanities and social studies only to discover that what the society really wants out of its schools is technicians, not philosophers. In Britain, this strong trend away from the sciences over the past four years continues to provoke annoyed concern from public figures who

[10] The rapid growth of the college population is an international phenomenon, with Germany, Russia, France, Japan, and Czechoslovakia (among the developed countries) equaling or surpassing the increase of the United States. UNESCO statistics for the period 1950–64 are as follows:

	1950	1964	Increase
U.S.A.	2.3 million	5 million	2.2x
U.K.	133,000	211,000	1.6x
U.S.S.R.	1.2 million	3.6 million	3.0x
Italy	192,000	262,000	1.3x
France	140,000	455,000	3.3x
W. Germany	123,000	343,000	2.8x
W. Berlin	12,000	31,000	2.6x
Czechoslovakia	44,000	142,000	3.2x
Japan	391,000	917,000	2.3x
India	404,000	1.1 million	2.2x

are not the least bit embarrassed to reveal their good bourgeois philistinism by loudly observing that the country is not spending its money to produce poets and Egyptologists—and then demanding a sharp cut in university grants and stipends.[11]

Yet at the same time, these non-technicians know that the society cannot do without its universities, that it cannot shut them down or brutalize the students without limit. The universities produce the brains the technocracy needs; therefore, making trouble on the campus is making trouble in one of the economy's vital sectors. And once the graduate students—many of whom may be serving as low-level teaching assistants —have been infected with qualms and aggressive discontents, the junior faculty, with whom they overlap, may soon catch the fevers of dissent and find themselves drawn into the orbit of "youth."

The troubles at Berkeley in late 1966 illustrate the expansiveness of youthful protest. To begin with, a group of undergraduates stages a sit-in against naval recruiters at the Student Union. They are soon joined by a contingent of non-students, whom the administration then martyrs by selective arrest. A non-student of nearly thirty—Mario Savio, already married and a father—is quickly adopted as spokesman for the protest. Finally, the teaching assistants call a strike in support of the menaced demonstration. When at last the agitation comes to its ambiguous conclusion, a rally of thousands gathers outside Sproul Hall, the central administration building, to sing the Beatles' "Yellow Submarine"— which happens to be the current hit on all the local high-school campuses. If "youth" is not the word we are going to use to cover this obstreperous population, then we may have to coin another. But undeniably the social grouping exists with a self-conscious solidarity.

If we ask who is to blame for such troublesome children, there can be only one answer: it is the parents who have equipped them with an anemic superego. The current generation of students is the beneficiary of the particularly permissive child-rearing habits that have been a feature of our postwar society. Dr. Spock's endearing latitudinarianism (go easy on the toilet training, don't panic over masturbation, avoid the heavy discipline) is much more a reflection than a cause of the new (and wise) conception of proper parent-child relations that prevails in our middle class. A high-consumption, leisure-wealthy society simply doesn't need contingents of rigidly trained, "responsible" young workers. It cannot employ more than a fraction of untrained youngsters fresh out of high school. The middle class can therefore afford to prolong the ease and drift of childhood, and so it does. Since nobody expects a child

---

[11] In his 1967 Reith Lectures, Dr. Edmund Leach seeks to account for the steady swing from the sciences. See his *Runaway World*, British Broadcasting Company, 1968. For reflections on the same phenomenon in Germany, see Max Beloff's article in *Encounter*, July, 1968, pp. 28–33.

to learn any marketable skills until he gets to college, high school becomes a country club for which the family pays one's dues. Thus the young are "spoiled," meaning they are influenced to believe that being human has something to do with pleasure and freedom. But unlike their parents, who are also avid for the plenty and leisure of the consumer society, the young have not had to sell themselves for their comforts or to accept them on a part-time basis. Economic security is something they can take for granted—and on it they build a new, uncompromised personality, flawed perhaps by irresponsible ease, but also touched with some outspoken spirit. Unlike their parents, who must kowtow to the organizations from which they win their bread, the youngsters can talk back at home with little fear of being thrown out in the cold. One of the pathetic, but, now we see, promising characteristics of postwar America has been the uppityness of adolescents and the concomitant reduction of the paterfamilias to the general ineffectuality of a Dagwood Bumstead. In every family comedy of the last twenty years, dad has been the buffoon.

The permissiveness of postwar child-rearing has probably seldom met A. S. Neill's standards—but it has been sufficient to arouse expectations. As babies, the middle-class young got picked up when they bawled. As children, they got their kindergarten finger paintings thumbtacked on the living room wall by mothers who knew better than to discourage incipient artistry. As adolescents, they perhaps even got a car of their own (or control of the family's), with all of the sexual privileges attending. They passed through school systems which, dismal as they all are in so many respects, have nevertheless prided themselves since World War II on the introduction of "progressive" classes having to do with "creativity" and "self-expression." These are also the years that saw the proliferation of all the mickey mouse courses which take the self-indulgence of adolescent "life problems" so seriously. Such scholastic pap mixes easily with the commercial world's effort to elaborate a total culture of adolescence based on nothing but fun and games. (What else could a culture of adolescence be based on?) The result has been to make of adolescence, not the beginning of adulthood, but a status in its own right: a limbo that is nothing so much as the prolongation of an already permissive infancy.

To be sure, such an infantization of the middle-class young has a corrupting effect. It ill prepares them for the real world and its unrelenting if ever more subtle disciplines. It allows them to nurse childish fantasies until too late in life; until there comes the inevitable crunch. For as life in the multiversity wears on for these pampered youngsters, the technocratic reality principle begins grimly to demand its concessions. The young get told they are now officially "grown up," but they have been left too long without any taste for the rigidities and hypocrisies that adulthood is supposed to be all about. General Motors all of a sudden wants barbered hair, punctuality, and an appropriate reverence for the conformities of the organizational hierarchy. Washington wants patriotic cannon fodder with no questions asked. Such prospects do not look like fun from the vantage point of between eighteen and twenty years of relatively carefree drifting.[12]

Some of the young (most of them, in fact) summon up the proper sense of responsibility to adjust to the prescribed patterns of adulthood; others, being incorrigibly childish, do not. They continue to assert pleasure and freedom as human rights and begin to ask aggressive questions of those forces that insist, amid obvious affluence, on the continued necessity of discipline, no matter how subliminal. This is why, for example, university administrators are forced to play such a false game with their students, insisting on the one hand that the students are "grown-up, responsible men and women," but on the other hand knowing full well that they dare not entrust such erratic children with any power over their own education. For what can one rely upon them to do that will suit the needs of technocratic regimentation?

The incorrigibles either turn political or drop out. Or perhaps they fluctuate between the two, restless, bewildered, hungry for better ideas about grown-upness than GM or IBM . . . seems able to offer. Since they are improvising their own ideal of adulthood—a task akin to lifting oneself by one's bootstraps—it is all too easy to go pathetically wrong. Some become ne'er-do-well dependents, bumming about the bohemias of America and Europe on money from home; others simply bolt. The FBI reports the arrest of over ninety thousand juvenile runaways in 1966; most of those who flee well-off middle-class homes get picked up by the thousands each current year in the big-city bohemias, fending off malnutrition and venereal disease. The immigration departments of Europe record a constant level over the past few years of something like ten thousand disheveled "flower children" (mostly American, British, German, and Scandinavian) migrating to the Near East and India—usually toward Katmandu (where drugs are cheap and legal) and a deal of hard knocks along the way. The influx has been sufficient to force Iran and Afghanistan to substantially boost the "cash in hand" requirements of prospective tourists. And the British consul-general in Istanbul officially requested Parliament in late 1967 to grant him increased accommodations for the "swarm" of penniless young Englishmen who have been cropping up at the consulate on their way east,

[12] Even the Young Americans for Freedom, who staunchly champion the disciplined virtues of the corporate structure, have become too restive to put up with the indignity of conscription. With full support from Ayn Rand, they have set the draft down as "selective slavery." How long will it be before a conservatism that perceptive recognizes that the ideal of free enterprise has nothing to do with technocratic capitalism?

seeking temporary lodgings or perhaps shelter from Turkish narcotics authorities.[13]

One can flippantly construe this exodus as the contemporary version of running off with the circus; but the more apt parallel might be with the quest of third-century Christians (a similarly scruffy, uncouth, and often half-mad lot) for escape from the corruptions of Hellenistic society: it is much more a flight from than toward. Certainly for a youngster of seventeen, clearing out of the comfortable bosom of the middle-class family to become a beggar is a formidable gesture of dissent. One makes light of it at the expense of ignoring a significant measure of our social health.

So, by way of a dialectic Marx could never have imagined, technocratic America produces a potentially revolutionary element among its own youth. The bourgeoisie, instead of discovering the class enemy in its factories, finds it across the breakfast table in the person of its own pampered children. To be sure, by themselves the young might drift into hopeless confusion and despair. But now we must add one final ingredient to this ebullient culture of youthful dissent, which gives it some chance of achieving form and direction. This is the adult radical who finds himself in a plight which much resembles that of the bourgeois intellectual in Marxist theory. In despair for the timidity and lethargy of his own class, Marx's middle-class revolutionary was supposed at last to turn renegade and defect to the proletariat. So in postwar America, the adult radical, confronted with a diminishing public among the "cheerful robots" of his own generation, naturally gravitates to the restless middle-class young. Where else is he to find an audience? The working class, which provided the traditional following for radical ideology, now neither leads nor follows, but sits tight and plays safe: the stoutest prop of the established order. If the adult radical is white, the ideal of Black Power progressively seals off his entrée to Negro organizations. As for the exploited masses of the Third World, they have as little use for white Western ideologues as our native blacks—and in any case they are far distant. Unless he follows the strenuous example of a Regis Debray, the white American radical can do little more than sympathize from afar with the revolutionary movements of Asia, Africa, and Latin America.

On the other hand, the disaffected middle-class young are at hand, suffering a strange new kind of "immiserization" that comes of being stranded between a permissive childhood and an obnoxiously conformist adulthood, experimenting desperately with new ways of growing up self-respectfully into a world they despise, calling for help. So the radical

[13] For the statistic mentioned, see *Time,* September 15, 1967, pp. 47–49; *The Observer* (London), September 24, 1967; and *The Guardian* (London), November 18, 1967.

adults bid to become gurus to the alienated young or perhaps the young draft them into service.

Of course, the young do not win over all the liberal and radical adults in sight. From more than a few their readiness to experiment with a variety of dissenting life styles comes in for severe stricture—which is bound to be exasperating for the young. What are they to think? For generations, left-wing intellectuals have lambasted the bad habits of bourgeois society. "The bourgeoisie" they have insisted, "is obsessed by greed; its sex life is insipid and prudish; its family patterns are debased; its slavish conformities of dress and grooming are degrading; its mercenary routinization of existence is intolerable; its vision of life is drab and joyless; etc., etc." So the restive young, believing what they hear, begin to try this and that, and one by one they discard the vices of their parents, preferring the less structured ways of their own childhood and adolescence—only to discover many an old-line dissenter, embarrassed by the brazen sexuality and unwashed feet, the disheveled dress and playful ways, taking up the chorus, "No, that is not what I meant. That is not what I meant at all."

For example, a good liberal like Hans Toch invokes the Protestant work ethic to give the hippies a fatherly tonguelashing for their "consuming but noncontributing" ways. They are being "parasitic," Professor Toch observes, for "the hippies, after all accept—even demand—social services, while rejecting the desirability of making a contribution to the economy." [14] But *of course* they do. Because we have an economy of cybernated abundance that does not need their labor, that is rapidly severing the tie between work and wages, that suffers from hard-core poverty due to maldistribution, not scarcity. From this point of view, why is the voluntary dropping-out of the hip young any more "parasitic" than the enforced dropping-out of impoverished ghetto dwellers? The economy can do abundantly without all this labor. How better, then, to spend our affluence than on those minimal goods and services that will support leisure for as many of us as possible? Or are these hippies reprehensible because they seem to enjoy their mendicant idleness, rather than feeling, as the poor apparently should, indignant and fighting mad to get a good respectable forty-hour-week job? There are criticisms to be made of the beat-hip bohemian fringe of our youth culture—but this is surely not one of them.

It would be a better general criticism to make of the young that they

[14] Hans Toch, "The Last Word on the Hippies," *The Nation,* December 4, 1967. See also the jaundiced remarks of Eric Hoffer in the *New York Post Magazine,* September 23, 1967, pp. 32-33; Milton Mayer writing in *The Progressive,* October 1967; and Arnold Wesker's "Delusions of Floral Grandeur" in the English magazine *Envoy,* December 1967.

have done a miserably bad job of dealing with the distortive publicity with which the mass media have burdened their embryonic experiments. Too often they fall into the trap of reacting narcissistically or defensively to their own image in the fun-house mirror of the media. Whatever these things called "beatniks" and "hippies" originally were, or still are, may have nothing to do with what *Time, Esquire, Cheeta,* CBSNBCABC, Broadway comedy, and Hollywood have decided to make of them. Dissent, the press has clearly decided, is hot copy. But if anything, the media tend to isolate the weirdest aberrations *and* consequently to attract to the movement many extroverted poseurs. But what does bohemia do when it finds itself massively infiltrated by well-intentioned sociologists (and we now all of a sudden have specialized "sociologists of adolescence"), sensationalizing journalists, curious tourists, and weekend fellow travelers? What doors does one close on them? The problem is a new and tough one: a kind of cynical smothering of dissent by saturation coverage, and it begins to look like a far more formidable weapon in the hands of the establishment than outright suppression.

Again, in his excellent article on the Italian students quoted above, Nicola Chiaromonte tells us that dissenters

> . . . must detach themselves, must become resolute "heretics." They must detach themselves quietly, without shouting or riots, indeed in silence and secrecy; not alone but in groups, in real "societies" that will create, as far as possible, a life that is independent and wise. . . . It would be . . . a nonrhetorical form of "total rejection."

But how is one to develop such strategies of dignified secrecy when the establishment has discovered exactly the weapon with which to defeat one's purposes: the omniscient mass media? The only way anybody or anything stays underground these days is by trying outlandishly hard—as when Ed Saunders and a group of New York poets titled a private publication *Fuck You* to make sure it stayed off the newsstands. But it can be quite as distortive to spend all one's time evading the electronic eyes and ears of the world as to let oneself be inaccurately reported by them.

Yet to grant the fact that the media distort is not the same as saying that the young have evolved no life style of their own, or that they are unserious about it. We would be surrendering to admass an absolutely destructive potential if we were to take the tack that whatever it touches is automatically debased or perhaps has no reality at all. In London today at some of the better shops one can buy a Chinese Army-style jacket, advertised as "Mao Thoughts in Burberry Country: elegant navy flannel, revolutionary with brass buttons and Mao collar." The cost: £28 . . . a mere $68. Do Mao and the cultural revolution suddenly become mere figments by virtue of such admass larks?

Commercial vulgarization is one of the endemic pests of twentieth-century Western life, like the flies that swarm to sweets in the summer. But the flies don't create the sweets (though they may make them less palatable); nor do they make the summer happen. It will be my contention that there is, despite the fraudulence and folly that collect around its edges, a significant new culture a-borning among our youth, and that this culture deserves careful understanding, if for no other reason than the sheer size of the population it potentially involves.

But there *are* other reasons, namely, the intrinsic value of what the young are making happen. If, however, we want to achieve that understanding, we must insist on passing over the exotic tidbits and sensational case histories the media offer us. Nor should we resort to the superficial snooping that comes of cruising bohemia for a few exciting days in search of local color and the inside dope, often with the intention of writing it all up for the slick magazines. Rather, we should look for major trends that seem to outlast the current fashion. We should try to find the most articulate public statements of belief and value the young have made or have given ear to; the thoughtful formulations, rather than the off-hand gossip. Above all, we must be willing, in a spirit of critical helpfulness, to sort out what seems valuable and promising in this dissenting culture, as if indeed it mattered to us whether the alienated young succeeded in their project.

Granted this requires a deal of patience. For what we are confronted with is a progressive "adolescentization" of dissenting thought and culture, if not on the part of its creators, then on the part of much of its audience. And we should make no mistake about how far back into the early years of adolescence these tastes now reach. Let me offer one illuminating example. In December of 1967, I watched a group of thirteen-year-olds from a London settlement house perform an improvised Christmas play as part of a therapeutic theater program. The kids had concocted a show in which Santa Claus had been imprisoned by the immigration authorities for entering the country without proper permission. The knock at official society was especially stinging, coming as it did instinctively from some very ordinary youngsters who had scarcely been exposed to any advanced intellectual influences. And whom did the thirteen-year-olds decide to introduce as Santa's liberators? An exotic species of being known to them as "the hippies," who shiva-danced to the jailhouse and magically released Father Christmas, accompanied by strobelights and jangling sitars.

However lacking older radicals may find the hippies in authenticity or revolutionary potential, they have clearly succeeded in embodying radical disaffiliation—what Herbert Marcuse has called the Great Refusal—in a form that captures the need of the young for unrestricted joy. The hippy, real or as imagined, now seems to stand as one of the few images toward which the very young can grow without having to give up the childish sense of enchantment and playfulness, perhaps because the hippy keeps one foot in his childhood. Hippies who may be pushing thirty wear buttons that read "Frodo Lives" and decorate their pads with maps of Middle Earth (which happens to be the name of one of London's rock clubs). Is it any wonder that the best and brightest youngsters at Berkeley High School (just to choose the school that happens to be in my neighborhood) are already coming to class barefoot, with flowers in their hair, and ringing with cowbells?

Such developments make clear that the generational revolt is not likely to pass over in a few years' time. The ethos of disaffiliation is still in the process of broadening down through the adolescent years, picking up numbers as time goes on. With the present situation we are perhaps at a stage comparable to the Chartist phase of trade unionism in Great Britain, when the ideals and spirit of a labor movement had been formulated but had not reached anything like class-wide dimensions. Similarly, it is still a small, if boisterous minority of the young who now define the generational conflict. But the conflict will not vanish when those who are now twenty reach thirty; it may only reach its peak when those who are now eleven and twelve reach their late twenties. (Say, about 1984.) We then may discover that what a mere handful of beatniks pioneered in Allen Ginsberg's youth will have become the life-style of millions of college-age young. Is there any other ideal toward which the young can grow that looks half so appealing?

"Nothing," Goethe observed, "is more inadequate than a mature judgment when adopted by an immature mind." When radical intellectuals have to deal with a dissenting public that becomes this young, all kinds of problems accrue. The adolescentization of dissent poses dilemmas as perplexing as the proletarianization of dissent that bedeviled left-wing theorists when it was the working class they had to ally with in their effort to reclaim our culture for the good, the true, and the beautiful. Then it was the horny-handed virtues of the beer hall and the trade union that had to serve as the medium of radical thought. Now it is the youthful exuberance of the rock club, the love-in, the teach-in.

The young, miserably educated as they are, bring with them almost nothing but healthy instincts. The project of building a sophisticated framework of thought atop those instincts is rather like trying to graft an oak tree upon a wildflower. How to sustain the oak tree? More important, how to avoid crushing the wildflower? And yet such is the project that confronts those of us who are concerned with radical social change. For the young have become one of the very few social levers dissent has to work with. This is that "significant soil" in which the Great Refusal has begun to take root. If we reject it in frustration for the youthful follies that also sprout there, where then do we turn?

CHAPTER 4

I ONLY WORK HERE

PHILIP SLATER

Presented in a dispassionate, almost ironic style Philip Slater's essay "I Only Work Here" takes a look at life in contemporary America. In the preface to the book in which it originally appeared, Slater states that his reason for writing the book was to reach some understanding of the social and psychological forces and strains that are ripping our society apart—to call our attention to what people are doing to themselves and each other. Like other selections in this volume, the essay examines the relationship among technology, society, and the quality of life. Slater is vitally concerned about the life-style that so many modern Americans find themselves following because of self-imposed subservience to technology. In the face of today's problems, neither our solutions nor our basic values seem to be working. Instead, we have what Slater sees as a severe gap separating the fantasies Americans live by from the realities amid which they live. Although people seem to know what "happiness" is supposed to look or feel like, and what they must do or buy to achieve it, the goal eludes them. The roots of this condition are planted firmly in the culture and history of the nation. Our present condition is perhaps perceived by most as only a vague feeling of uneasiness—something is not quite right; things just aren't *really* the way they should (or used to) be. While answers appear to be slow in coming, the questions—and more important, the anxiety—persist.

Using this theme as a point of departure, Slater asserts that the inflated fear of radicalism in the United States today is an indication of this unvoiced anxiety. Radical activities are disturbing not because they actually pose a physical threat (in the same way as, say, automobiles do) but because we fear having our innermost doubts about the viability of our socal system and way of life voiced aloud. While our life-style is undoubtedly among the most materially wealthy in the world today, we suffer from a "spiritual impoverishment." Something, Slater suggests, about the social system almost entirely frustrates our efforts to satisfy three basic desires:

1. The desire for community
2. The desire for engagement
3. The desire for dependence

Let us briefly examine each of these and see how the culture has blocked our access to them.

Because of the fierce competition built into the American way of life, the possibility of creating a stable, satisfying community is diminished. Owing to technological change, the extended family and stable neighborhood—two of the social cornerstones of the community—have ceased to have meaning for the majority of Americans. The quality of our social interactions becomes increasingly brittle and abrasive as a larger number of people compete for already scarce resources. The result, predictably, is the lengthening of the social distance already separating people and the encouragement of even more formidable barriers to interaction and concern. This social isolation is most dramatically seen where people appear indifferent to the troubles of their fellows. The case of Kitty Genovese, a young woman who was stabbed to death while a score of people watched and did not even call the police, well illustrates this. Where no feeling of community exists, concern and involvement are, at best, problematic.

This lack of commitment can be linked to our consistent tendency to avoid any real confrontation with persistent social problems. Rather cynically, Slater suggests that many of the people who established and populated America had opted for settlement on a new continent rather than for personal and collective confrontation with the social conditions prevalent in their homelands.

Today, social problems are typically denied and people whose behavior belies our denial are labeled deviant or in some cases, when a law is considered to be breached, quietly removed to an institution. Dealing with problems in this way ensures that we will seldom if ever have the satisfaction of knowing that something was really accomplished. Instead, a process that ultimately takes more than it gives is sustained.

In the interest of rational productivity our society has had to ensure the mobility and dependability of its members. Traditionally, these control functions were assumed and satisfied by the family, religion, and the community. These structures, however, proved counterproductive for the rational society and were replaced by the more mobile nuclear family inhabiting an anonymous neighborhood. Similarly, control of impulse and emotion had to be internalized to ensure that the individual would operate in a predictable way regardless of setting. The complete internalization of the control function can have the effect of stifling the individual from within—of so curbing his emotions that, even when he wants to, he finds that he cannot spontaneously abandon himself to the moment. For such a person, both elation and grief have to be experienced alone. This process of control, Slater suggests, is responsible for the last of the desires—that for dependence. Emotional isolation is as bad as social isolation—the individual very much wants to share responsibility for the control of his impulses and the direction of his life.

American culture, it appears, is rapidly approaching the breaking point. For many, life is becoming increasingly meaningless; simply to "get through the day" requires more self-sacrifice; and the range of alternatives, while seemingly greater, seems to offer even fewer satisfactions. The troublesome presence of today's radicals, malcontents in a land of plenty, propels these feelings into our consciousness. It is not the handful of radicals that troubles us but the knowledge that perhaps, even if in only a small way, they may be *right*.

Philip Slater was born in 1927. He received his higher education at Harvard University, earning a Ph. D. degree in 1955, and has written numerous books and scholarly papers.

> *It's getting hard to be someone,*
> *But it all works out,*
> *It doesn't matter much to me.*
> LENNON AND MCCARTNEY

> *All the lonely people—*
> *Where do they all come from?*
> LENNON AND MCCARTNEY

> *He said his name was Columbus,*
> *And I just said, "good luck."*
> DYLAN

One of the functions of a society is to make its inhabitants feel safe, and Americans devote more of their collective resources to security than to any other need. Yet Americans do not feel safe, despite (or because of) shotguns in the closet and nuclear bombers patrolling overhead. With each decade we seem to accumulate more fears, and most of these fears seem to be about each other. In the fifties we were afraid of native Communists, and although we now feel sheepish about *that* moment of panic we express today the same kinds of fear toward blacks, hippies,

"I Only Work Here" by Philip Slater, pp. 1–29 in *The Pursuit of Loneliness: American Culture at the Breaking Point,* 1970, is reprinted by permission of the publisher, Beacon Press.

and student radicals; and in our reactions to all of those fears we have created some very real dangers.

The contrast between our intense fear of small and comparatively unarmed minorities and the Dawn Patrol bravado with which we respond to serious threats of total extinction is rather striking. During the Cuban missile crisis, for example, people interviewed on the street combined a clear awareness that "this may be World War III" with the kind of cheery blandness that psychiatrists label "schizoid" and "inappropriate" when it occurs in a personal context. Given this lack of concern for an overwhelming threat, how can we account for the exaggerated fear of domestic minorities?

From Freud we learned long ago to suspect, when a fear seems out of proportion, that it has been bloated by a wish; and this seems particularly likely when the danger is defined as a psychological one—an evil influence. We fear storms and wild beasts, but we do not censor them. If we must guard ourselves against evil influences we thereby admit their seductive appeal. Thus the McCarthy era reached its peak after the discovery that a few Americans had responded to Chinese "brainwashing" efforts, and the fear of conversion to Communism was quite explicit in public statements and popular surveys. One survey respondent, for example, made the revealing statement that "so many people in America *are eager* like those soldiers of ours in Korea to fall into the trap set by Communist propaganda." [1] The anticommunism of that period and its institutional residues have served as a kind of political fig leaf.

The same emphasis surrounds our fears of radicalism today. Draft resistance, peace demonstrations, black militance, hippie communes, and student protest are disturbing not because they provide a serious physical danger (equivalent to, say, driving a car), but because we fear having our secret doubts about the viability of our social system voiced aloud. It is not what happens abroad that generates hysteria, but rather what appears to be happening within ourselves. This is why force must be used against the expression of certain ideas—if the ideas pluck a responsive chord counterarguments are difficult to remember, and one must fall back on clubs and tear gas.

But what is the nature of the attraction exerted by radical ideas on unwilling conservatives? We know something about the hopes that tinge the old maid's search for a ravisher under her bed, but we need to understand the seductive impact that informs our enraged fascination with the revolutionary currents of American society. Since the very form of this question rests on certain assumptions about culture and personality, however, let me first make these explicit.

The emotional repertory of human beings is limited and standard. We are built to feel warm, happy, and contented when caressed, to feel angry when frustrated, frightened when attacked, offended when insulted, jealous when excluded, and so on. But every culture holds some of these human reactions to be unacceptable and attempts to warp its participants into some peculiar specialization. Since human beings are malleable within limits, the warping is for the most part successfully achieved, so that some learn not to laugh, some not to cry, some not to love, and some not to hate in situations in which these reactions might appropriately be expressed.

This cultural warping of human emotionality is eased by compartmentalization: there are special times and places and situations where the disparaged responses are permitted, or classes of people who can provide vicarious satisfaction through a conspicuous performance of some kind.

Yet there are always a few of these responses with which every society and every individual has trouble. They must be shouted down continually, although they are usually visible to the outsider. Thus although the Germans, for example, have always placed great stress on order, precision, and obedience to authority, they periodically explode into revolutionary chaos and are driven by romantic *Götterdämmerung* fantasies. In the same way there is a cooperative underside to competitive America, a rich spoofing tradition in ceremonious England, an elaborated pornography in all prudish societies, and so on. Rather than saying Germans are obedient or Anglo-Saxon societies stuffy or puritanical, it is more correct to say that Germans are preoccupied with issues of authority, Anglo-Saxons with the control of emotional and sexual expression, and so forth. Those issues about which members of a given society seem to feel strongly all reveal a conflict one side of which is strongly emphasized, the other side as strongly (but not quite successfully) suppressed.*

These opposing forces are much more equally balanced than the society's participants like to recognize—were this not true there would be no need for suppression. Life would indeed be much less frantic if we were all able to recognize the diversity of responses and feelings within ourselves, and could abandon our somewhat futile efforts to present a monolithic self-portrait to the world. Probably some exaggeration of uniformity is necessary, however, in order for us to act at all, or at least with enough consistency to permit smooth social functioning.

* This kind of thing has been a great boon to literary criticism and biography over the years. Generations of humanists have excited themselves and their readers by showing "contradictions" and "paradoxes" in some real or fictional person's character, simply because a trait and its opposite coexisted in the same person. But in fact traits and their opposites always coexist if the traits are of any intensity, and the whole tradition of cleverly ferreting out paradoxes of character depends upon the psychological naïveté of the reader for its impact. Inadequate psychologies have always been good for business in the academic world.

On the individual level the delicate balance reveals itself through conversion. An individual who "converts" from one orientation to its exact opposite appears to himself and others to have made a gross change, but actually it involves only a very small shift in the balance of a focal and persistent conflict. Just as only one percent of the voting population is needed to reverse the results of an American election, so only one percent of an individual's internal "constituencies" need shift in order to transform him from voluptuary to ascetic, from policeman to criminal, from Communist to anticommunist, or whatever. The opposite sides are as evenly matched as before, and the apparent change merely represents the desperate efforts made by the internal "majority" to consolidate its shaky position of dominance. The individual must expend just as much energy shouting down the new "minority" as he did the old; some of the most dedicated witch hunters of the 1950s, for example, were ex-Communists.

On the societal level there are more outlets for the expression of "minority" themes and sentiments, and reversals of emphasis involve more overlap between the opposing trends. The United States, for example, traditionally one of the most prudish societies in the world, has also long displayed, in a somewhat warped and mechanical way, the greatest profusion of sexual stimuli.

These considerations suggest that the fear of radical movements in America derives much of its intensity from the attraction that such movements have for their opponents—an attraction that must be stifled. But what is it? What is so severely lacking in our society that the assertion of an alternative life style throws so many Americans into panic and rage?

I would like to suggest three human desires that are deeply and uniquely frustrated by American culture:

1. The desire for *community*—the wish to live in trust and fraternal cooperation with one's fellows in a total and visible collective entity
2. The desire for *engagement*—the wish to come directly to grips with social and interpersonal problems and to confront on equal terms an environment which is not composed of ego-extensions
3. The desire for *dependence*—the wish to share responsibility for the control of one's impulses and the direction of one's life

When I say that these three desires are frustrated by American culture, this need not conjure up romantic images of the individual struggling against society. In every case it is fair to say that we participate eagerly in producing the frustration we endure—it is not something merely done to us. For these desires are in each case subordinate to their opposites in that vague entity called the American Character. The thesis . . . is that

Americans have voluntarily created and voluntarily maintain a society which increasingly frustrates and aggravates these secondary yearnings, to the point where they threaten to become primary. Groups that in any way personify this threat are therefore feared in an exaggerated way, and will be until Americans as a group are able to recognize and accept those needs within themselves.

I. COMMUNITY AND COMPETITION

We are so accustomed to living in a society that stresses individualism that we need to be reminded that "collectivism" in a broad sense has always been the more usual lot of mankind, as well as of most other species. Most people in most societies have been born into and died in stable communities in which the subordination of the individual to the welfare of the group was taken for granted, while the aggrandizement of the individual at the expense of his fellows was simply a crime.

This is not to say that competition is an American invention—all societies involve some sort of admixture of cooperative and competitive institutions. But our society lies near or on the competitive extreme, and although it contains cooperative institutions I think it is fair to say that Americans suffer from their relative weakness and peripherality. Studies of business executives have revealed, for example, a deep hunger for an atmosphere of trust and fraternity with their colleagues (with whom they must, in the short run, engage in what Riesman calls "antagonistic cooperation"). The competitive life is a lonely one, and its satisfactions are very short-lived indeed, for each race leads only to a new one.

In the past, as so many have pointed out, there were in our society many oases in which one could take refuge from the frenzied invidiousness of our economic system—institutions such as the extended family and the stable local neighborhood in which one could take pleasure from something other than winning a symbolic victory over one of his fellows. But these have disappeared one by one, leaving the individual more and more in a situation in which he must try to satisfy his affiliative and invidious needs in the same place. This has made the balance a more brittle one—the appeal of cooperative living more seductive, and the need to suppress our longing for it more acute.

In recent decades the principal vehicle for the tolerated expression of this longing has been the mass media. Popular songs and film comedies have continually engaged in a sentimental rejection of the dominant mores, maintaining that the best things in life are free, that love is more important than success, that keeping up with the Joneses is absurd, that personal integrity should take precedence over winning, and so on. But these protestations must be understood for what they are: a safety valve for the dissatisfactions that the modal American experiences when he behaves as he thinks he should. The same man who chuckles and sentimentalizes over a happy-go-lucky hero in a film would view his real-life counterpart as frivolous and irresponsible, and suburbanites who philosophize over their back fence with complete sincerity about their "dog-eat-dog-world," and what-is-it-all-for, and you can't-take-it-with-you, and success-doesn't-make-you-happy-it-just-gives-you-ulcers-and-a-heart-condition—would be enraged should their children pay serious attention to such a viewpoint. Indeed, the degree of rage is, up to a point, a function of the degree of sincerity: if the individual did not feel these things he would not have to fight them so vigorously. The peculiarly exaggerated hostility that hippies tend to arouse suggests that the life they strive for is highly seductive to middle-aged Americans.

The intensity of this reaction can in part be attributed to a kind of circularity that characterizes American individualism. When a value is as strongly held as is individualism in America the illnesses it produces tend to be treated by increasing the dosage, in the same way an alcoholic treats a hangover or a drug addict his withdrawal symptoms. Technological change, mobility, and the individualistic ethos combine to rupture the bonds that tie each individual to a family, a community, a kinship network, a geographical location—bonds that give him a comfortable sense of himself. As this sense of himself erodes, he seeks ways of affirming it. But his efforts at self-enhancement automatically accelerate the very erosion he seeks to halt.

It is easy to produce examples of the many ways in which Americans attempt to minimize, circumvent, or deny the interdependence upon which all human societies are based. We seek a private house, a private means of transportation, a private garden, a private laundry, self-service stores, and do-it-yourself skills of every kind. An enormous technology seems to have set itself the task of making it unnecessary for one human being ever to ask anything of another in the course of going about his daily business. Even within the family Americans are unique in their feeling that each member should have a separate room, and even a separate telephone, television, and car, when economically possible. We seek more and more privacy, and feel more and more alienated and lonely when we get it. What accidental contacts we do have, furthermore, seem more intrusive, not only because they are unsought but because they are unconnected with any familiar pattern of interdependence.

Most important, our encounters with others tend increasingly to be competitive as a result of the search for privacy. We less and less often meet our fellow man to share and exchange, and more and more often encounter him as an impediment or a nuisance: making the highway crowded when we are rushing somewhere, cluttering and littering the beach or park or wood, pushing in front of us at the supermarket, taking the last parking place, polluting our air and water, building a highway through our house, blocking our view, and so on. Because we have cut off so much communication with each other we keep bumping into each other, and thus a higher and higher percentage of our interpersonal contacts are abrasive.

We seem unable to foresee that the gratification of a wish might turn out to be something of a monkey's paw if the wish were shared by many others. We cheer the new road that initially shaves ten minutes off the drive to our country retreat but ultimately transforms it into a crowded resort and increases both the traffic and the time. We are continually surprised to find, when we want something, that thousands or millions of others want it, too—that other human beings get hot in summer and cold in winter. The worst traffic jams occur when a mass of vacationing tourists departs for home early to "beat the traffic." We are too enamored of the individualistic fantasy that everyone is, or should be, different—that each person could somehow build his entire life around some single, unique eccentricity without boring himself and everyone else to death. Each of us of course has his quirks, which provide a surface variety that is briefly entertaining, but aside from this human beings have little basis for their persistent claim that they are not all members of the same species.

Since our contacts with others are increasingly competitive, unanticipated, and abrasive, we seek still more apartness and accelerate the trend. The desire to be somehow special inaugurates an even more competitive quest for progressively more rare and expensive symbols—a quest that is ultimately futile since it is individualism itself that produces uniformity.

This is poorly understood by Americans, who tend to confuse uniformity with "conformity," in the sense of compliance with or submission to group demands. Many societies exert far more pressure on the individual to mold himself to fit a particularized segment of a total group pattern, but there is variation among these circumscribed roles. Our society gives far more leeway to the individual to pursue his own ends, but, since *it* defines what is worthy and desirable, everyone tends, independently but monotonously, to pursue the same things in the same way. The first pattern combines cooperation, conformity, and variety; the second, competition, individualism, and uniformity.

These relationships are exemplified by two familiar processes in contemporary America: the flight to the suburb and the do-it-yourself movement. Both attempt to deny human interdependence and pursue unrealistic fantasies of self-sufficiency. The first tries to overlook our dependence upon the city for the maintenance of the level of culture we demand. "Civilized" means, literally, "citified," and the state of the city is an accurate index of the condition of the culture as a whole. We behave toward our cities like an irascible farmer who never feeds his cow and then kicks her when she fails to give enough milk. But the flight to the suburb is in any case self-defeating, its goals subverted by the mass quality of the exodus. The suburban dweller seeks peace, privacy, nature, community, and a child-rearing environment which is healthy and culturally optimal. Instead he finds neither the beauty and serenity of the countryside, the stimulation of the city, nor the stability and sense of community of the small town, and his children are exposed to a cultural deprivation equaling that of any slum child with a television set. Living in a narrow age-graded and class-segregated society, it is little wonder that suburban families have contributed so little to the national talent pool in proportion to their numbers, wealth, and other social advantages.* And this transplantation, which has caused the transplants to atrophy, has blighted the countryside and impoverished the city. A final irony of the suburban dream is that, for many Americans, reaching the pinnacle of one's social ambitions (owning a house in the suburbs) requires one to perform all kinds of menial tasks (carrying garbage cans, mowing lawns, shoveling snow, and so on) that were performed for him when he occupied a less exalted status.

Some of this manual labor, however, is voluntary—an attempt to deny the elaborate division of labor required in a complex society. Many Americans seem quite willing to pay this price for their reluctance to engage in interpersonal encounters with servants and artisans—a price which is rather high unless the householder particularly relishes the work (some find in it a tangible relief from the intangibles they manipulate in their own jobs) or is especially good at it, or cannot command a higher rate of pay in the job market than the servant or artisan.

The do-it-yourself movement has accompanied, paradoxically, increasing specialization in the occupational sphere. As one's job narrows, perhaps, one seeks the challenge of new skill-acquisition in the home. But specialization also means that one's interpersonal encounters with artisans in the home proliferate and become more impersonal. It is not a matter of a familiar encounter with the local smith or grocer—a few well-known individuals performing a relatively large number of functions, and with whom one's casual interpersonal contacts may be a source of satisfaction, and are in any case a testimony to the stability and

---

* Using cities, small towns, and rural areas for comparison. The small Midwestern town achieves its legendary dullness by a process akin to evaporation—all the warm and energetic particles depart for coastal cities, leaving their place of origin colder and flatter than they found it. But the restless spirit in a small town knows he lives in the sticks and has a limited range of experience, while his suburban counterpart can sustain an illusion of cosmopolitanism in an environment which is far more constricted (a small town is a microcosm, a suburb merely a layer).

meaningful interrelatedness of human affairs. One finds instead a multiplicity of narrow specialists—each perhaps a stranger (the same type of repair may be performed by a different person each time). Every relationship, such as it is, must start from scratch, and it is small wonder that the householder turns away from such an unrewarding prospect in apathy and despair.

Americans thus find themselves in a vicious circle, in which their extrafamilial relationships are increasingly arduous, competitive, trivial, and irksome, in part as a result of efforts to avoid or minimize potentially irksome or competitive relationships. As the few vestiges of stable and familiar community life erode, the desire for a simple, cooperative life style grows in intensity. The most seductive appeal of radical ideologies for Americans consists in the fact that all in one way or another attack the competitive foundations of our society. Each touches a responsive doubt, and the stimuli arousing this doubt must be carefully unearthed and rooted out, just as the Puritan must unearth and root out the sexual stimuli that excite him.*

Now it may be objected that American society is far less competitive than it once was, and the appeal of radical ideologies should hence be diminished. A generation of critics has argued that the entrepreneurial individualist of the past has been replaced by a bureaucratic, security-minded, Organization Man. Much of this historical drama was written through the simple device of comparing yesterday's owner-president with today's assistant sales manager; certainly these nostalgia-merchants never visited a nineteenth-century company town. Another distortion is introduced by the fact that it was only the most ruthlessly competitive robber barons who survived to tell us how it was. Little is written about the neighborhood store that extended credit to the poor, or the small town industry that refused to lay off local workers in hard times—they all went under together. And as for the organization men—they left us no sagas.

Despite these biases real changes have undoubtedly occurred, but even if we grant that the business world as such was more competitive, the total environment contained more cooperative, stable, and personal elements. The individual worked in a smaller firm with lower turnover in which his relationships were more enduring and less impersonal, and in which the ideology of Adam Smith was tempered by the fact

---

* Both efforts are ambivalent, since the "seek and destroy" process is in part a quest for the stimulus itself. The Puritanical censor both wants the sexual stimulus and wants to destroy it, and his job enables him to gratify both of these "contradictory" desires. There is a similar prurience in the efforts of groups such as the House Un-American Activities Committee to "uncover subversion." Just as the censor gets to experience far more pornography than the average man, so the Congressional red-baiter gets to hear as much Communist ideology as he wants, which is apparently quite a lot.

that the participants were neighbors and might have been childhood playmates. Even if the business world was as "dog-eat-dog" as we imagine it (which seems highly unlikely), one encountered it as a deviant episode in what was otherwise a more comfortable and familiar environment that the organization man can find today in or out of his office. The organization man complex is simply an attempt to restore the personal, particularistic, paternalistic environment of the family business and the company town; and the other-directed "group-think" of the suburban community is a desperate attempt to bring some old-fashioned small-town collectivism into the transient and impersonal life-style of the suburb. The social critics of the 1950s were so preoccupied with assailing these rather synthetic substitutes for traditional forms of human interdependence that they lost sight of the underlying pathogenic forces that produced them. Medical symptoms usually result from attempts made by the body to counteract disease, and attacking such symptoms often aggravates and prolongs the illness. This appears to be the case with the feeble and self-defeating efforts of twentieth-century Americans to find themselves a viable social context.

II. ENGAGEMENT AND UNINVOLVEMENT

Many of the phenomena we have discussed can also be linked to a compulsive American tendency to avoid confrontation of chronic social problems. This avoiding tendency often comes as a surprise to foreigners, who tend to think of Americans as pragmatic and down-to-earth. But while trying to solve long-range social problems with short-run "hardware" solutions produces a lot of hardware—a down-to-earth result, surely—it can hardly be considered practical when it aggravates the problems, as it almost always does. American pragmatism is deeply irrational in this respect, and in our hearts we have always known it. One of the favorite themes of American cartoonists is the man who paints himself into a corner, saws off the limb he is sitting on, or runs out of space on the sign he is printing. The scientist of science-fiction and horror films, whose experimentation leads to disastrously unforeseen consequences, is a more anxious representation of this same awareness that the most future-oriented nation in the world shows a deep incapacity to plan ahead. We are, as a people, perturbed by our inability to anticipate the consequences of our acts, but we still wait optimistically for some magic telegram, informing us that the tangled skein of misery and self-deception into which we have woven ourselves has vanished in the night. Each month popular magazines regale their readers with such telegrams: announcing that our transportation crisis will be solved by a bigger plane or a wider road, mental illness with a pill, poverty with a law, slums with a bulldozer, urban conflict with a gas, racism with a goodwill gesture. Perhaps the most grotesque of all these telegrams was an article in *Life* showing a group of suburbanites participating in a "Clean-Up Day" in an urban slum. Foreigners are surprised when Americans exhibit this kind of naïveté and/or cynicism about social problems, but their surprise is inappropriate. Whatever realism we may display in technical areas, our approach to social issues inevitably falls back on cinematic tradition, in which social problems are resolved by gesture. Deeply embedded in the somnolent social consciousness of the broomwielding suburbanites is a series of climactic movie scenes in which a long column of once surly natives, marching in solemn silence and as one man, framed by the setting sun, turn in their weapons to the white chief who has done them a good turn, or menace the white adventurer's enemy (who turns pale at the sight), or rebuild the missionary's church, destroyed by fire.

When a social problem persists (as they tend to do) longer than a few days, those who call attention to its continued presence are viewed as "going too far" and "causing the pendulum to swing the other way." We can make war on poverty but shrink from the extensive readjustments required to stop breeding it. Once a law is passed, a commission set up, a study made, a report written, the problem is expected to have been "wiped out" or "mopped up." Bombs abroad are matched by "crash programs" at home—the terminological similarity reveals a psychological one. Our approach to transportation problems has had the effect, as many people have observed, of making it easier and easier to travel to more and more places that have become less and less worth driving to. Asking us to consider the manifold consequences of chopping down a forest, draining a swamp, spraying a field with poison, making it easier to drive into an already crowded city, or selling deadly weapons to everyone who wants them arouses in us the same impatience as a chess problem would in a hyperactive six-year-old.

The avoiding tendency lies at the very root of American character. This nation was settled and continuously repopulated by people who were not personally successful in confronting the social conditions obtaining in their mother country, but fled these conditions in the hope of a better life. This series of choices (reproduced in the westward movement) provided a complex selection process—populating America disproportionately with a certain kind of person.

In the past we have always, explicitly or implicitly, stressed the positive side of this selection, implying that America thereby found itself blessed with a unusual number of energetic, mobile, ambitious, daring, and optimistic persons. Now there is no reason to deny that a number of traits must have helped to differentiate those who chose to come from those who chose to stay, nor that these differences must have generated social institutions and habits of mind that tended to preserve and reproduce these characteristics. But very little attention has been paid to the more negative aspects of the selection. If we gained the energetic and daring we also gained the lion's share of the rootless, the unscrupulous, those who value money over relationships, and those who put self-aggrandizement ahead of love and loyalty. And most of all, we gained a critically undue proportion of persons who, when faced with a difficult situation, tended to chuck the whole thing and flee to a new environment. Escaping, evading and avoiding are resonses which lie at the base of much that is peculiarly American —the suburb, the automobile, the self-service store, and so on.

These responses also contribute to the appalling discrepancy between our material resources and our treatment of those who cannot adequately care for themselves. This is not an argument against institutionalization: American society is not geared to handle these problems in any other way, and this is in fact the point I wish to make. One cannot successfully alter one facet of a social system if everything else is left the same, for the patterns are interdependent and reinforce one another. In a cooperative, stable society the aged, infirm, or psychotic person can be absorbed by the local community, which knows and understands him. He presents a difficulty which is familiar and which can be confronted daily and directly. This condition cannot be reproduced in our society today—the burden must be carried by a small, isolated, mobile family unit that is not really equipped for it.

But understanding the forces that require us to incarcerate those who cannot function independently in our society does not give us license to ignore the significance of doing so. The institutions we provide for those who cannot care for themselves are human garbage heaps—they result from and reinforce our tendency to avoid confronting social and interpersonal problems. They make life "easier" for the rest of society, just as does the automobile. And just as we find ourselves having to devise ridiculous exercises to counteract the harmful effects of our dependence upon the automobile, so the "ease" of our non-confronting social technology makes us bored, flabby, and interpersonally insensitive, and our lives empty and mechanical.

Our ideas about institutionalizing the aged, psychotic, retarded, and infirm are based on a pattern of thought that we might call the Toilet Assumption—the notion that unwanted matter, unwanted difficulties, unwanted complexities and obstacles will disappear if they are removed from our immediate field of vision. We do not connect the trash we throw from the car window with the trash in our streets, and we assume that replacing old buildings with new expensive ones will alleviate poverty in the slums. We throw the aged and psychotic into institutional holes where they cannot be seen. Our approach to social problems is to decrease their visibility: out of sight, out of mind. This is the real foundation of racial segregation, especially its most extreme case, the Indian "reservation." The result of our social efforts has been to remove the underlying problems of our society farther and farther from daily experience and daily consciousness, and hence to decrease, in the mass of the population, the knowledge, skill, resources, and motivation necessary to deal with them.

When these discarded problems rise to the surface again—a riot, a protest, an exposé in the mass media—we react as if a sewer had backed up. We are shocked, disgusted, and angered, and immediately call for the emergency plumber (the special commission, the crash program) to ensure that the problem is once again removed from consciousness.

The Toilet Assumption is not merely a facetious metaphor. Prior to the widespread use of the flush toilet all of humanity was daily confronted with the immediate reality of human waste and its disposal. They knew where it was and how it got there. Nothing miraculously vanished. Excrement was conspicuously present in the outhouse or chamber pot, and the slops that went out the window went visibly and noticeably into the street. The most aristocratic Victorian ladies strolling in fashionable city parks thought nothing of retiring to the bushes to relieve themselves. Similarly, garbage did not disappear down a disposal unit—it remained nearby.

As with physical waste, so with social problems. The biblical adage, "the poor are always with us," had a more literal meaning before World War I. The poor were visible and all around. Psychosis was not a strange phenomenon in a textbook but a familiar neighbor or village character. The aged were in every house. Everyone had seen animals slaughtered and knew what they were eating when they ate them; illness and death were a part of everyone's immediate experience.

In contemporary life the book of experience is filled with blank and mysterious pages. Occupational specialization and plumbing have exerted a kind of censorship over our understanding of the world we live in and how it operates. And when we come into immediate contact with anything that does not seem to fit into the ordinary pattern of our somewhat bowdlerized existence our spontaneous reaction is to try somehow to flush it away, bomb it away, throw it down the jail.

But in some small degree we also feel bored and uneasy with the orderly chrome and porcelain vacuum of our lives, from which so much of life has been removed. Evasion creates self-distaste as well as comfort, and radical confrontations are exciting as well as disruptive. The answering chord that they produce within us terrifies us, and although we cannot entirely contain our fascination, it is relatively easy to project our self-disgust onto the perpetrators of the confrontations.

This ambivalence is reflected in the mass media. The hunger for confrontation and experience attracts a lot of attention to social problems, but these are usually dealt with in such a way as to reinforce the avoidance process. The TV documentary presents a tidy package with opposing views and an implication of progress. Reports in popular magazines attempt to provide a substitute for actual experience. Important book and film reviews, for example, give just the blend of titillation and condescension to make the reader imagine that he is already "in" and need not undergo the experience itself—that he has not only participated in the novel adventure but already outgrown it. Thus the ultimate effect of the media is to reinforce the avoiding response by providing an effigy of confrontation and experience. There is always the danger with such insulating mechanisms, however, that they at times get overloaded, like tonsils, and become carriers of precisely the agents against which they are directed. This is an increasingly frequent event in our society today.

A corollary of this latent desire for social confrontation is the desire for an incorruptible man—a man who cannot be bribed, who does not have his price. Once again this desire is a recessive trait, relegated largely to the realm of folk drama and movie script, but it exists nonetheless, as a silent rebellion against the oppressive democratic harmony of a universal monetary criterion.

In the hard reality of everyday life, however, the incorruptible man is at best an inconvenience, an obstacle to the smooth functioning of a vast institutional machinery. Management leaders, for example, tend to prefer corrupt union leaders—"people you can do business with"—to those who might introduce questions and attitudes lying outside the rules of a monetary game. The man who cannot be bought tends to be mistrusted as a fanatic, and the fact that incorruptible men are so often called Communists may be understood in the same light. As in the case of the mass media, however, this mechanism has become overloaded, so that having been jailed and/or called a Communist or traitor is now regarded by young adults as a medal attesting to one's social concern.

Also closely related to the latent desire for confrontation is an inarticulate wish to move in an environment consisting of something other than our own creations. Human beings evolved as organisms geared to mastery of the natural environment. Within the past few thousand years we have learned to perform this function so well that the natural environment poses very little threat to civilized peoples. Our dangers are self-made ones—subtle, insidious, and meaningless. We die from our machines, our own poisons, our own weapons, our own despair. Furthermore, we are separated from primitive conditions by too few millennia to have evolved any comfortable adaptation to a completely man-made environment. We still long for and enjoy struggling against the elements, even though such activity can only occasionally be considered meaningful of functional.* We cross the ocean in artificially primitive boats, climb mountains we could fly over, kill animals we do not eat. Natural disasters, such as floods, hurricanes, blizzards, and so on, generate a cheerfulness which would seem inappropriate if we did not all share it. It is as if some balance between man and nature had been restored, and with it man's "true function." Like the cat that prefers to play with a ball around the obstacle of a chair leg, so man seems to derive some perverse joy from having a snowstorm force him to use the most primitive mode of transportation. It is particularly amusing to observe people following the course of an approaching hurricane and affecting a proper and prudent desire that it veer off somewhere, in the face of an ill-concealed craving that it do nothing of the kind. There is a satisfaction that comes from relating to nature on equal terms, with respect and even deference to forms of life different from ourselves—as the Indian respects the deer he kills for food and the tree that shields him from the sun.

We interact largely with extensions of our own egos. We stumble over the consequences of our past acts. We are drowning in our own excreta (another consequence of the Toilet Assumption). We rarely come into contact with a force which is clearly and cleanly Not-Us. Every struggle is a struggle with ourselves, because there is a little piece of ourselves in everything we encounter—houses, clothes, cars, cities, machines, even our foods. There is an uneasy, anesthetized feeling about this kind of life—like being trapped forever inside an air-conditioned car with power steering and power brakes and only a telephone to talk to. Our world is only a mirror, and our efforts mere shadowboxing—yet shadowboxing in which we frequently manage to hurt ourselves.

Even that part of the world which is not man-made impinges upon us through a symbolic network we have created. We encounter primarily our own fantasies: we have a concept and image of a mountain, a lake, or a forest almost before we ever see one. Travel posters tell us what it means to be in a strange land, the events of life become news

---

* The cholesterol problem provides an illustration: one theory proposes that the release of cholesterol into the bloodstream was functional for hunting large animals with primitive weapons. Since the animal was rarely killed but only wounded, he had to be followed until he dropped, and this was a matter of walking or running for several days without food or rest. A similar response would be activated today in fields such as advertising, in which a sustained extra effort over a period of time (to obtain a large contract, for example) is periodically required. But these peak efforts do not involve any physical release—the cholesterol is not utilized.

items before they actually happen—all experience receives preliminary structure and interpretation. Public relations, television drama, and life become indistinguishable.

The story of Pygmalion is thus the story of modern man, in love with his own product. But like all discreet fairly tales, that of Pygmalion stops with the consummation of his love. It does not tell us of his ineffable boredom at having nothing to love but an excrescence of himself. But we know that men who live surrounded by that which and those whom they have molded to their desires—from the Caliph of Baghdad to Federico Fellini—suffer from a fearsome ennui. The minute they assume material form our fantasies cease to be interesting and become mere excreta.

III. DEPENDENCE AND INDEPENDENCE

Independence training in American society begins almost at birth —babies are held and carried less than in most societies and spend more time in complete isolation—and continues, despite occasional parental ambivalence, throughout childhood and adolescence. When a child is admonished to be a "big boy" or "big girl" this usually means doing something alone or without help (the rest of the time it involves strangling feelings, but this norm seems to be on the wane). Signs of independence are usually rewarded, and a child who in too obvious a manner calls attention to the fact that human intelligence is based almost entirely on the process of imitation is ridiculed by calling him a copycat or a monkey (after the paradoxical habit humans have of projecting their most uniquely human attributes onto animals).

There have been many complaints in recent years that independence training is less rigorous than it once was, but again, as in the case of competitiveness, this is hard to assess. To be on one's own in a simple, stable, and familiar environment requires a good deal less internal "independence" than to be on one's own in a complex, shifting, and strange one. Certainly a child could run about more freely a century ago without coming to harm, and his errors and misdeeds had far more trivial consequences than today; but this decline in the child's freedom of movement says nothing about the degree to which the child is asked to forgo the pleasures of depending upon his parents for nurturance and support. If the objective need is greater, it may offset a small increase in parental tolerance for dependent behavior, and cause the child to experience the independence training as more severe rather than less.

In any case, American independence training is severe relative to most of the rest of the world, and we might assume this to have emotional consequences. This is not to say that such training is not consonant with the demands of adult society: the two are quite in accord. Sociologists and anthropologists are often content to stop at this point and say that as long as this accord exists there is no problem worth discussing. But the frustration of any need has its effects (one of them being to increase the society's vulnerability to social change) and these should be understood.

An example might help clarify this issue. Ezra and Suzanne Vogel observe that Japanese parents encourage dependency as actively as American parents push independence, and that healthy children and adults in Japan rely heavily on others for emotional support and decisions about their lives. A degree of dependence on the mother which in America would be considered "abnormal" prepares the Japanese for a society in which far more dependency is expected and accepted than in ours. The Japanese firm is highly paternalistic and takes a great deal of responsibility for making the individual employee secure and comfortable. The Vogels observe, however, that just as the American mother tends to complain at the success of her efforts and feel that her children are *too* independent, so the Japanese mother tends to feel that her children are too *dependent,* despite the fact that she has trained them this way.[2]

What I am trying to point out is that regardless of the congruence between socialization practices and adult norms, any extreme pattern of training will produce stresses for the individuals involved. And just as the mothers experience discomfort with the effects of these patterns, so do the children, although barred by cultural values from recognizing and naming the nature of their distress, which in our society takes the form of a desire to relinquish responsibility for control and decision-making in one's daily life. Deeply felt democratic values usually stand in the way of realizing this goal through authoritarian submission, although our attitudes toward democracy are not without ambivalence, as has been suggested elsewhere; [3] but the temptation to abdicate self-direction in more subtle ways is powerful indeed. Perhaps the major problem for Americans is that of choice: Americans are forced into making more choices per day, with fewer "givens," more ambiguous criteria, less environmental stability, and less social structural support, than any people in history.

Many of the mechanisms through which dependency is counteracted in our society have already been discussed in the preceding sections, but a word should be said about the complex problem of internalized controls. In stable societies, as many authors have pointed out, the control of human impulses is usually a collective responsibility. The individual is viewed as not having within himself the controls required to guarantee that his impulses will not break out in ways disapproved by the community. But this matters very little, since the group is always near at hand to stop him or shame him or punish him should he forget himself.

In more fluid, changing societies we are more apt to find controls that are internalized—that do not depend to so great an extent on control and enforcement by external agents. This has long been characteristic of American society—de Tocqueville observed in 1830 that American women were much more independent that European women, freer from chaperonage, and able to appear in what a European would consider "compromising" situations without any sign of sexual involvement.

Chaperonage in in fact the simplest way to illustrate the difference between external and internalized controls. In chaperon cultures—such as traditional Middle-Eastern and Latin societies—it simply did not occur to anyone that a man and woman could be alone together and not have sexual intercourse. In America, which represents the opposite extreme, there is almost no situation in which a man and a woman could find themselves in which sexual intercourse could not at least be considered problematic (Hollywood comedies have exploited this phenomenon—well past the point of exhaustion and nausea—over the past 35 years). Americans are virtuosi of internalized control of sexual expression (the current relaxation of sexual norms in no way changes this), and this has caused difficulties whenever the two systems have come into contact. An unchaperoned girl in a bikini or mini-skirt means one thing in America, another in Baghdad. It is a mistake to consider a chaperon society more prudish—the compliment is likely to be returned when the difference is understood. Even Americans consider some situations inherently sexual: if a girl from some mythical culture came to an American's house, stripped, and climbed into bed with him, he would assume she was making a sexual overture and would be rather indignant if he found that she was merely expressing casual friendship according to her native customs. He would also be puzzled if *he* were called prudish, and we need not speculate as to what he would call *her*.

But how are internalized controls created? We know that they are closely tied to what are usually called "love-oriented" techniques of discipline in childhood. These techniques avoid physical punishment and deprivation of privileges and stress reasoning and the withdrawal of parental affection. The basic difference between "love-oriented" and "fear-oriented" techniques (such as physical punishment) is that in the latter case the child simply learns to avoid punishment while in the former he tends to incorporate parental values as his own in order to avoid losing parental love and approval. When fear-oriented techniques prevail, the child is in the position of inhabitants of an occupied country, who obey to avoid getting hurt but disobey whenever they think they can get away with it. Like them, the child does not have any emotional commitment to his rulers—he does not fear losing their love.

Love-oriented techniques require by definition that love and discipline emanate from the same source. When this happens it is not merely a question of avoiding the punisher: the child wishes to anticipate the displeasure of the loved and loving parent, wants to be like the parent, and takes into himself as a part of himself the values and attitudes of the parent. He wants to please, not placate, and because he has taken the parent's attitudes as his own, pleasing the parent comes to mean making him feel good about himself. Thus while individuals raised with fear-oriented techniques tend to direct anger outward under stress, those raised with love-oriented techniques tend to direct it inward in the form of guilt—a distinction that has important physiological correlates.[4]

Under stable conditions external controls work perfectly well. Everyone knows his own place and his neighbor's, and deviations from expected behavior will be quickly met from all sides. When social conditions fluctuate, social norms change, and people move frequently from one social setting to another and are often among strangers, this will no longer do. An individual cannot take his whole community with him wherever he goes, and in any case the rules differ from place to place. The mobile individual must travel light, and internalized controls are portable and transistorized, as it were.

Anger directed inward is also made for mobile conditions. In a stable community two youths who start to get into a fight will be held back by their friends—they depend upon this restraint and can abandon themselves to their passion, knowing that it will not produce harmful consequences. But where one moves among strangers it becomes increasingly important to have other mechanisms for handling aggression. In situations of high mobility and flux the individual must have a built-in readiness to feel himself responsible when things go wrong.

Most modern societies are a confused mixture of both systems, a fact that enables conservative spokesmen to attribute rising crime rates to permissive child-rearing techniques. The overwhelming majority of ordinary crimes, however, are committed by individuals who have *not* been reared with love-oriented techniques, but, insofar as the parent or parents have been able to rear them at all, by the haphazard use of fear-oriented discipline. Love-oriented child-rearing techniques are a luxury that slum parents, for example, can seldom afford.

Furthermore, it is rather misleading to refer to the heavily guilt-inducing socialization techniques of middle-class parents as "permissive." Misbehavior in a lower-class child is more often greeted with a cuff, possibly accompanied by some non-informative response such as "stop that!" But it may not be at all clear to the child which of the many motions he is now performing "that" is; and, indeed, "that" may be punished only when the parent is feeling irritable. A child would have to have achieved an enormously high intelligence level (which, of course, it has not, for this very reason) to be able to form a moral concept out of a hundred irritable stop-that's. What he usually forms is merely a crude sense of when the "old man" or the "old lady" is to be avoided. The self-conscious, highly verbal, middle-class parent is at the opposite extreme. He or she feels that discipline should relate to the child's act, not the parent's own emotional state, and is very careful to emphasize verbally the principle involved in the misbehavior ("it's bad to hit people" or "we have to share with guests"). Concept-formation is made very easy for the middle-class child, and he tends to think of moral questions in terms of principles.

As he grows older this tendency is reinforced by his encounter with different groups with different norms. In a mobile society, one cannot simply accept the absolute validity of any rule because one experiences competing moral codes. As a result the middle-class child tends to evolve a system of meta-rules, that is, rules for assessing the relative validity of these codes. The meta-rules tend to be based upon the earliest and most general principles expressed by the parents; such as prohibitions on violence against others, egalitarianism, mutuality, and so on. This ability to treat rules in a highly secular fashion while maintaining a strong moral position is baffling to those whose control mechanisms are more primitive, but it presupposes a powerful and articulate conscience. Such an individual can expose himself to physical harm and to violence-arousing situations without losing control and while maintaining a moral position. This may seem inconceivable to an uneducated working-class policeman whose own impulses are barely held in line by a jerry-built structure of poorly articulated and mutually contradictory moral absolutes. Hence he tends to misinterpret radical middle-class behavior as a hypocritical mask for mere delinquency.

The point of this long digression, however, is that internalization is a mixed blessing. It may enable one to get his head smashed in a good cause, but the capacity to give oneself up completely to an emotion is almost altogether lost in the process. Where internalization is high there is often a feeling that the controls themselves are out of control—that emotion cannot be expressed when the individual would like to express it. Life is muted, experience filtered, emotion anesthetized, affective discharge incomplete. Efforts to shake free from this hypertrophied control system include not only drugs, and sensation-retrieval techniques such as those developed at the Esalen Institute in California, but also confused attempts to reestablish external systems of direction and control—the vogue currently enjoyed by astrology is an expression of this. The simplest technique, of course, would be the establishment of a more authoritarian social structure, which would relieve the individual of the great burden of examining and moderating his own response. He could become as a child, lighthearted, spontaneous, and passionate, secure in the knowledge that others would prevent his impulses from causing harm.

Realization of this goal is prevented by democratic values and the social conditions that foster them (complexity, fluidity, change). But the desire plays a significant part in conventional reactions to radical minorities, who are all felt to be seeking the abandonment of self-restraints of one kind or another and at the same time demanding *more* responsible behavior from the establishment. This is both infuriating and contagious to white middle-class adults, who would like very much to do the same, and their call for "law and order" (that is, more *external* control) is an expression of that desire as well as an attempt to smother it. This conflict over dependency and internalization also helps explain why official American anticommunism always lays so much stress on the authoritarian (rather than the socialistic) aspects of Communist states.

INDIVIDUALISM REASSESSED

The three variables we have been discussing—community, engagement, dependency—can all trace their suppression in American society to our commitment to individualism. The belief that everyone should pursue autonomously his own destiny has forced us to maintain an emotional detachment (for which no amount of superficial gregariousness can compensate) from our social and physical environment, and aroused a vague guilt about our competitiveness and indifference to others; for, after all, our earliest training in childhood does not stress competitiveness, but cooperation, sharing, and thoughtfulness—it is only later that we learn to reverse these priorities. Radical challenges to our society, then, always tap a confused responsive chord within us that is far more disturbing than anything going on outside. They threaten to reconnect us with each other, with nature, and with ourselves, a possibility that is thrilling but terrifying—as if we had grown a shell-like epidermis and someone was threatening to rip it off.

Individualism finds its roots in the attempt to deny the reality and importance of human interdependence. One of the major goals of technology in America is to "free" us from the necessity of relating to, submitting to, depending upon, or controlling other people.* Unfortunately, the more we have succeeded in doing this the more we have felt disconnected, bored, lonely, unprotected, unnecessary, and unsafe.

Individualism has many expressions: free enterprise, self-service, academic freedom, suburbia, permissive gun-laws, civil liberties, do-it-yourself, oil-depletion allowances. Everyone values some of these expressions and condemns others, but the principle is widely shared. Criticisms of our society since World War II have almost all embraced this value and expressed fears for its demise—the organization man, the other-directed man, conformity, "group-think," and so on. In general these critics have failed to see the role of the value they embrace so fervently in generating the phenomena they so detest.

The most sophisticated apologist for individualism is David Riesman, who recognizes at least that uniformity and community are not the same thing, and does not shrink from the insoluble dilemmas that these issues create. Perhaps the definitive and revealing statement of what individualism is all about is his: "I am insisting that no ideology, however noble, can justify the sacrifice of an individual to the needs of the group." [5]

Whenever I hear such sentiments I recall Jay Haley's discussion of the kind of communication that characterizes the families of schizophrenics. He points out that people who communicate with one another necessarily govern each other's behavior—set rules for each other. But an individual may attempt to avoid this human fate—to become independent, uninvolved: "He may choose the schizophrenic way and indicate that nothing he does is done in relationship to other people." The family of the schizophrenic establishes a system of rules like all families, but also has "a prohibition on any acknowledgement that a family member is setting rules. Each refuses to concede that he is circumscribing the behavior of others, and each refuses to concede that any other family member is governing him." The attempt, of course, fails. "The more a person tries to avoid being governed or governing others, the more helpless he becomes and so governs others by forcing them

---

*The peculiar germ-phobia that pervades American life (and supports several industries) owes much to this insulation machinery. So far have we carried the fantasy of individual autonomy that we imagine each person to have his own unique species of germs, which must therefore not be mixed and confused with someone else's. We are even disturbed at the presence of the germs themselves: despite the fact that many millions of them inhabit every healthy human body from the cradle to the grave we regard them as trespassers. We feel that nature has no business claiming a connection with us, and perhaps one day we will prove ourselves correct.

to take care of him." [6] In our society as a whole this caretaking role is assigned to technology, like so much else.

Riesman overlooks the fact that the individual is sacrificed either way. If he is never sacrificed to the group the group will collapse and the individual with it. Part of the individual is, after all, committed to the group. Part of him wants what "the group" wants, part does not. No matter what is done some aspect of the individual—id, ego, or whatever—will be sacrificed.

An individual, like a group, is a motley collection of ambivalent feelings, contradictory needs and values, and antithetical ideas. He is not, and cannot be, a monolithic totality, and the modern effort to bring this myth to life is not only delusional and ridiculous, but also acutely destructive, both to the individual and to his society.

Recognition of this internal complexity would go a long way toward resolving the dilemma Riesman implicitly poses. For the reason a group needs the kind of creative deviant Riesman values is the same reason it needs to sacrifice him: the failure of the group members to recognize the complexity and diversity and ambivalence within themselves. Since they have oversimplified and rejected parts of themselves, they not only lack certain resources but also are unable to tolerate their naked exposure by others. The deviant is a compensatory mechanism to mitigate this condition. He comes along and tries to provide what is "lacking" in the group (that is, what is present but denied, suppressed). His role is like that of the mutant—most are sacrificed but a few survive to save the group from itself in times of change. Individualism is a kind of desperate plea to save all mutants, on the grounds that we do not know what we are or what we need. As such it is horribly expensive—a little like setting a million chimps to banging on a typewriter on the grounds that eventually one will produce a masterpiece.

But if we abandon the monolithic pretense and recognize that any group sentiment, and its opposite, represents a part of everyone but only a part, then the prophet is unnecessary since he exists in all of us. And should he appear it will be unnecessary to sacrifice him since we have already admitted that what he is saying is true. And in the meantime we would be able to exercise our humanity, governing each other and being governed, instead of encasing ourselves in the leaden armor of our technological schizophrenia.

NOTES

1. S. A. Stouffer, *Communism, Conformity, and Civil Liberities* (New York: Wiley, 1966), p. 164. Italics mine.
2. Ezra F. Vogel and Suzanne H. Vogel, "Permissive Dependency in Ja-

pan," in H. Kent Geiger (ed.), *Comparative Perspectives on Marriage and the Family* (Boston: Little, Brown, 1968), pp. 68–77.

3. See Erich Fromm, *Escape from Freedom* (New York: Rinehart, 1941); W. G. Bennis and P. E. Slater, *The Temporary Society* (New York: Harper and Row, 1968) Chapter 1. Bennis and I attempt to show that the "efficiency" Americans attribute to autocratic systems applies only to situations involving simple, routine tasks. Such systems function poorly under conditions of change and complexity. They have an awkward tendency to run a "tight ship" which nevertheless sinks.

4. S. H. King and A. F. Henry, "Aggression and Cardiovascular Reactions Related to Parental Control over Behavior," *Journal of Abnormal and Social Psychology,* LIII, 1955, pp. 206–210.

5. David Riesman, *Individualism Reconsidered* (Garden City, New York: Doubleday Anchor, 1954), p. 27. This is a principle for which nature has shown a fine disregard—evolution proceeds on a diametrically opposite principle.

6. Jay Haley, "The Family of the Schizophrenic: A Model System," in G. Handel (ed.), *The Psychosocial Interior of the Family* (Chicago: Aldine, 1967), pp. 271–272.

CHAPTER 5

URBANIZATION AND SOCIAL CHARACTER

SCOTT GREER

Perhaps one of the thorniest problems considered by sociologists has been determination of the relationship between character—both individual and cultural—and the structure of society. In "Urbanization and Social Character," Scott Greer considers some of the aspects of the emergence and perseverance of an urban social character.

This article is one of the oldest to appear in the book. Therefore, some of its language and observations might appear somewhat dated when compared to, say, the extract from *The Greening of America*. The strength of this article, however, lies in its ability to focus our attention on certain social and cultural processes and their consequences. The *process* of urbanization is considered in a global context, so that we begin to consider the process in terms of a pervasive "system." The modern city in this context is part of a much larger, more inclusive national system that is inextricably linked economically, politically, and socially with other national systems. Technology, both material and social, has ensured the complete interdependence of all components of these systems by establishing a highly specialized man-machine-resource nexus that demands the utilization of large groups working in concert.

This sets the modern city off from its predecessors. Urban man is no longer so radically different from his "nonurban" counterpart. Both, for instance, look to the same national centers for political leadership, both are exposed to the same information via the mass media, and both have access to the same technology. So both can be said to live within the same culture.

The individual's character as a social actor in this context will be related to the same culture. Social character, as Greer sees it, is the probable behavior of the individual in a given situation. The move toward urbanization, because of its reliance upon technology, demanded a high degree of rationalism and self-control. Men had to fit themselves into the process of production and make adjustments in their life-styles that facilitated economic and social productivity. In the process, much was gained; yet, unfortunately, something was lost.

New life-styles, fuller political participation, the extension of education and prosperity—all accompanied the societal change. Along with these, though, came a breakdown of traditional structures and norms that gave meaning to men's lives. Work, for example, ceased to be satisfying in itself, becoming, instead, simply a means to an end. Hence the worker found himself to be alienated from the fruits of his labor and totally dependent on income to enrich his life. The extended family, composed of several generations living together, gave way to the more mobile nuclear family. This shift almost ensured that children would have fewer examples, or role models, besides their parents, on which to pattern their behavior or attitudes. The "community," as a social entity, lost significance as people shifted their focus of interest and activity to narrowly defined jobs geographically removed from their place of residence.

Curiously, however, the process has proved to be an uneven one. Not all parts of the culture, especially its social character, change at the same pace—material aspects far outstrip the social ones. People tend to be highly rational (in the sense of efficiency) about certain things and yet unseeing and intransigent about others; this may have long-term implications for the system. Societal or social problems are often defined in such narrow terms that the system seems to be working against itself. Technological rationality, for example, simply sees machines as more efficient than human workers. Therefore, the process of automation continues to destroy jobs. We as a people have not (although some individuals have) yet come to grips with this problem either by providing alternative jobs for those displaced or by establishing an economic order that guarantees our fellow citizens a measure of security. Such contradictions can be expected to continue—perhaps even get worse—until the various parts of our culture are brought back into harmony.

The problem, as Professor Greer sees it, is that the existent social character is not fully equipped to deal with a large society. People today, as never before, are preoccupied with the search for a realistic understanding of the world around them. The answer may lie in knowledge of the process by which social structures are created and modified; sociology is the discipline most likely to provide this knowledge.

Scott Greer is a Professor of Political Science and Sociology at Northwestern University. He received his Ph. D. degree from the

University of California at Los Angeles in 1952. He served as Research Director of the Laboratory in Urban Culture at Occidental College from 1952 to 1955 and as Chief Sociologist for the Metropolitan Saint Louis Survey from 1956 to 1957. The author of numerous books, including *Governing the Metropolis* (1962), *The Emerging City* (1962), *Metropolitics* (1963), and *Urban Renewal and American Cities* (1965), he has also contributed extensively to professional journals, including the *American Sociological Review*, the *American Journal of Sociology*, and *Social Forces*.

All of us are aware of the immense increase in the proportion of the population living in cities. Indeed, if we have paid attention to the literature on urbanization we have probably memorized the figures by now, realizing that the United States is over 70 percent urban, that the 64,000,000 new citizens expected by 1980 will be urban dwellers, and 80 percent of them suburbanites (Hauser, 1960: ch. 4). But the importance of this piling up of people in cities is by no means clear and the whole concept of "urbanization" obscures as much as it reveals the nature of our society. For our urbanization is not the dense concentration of the nineteenth century factory city—its growing edges are the open neighborhoods of suburbia. Nor is the way of urban man sharply dichotomized from that of his relative in the country—often he has moved directly from a village to a suburb, visually and socially little different from his previous home. "Urbanization" is a loose summary word, absorbing many meanings and pointing to different things. Let us see how it can be made into a working tool.

Cities are possible because of a geographical division of labor. Briefly, urban dwellers have not extracted the raw materials from the soil; they have bought, stolen, or taxed these resources from countrymen. Thus cities depend upon the agricultural hinterland. In the past they were never dominant, for the countrymen could not produce enough surplus; urbanites were a small class released from bondage to soil and the seasons by the work of their rural cousins. Our enormously increased urban population today rests upon the increased productivity of the extractive industries; this has allowed us to reverse, in less than one hundred years, the proportion of the American population dwelling in cities.

The building of cities does not, in itself, change the basic structure of human life (Greer, 1962). It is change in the basic political econ-

"Urbanization and Social Character: Notes on the American as Citizen," by Scott Greer, in H. J. Schmandt and W. Bloomberg, Jr. (eds.), *The Quality of Urban Life*, Vol. 3, *Urban Affairs Annual Reviews* (1969), pp. 95–127, is reprinted by permission of the publisher, Sage Publications, Inc.

omy of the society which allows—indeed forces—the creation and growth of cities. Two meanings wrapped up in the term "urbanization" can be separated in view of this fact: the first is simply the "concentration of people in cities." The second, and more basic, is the social transformation that releases manpower from an agriculture which remains adequate to sustain large and growing urban centers.

The release of labor from extractive industries is made possible by two intertwined developments. The first is the use of nonhuman energies harnessed to machines as substitutes for the human beast of burden. The second is the coordination of human behavior in larger and larger networks of interdependence. The two interact. Nonhuman energy makes possible the release of men from manual work and, equally important, the constraints of distance: it allows rapid communication and the coordination of behavior over greater spans than was possible before. This, in turn, allows for the development of giant armies, corporations, nations, and other functional groups. The latter hasten the tendency to exploit nonhuman energy and the machine. Thus, the two developments of technology, physical and social, result in an extension of the network of interdependence, the social interdependence of large groups cemented by a common dependence upon the man-machine-resource nexus sustaining the entire society. So close is this dependence that none of our great cities could survive more than a few weeks without the national market, while few (and deviant) are the individuals who could get a bare subsistence from the earth on their own.

These radical transformations of society have been given the summary name, "increase in societal scale" (Wilson, 1945). They have two major consequences for the ordinary citizen: they increase his dependence upon a large-scale system and they free him to a large degree from dependence upon the near-at-hand, the neighbors and neighborhood and parish of his immediate surroundings. But his freedom is not from the boundaries of social groups per se; it is simply a shift from the constraints of Main Street and the neighbors to the control system of the bureaucracy. For, with increasing scale the major work of the society is delegated to large task forces. These, formally organized and rationally oriented towards production, distribution, and survival, uniformly take the shape of bureaucracies. In them the citizen holds office, affirms norms, receives punishment and rewards, and achieves (or fails) his destiny. Upon them he is dependent.

Thus, underlying the process which concentrates people in cities is the major process of *organizational transformation*. This is a process which can best be measured by its effects upon a total society: cities and hinterlands are equally affected in the process. In setting the conditions within which one can earn a living, enjoy citizenship, procreate and be protected, the organizational structure is a major clue to the way people will behave. From interdependence among ourselves we learn to organize our actions, controlling ourselves and each other. The organizational system tells us, in short, what men must do if they are to hold a job in the society (Greer, 1955). (Thus we require of American workers a rigorous attention to chronological time, to efficiency, to the subtle cues of interpersonal blandishment and bargaining, with a weather eye to the "rules.") But beyond the requirements made upon the individual citizen are other constraints derived from our social organization: the mutual dependence of the economy, the polity and the family system, separately and interacting, set the limits of what we can and must do *collectively*. The Great Depression indicated the force the polity will exert upon the economy when unemployment grows to disastrous proportions, while the . . . "war on poverty" indicates the ways in which the economy *forces* issues upon the polity. At the juncture of the great organizational segments of the society, where the President treats with the directors of big steel and the United Steelworkers of America, the interdependence of giant organizations (and our common dependence on their coordination) is dramatic and clear.

Urbanization stands, then, for the concentration of people in cities and the processes which lead them there. Concealed in the term, however, and frequently assumed without being made explicit, is another meaning—a certain kind and quality of living which we call "urbanity." Derived from the same linguistic roots, "urbanity" indicates a life-style which was once automatically associated with the dwellers in cities. It meant that those who dwell in cities become more sophisticated, accustomed to variety and wont to see the world in a larger perspective. Contrasted with the peasant or countryman, the urbanite was free from the automatic demands of custom and habit, the brute pressure of "the nuzzling herd society of the village." Literate and exposed to literature, he was both more "rootless" and more "cosmopolitan" than the yokel. Urbanism, in this perspective, is the cultural parallel of increasing scale: the urbanite was envisioned as a citizen of a larger universe because he lived at the meeting place of many disparate and distant worlds.

In societies of the past, energy-poor and dependent upon the peasant village for surplus, the three meanings implied in "urbanization" were closely related in the empirical instant. The concentration of people in cities required a sufficient scale of organization and surplus energy to provide dependable fodder for Caesar's herds, and the people of the cities (the "urbs") did indeed become different in their culture and point of view from the "daemonic" universe of the peasant villager. They worked at the structure of controlling the larger area of city state or empire through the army, the state bureaucracy, the church, and the market. Their cities rose and collapsed with their varying success in controlling the peasants. But meanwhile, everywhere underlying the urban society, was the vast majority of mankind still chained to village, province, *latifundia*—a low energy source but the *sine qua non* for the entire system.

Today the matter is otherwise. As new sources of energy surplus have been harnessed to our machines, farming has become our most highly mechanized industry. The number of people actually working at agriculture is about the same as the number of the unemployed in the United States today, and only a small minority of the workforce stands for the tradition of village and country. The massive mode of the society is the employee of some exclusive membership organization, living in a giant metropolitan area and moving (or hoping to move) his residence towards its outskirts. We cannot define his way of life as "urbanity," for his country kin live in very much the same fashion as he does. All we can say is that the culture of urban man is radically transformed. All men are exposed to the communication flows of the urban society, a necessity flowing from their dependence upon the market and the state. Thus the city is no longer either the source of increasing societal scale, nor a prime shaper of the dominant culture. It is part of the more inclusive national system, and we must bear in mind its limits within, and its dependence upon, that system.

SOCIAL CHANGE AND SOCIAL CHARACTER

The culture of urban man is a major clue to his social character. For culture, that general agreement within a group concerning what the world is and what should be done in it, limits and determines the vocabulary in which he can communicate with others and formulate his own course of action. Its sources as diverse as dreams, images, logic, and misunderstanding, culture is a set of definitions which can be expressed symbolically with a common meaning among men. Of all the traits which could enter into the common storehouses, various and exotic as the findings of the anthropologists, only some can be accepted and used in any given cultural group. That which is accepted will pass through a history of natural selection. Favored by its resemblance to the existing culture, it will survive insofar as it is useful to the members of the group in playing their inescapable roles. As new traits are incorporated into the common culture, they add to the bases for communication and the ordering of individual behavior oriented to the rewards and punishments provided by the group; they become new limits.

The individual's character as a social actor will be intimately related to this preexisting common culture. For social character is nothing more than the probable behavior of an individual when confronted with a given kind of life situation. The Balinese go to sleep in the presence of overwhelming danger; the crew of the Texas City refineries remained at their station to maximize control for the common safety, though their entire environment might explode at any moment; the Hindu prays before the bayonet. However intertwined in the life and nervous system of the individual, each of these courses of action is a learned response to a kind of social situation, a statement of fact and of moral imperatives. Thus social character reflects the common culture, and can best be identified through social behavior, including verbal behavior. It is always a constructed pattern inferred from observations over time—as abstract as the id and as concrete as the prejudices which limit and frustrate our aims.

The basic importance of social character to the collective and its fortunes is this: it is one set of limits upon what men can understand and find it necessary to do. This means that the average social character of an aggregate tells us what can be assumed as common before clustered people form into a structured group. It provides the beads which can be strung on many different sorts of organizational wire. Social characters tolerating or condemning the game of gossip are major considerations in forming the kaffeeklatsch groups of Levittown, while the most scientific public administration practices fail in a society of feudal sheiks, whose nepotism is morally prescribed. Moore and Feldman have recently dramatized the consequences for economic development of a social character "uncommitted to labor" while those attempting to change fertility rates in traditional societies are well aware of the characterological barriers to sterility. Social character is a "lurking variable," an old palimpsest on the supposed tabula rasa which frequently makes nonsense of our efforts to rationalize the snarled affairs of a society.

While social character is a major basis for commonality in a social collective, it is more. Unlike the common culture, it points to patterns of *individual variation* in definitions and goals. In any collective large enough to be called a society there will be variation in the common culture, hence the character, of the important subgroups. Even in hunting and gathering societies the differences by age and sex are marked: the general unifying culture is subtly modified as it applies to the warrior, the old woman, the child. That which is accepted as general social fact and that which is a categorical imperative for action separate: the latter is specific oftentimes to the role. Thus a woman in New Guinea or the Tennessee hill country may know that blood revenge is required in a certain situation without feeling any compulsion to execute it. Social character varies enormously within a society—by one's subgroup, and by one's role within that subgroup.

This variation is a major resource for the society, for it supplies an array of alternative possibilities for social action. Small group research projects have made clear the variation in social types which take leadership roles under routine as against crisis conditions, while Pareto and Machiavelli speak of Lions versus the Foxes. And from another perspective, Levy points out the brilliant coup of the modernizing Japanese, who enrolled the Samurai estate, en masse, in the police force. This preexisting social character fitted nicely the requirements of the function, and the dangerous Samurai had a job in modern Japan.

Beyond the differentiation of social character brought on by variations in group and role, there are other processes tending to differentiate. It is important to remember that we have defined social character as the probability of an individual's acting a certain way *in a certain situation*. But the social situations any actor faces will vary enormously, and what holds for one in a given situation may not hold for another. Thus the "role-set," as Merton has called it, may include for an individual the roles of leader, follower, father, son, provider and client, ally and competitor—the list is nearly endless. Under the circumstances, there are many opportunities for error if the roles are not clearly defined and the situations [are not] clearly identified. The literature of the American frontier is replete with the pioneer father who treated his household as a factor of production, while Hughes underlines the temptation for French-Canadian foremen to treat their kinsmen as kin and *not* as factors of production (Hughes, 1943). The interaction of roles in the life-space of the same person may result in all kinds of "sports," while his effort to organize behavior with consistency from situation to situation may be still another dynamic. Fundamentalist in politics and religion, the small businessman is often the victim of consistency in his business policies, harvesting his marginal existence in the form of bankruptcy.

These are, then, some of the causes of variation in social character. As societies increase in scale, variation increases. The different kinds of work, of life-style, of ethnic background, tend to maximize the number and variety of subgroups which interact intensely among themselves and have little to do with other such groups. Massive migration into the larger society and within it, the fractionation of the job structure (from a few dozen titles to 40,000) and increasing choice resulting from leisure, wealth, and education, allow immense opportunities for variation in social character. At the same time, however, the increasing inclusion of the entire population in a large-scale national state and national market increases the uniformity of communications via the mass media and mass education. From variation among small groups segregated by region, class, race, and religion, we move to variations among segments of one integrated system. Integration is important; it is the necessary condition for the persistence of the entire social system.

The Distance from Past to Present

Robinson Jeffers says in one of his poems that he would have men keep apart from each other in small groups, so that occasional madness would not infect the whole. And for most of mankind, during most of its career on earth, this has been the pattern. The hunting and gathering societies that have dominated our history perforce had to stay apart; grazers, they literally lived from hand to mouth. With an energy source providing much less than one percent of that available to the average American today, they stayed in motion most of the time; like humming-birds, metabolism was their master. Only with the agricultural revolution of a few millennia past was it possible for man to settle down with a modicum of security and the resources to develop, eventually, city-states and empires.

It is important, therefore, to remember that most men, through most of our recent history, have spent their lives in what Turner calls "the daemonic world of the peasant village." They had, in a sense, a long childhood. Tied to the soil, illiterate, receiving the common culture by word of mouth from the older members, the individual was born, lived and died in a tiny circle of earth. With powerful traditions and a frozen technology suited to little more than a subsistence economy, he acted with fatalism, piety, and a superstitious fear of the unknown which hovered around him. Investing the world with magic powers, he believed implicitly in immanent justice—the automatic punishment of trans-gression by the very nature of things. When his limited expectations were fulfilled he was, presumably, content. When famine, war, and plague descended he accommodated, to persist or to perish.

To be sure, empires were erected upon the economy which the peasant maintained. Armies marched and countermarched, cities were built and looted, and high cultures were developed within their walls. But this involved only a few persons, at the most perhaps one out of ten. For most men the capital city was as far away as the moon. Neither the literate world of the high culture nor the role of responsible citizen and leader meant much to the traditional peasant villager. His character was to maintain the older traditions of work and family, and to accept, with piety or fatalism, the hardships imposed by armed men, believing it beyond his powers to control or destroy them. His religion justified some of the world's way with him (Turner, 1941, especially vol. 2, ch. 20).

This state of affairs persisted, with minor variations, among all the "higher civilizations" until a few hundred years ago. It is still the norm in much of the world—the 60,000,000 Indian villagers who live on no road are the thing itself, as are millions of others in Africa, Spain, South Asia, and Latin America. But in certain parts of the world non-human energy resources of enormous surplus, the fossil fuels, were discovered and harnessed to machines (Cottrell, 1955). Increased power allowed for the rapid extension of networks of interdependence; social organization increased in its extent and the intensity of control; the modern world emerged in western Europe and America. As it did so, the common culture changed from that of the peasant village to that of the rational, productive society.

From the peasant village to industrial society the distance was, for the ordinary man, probably as great as that from the Shoshone Indians to Imperial Rome. Among the western European nations where the change has been best documented, we see the complete destruction of the earlier world in a period of less than two hundred years. Beginning with the creation of national markets and the rationalization of agri-culture, the "great transformation" destroyed the subsistence econ-mies of the peasants through improvements in production which drove them from the land. Arriving in the cities, they provided immense pools of cheap labor useful for the rapidly developing factory and market system. The products of the latter, in turn, were traded back to the hinterland, joining city and country in an indissoluble link of economic interdependence. The bifurcated society of city and village was fused in a national whole.

The peasant villager was poorly prepared for this transition. It is doubtful that anything less violent than hunger could have driven so many into the chaotic social world of the cities, for that world took an immense toll of life, family security, health, and happiness. The casual-ties provide Marx's most vivid documentation of capital and its evils. But the destruction of the village as a social security system forced the peasantry to make their "great leap forward" into the world of rational production. It forced them to subsidize, through their weak bargaining position, the rapid expansion of European and American industrial society.

In the process the social character of the average man was forced to change, for he had to learn the common culture of city and factory in order to survive. He learned that work was instrumental, negotiable, and contractual. Beyond the bargain he had no protection. He learned that the public order was problematic; in the stews and sinks of London he learned to take account of the law and of that peculiarly urban social form, the police. (Not that he worried so much about lack of police protection; like the bottom dogs of our contemporary cities, his was the opposite need—protection *from* the police.) He learned to focus upon the market and its prices; his home, livelihood, family, and future depended upon the prices for labor and commodities.

In short, men became rational producers. The process of rationalization is, in this context, the separation of means from ends which allows one to estimate the fit between the two. Men moved from traditional, habit-bound, time-honored acts which guaranteed a livelihood, to rationally designed and prescribed acts which had an end reward—a paycheck. The reward of pleasure in the act itself frequently disappeared; what could be gotten from a tense and near-hysterical fourteen hour day of loom operation except the end reward, the paycheck (Frank, 1948)? This separation of the task into disvalued means and split ends was the source of Marx's concept of *alienation*, for it left the worker without pride or satisfaction in his work. From Durkheim's point of view, the rationalization of factory labor had another consequence; in destroying the value of the task as action in and for itself, rationalization destroyed the norms for behavior. "Anomie" means, precisely, the "lack of norms," or limits. The limits that remained were not visible in the rules for behavior during the performance of the task; they could only be inferred through foresight and planning. The net result was the devaluation of work as a good thing in itself and the definition of work as a *means* to an *end*.

The resulting social character of industrial man was one which fitted the task forces of production and a life in the city maze. From the functional requirement that men be coordinated in production developed the limited work role, the job. This required self-control, for one must be at work on time, must carry out his role on time and at given levels of accuracy, and must remain at work while the steam shafts rotate. From the requirement of balancing labor market and commodity market developed the household budget: week by week and year by year the necessary costs and income must be balanced on pain of hunger, disease, or the debtor's prison. And from the generally low level of income (one which rose little or not at all for decades) came the most rigid requirement of all, the necessity for parsimony. The norm of efficiency deified in mechanical production was thus translated into the everyday working rules of the household, exalting the cheapest articles of consumption. In brief, the social character of early industrial man was one emphasizing self-control and abnegation.

Much, however, did not really change. There is, after all, more to life than the acts of producing and consuming, the major spheres where new learning and a new character were required. There remained such various realms as public affairs, religion, the high culture, kinship, and social class. In these matters the social character of the peasant villager could and did persist in many ways.

Urbanization of his residence and mechanization of his job did not elevate the political role of the ordinary citizen. Illiterate and accustomed to compliance, he merely learned the self-controls necessary to avoid trouble with the police, the army, the wealthy, and others who dominated the urban scene. Having no tradition of public responsibility or participation, he became only a consumer of spectacles and a spectator of consumption. Nor was he able to participate in the high culture of the society. Uneducated, without security or leisure, he found his high culture in religion, where he was a poor consumer. Only in the deviant sects and cults did he find an opportunity and reward for active participation, and the reward was less intellectual than social. With his family he remained traditional and authoritarian, struggling to maintain the older kinship norms even though the network of kin was attenuated by migration and child labor. Nevertheless, his escape from the village probably facilitated his conservative authoritarianism in many ways, for he was free from the pressure of a close community and its public opinion.

The foregoing is a highly simplified view of social character in the early phases of industrial society. Emphasizing the mode, it does not do justice to the increasing differentiation of the population which followed upon the increasingly complex division of labor—a differentiation which resulted in the proliferation of social types. The peasants remained, a dwindling minority oriented to traditional, noncontractual, and habitual social roles, along with their reciprocal types, the landed gentry and the rentiers. In the cities the free professional man, expert and small businessman at once, became important, along with the salaried professional of government and private business. But cutting across all roles were the dominant concerns of the dominant organizations, the rapidly expanding empires of production and the market (Williams, 1960: 382).

The norms of production—self-control and enterprise—had some surprising consequences for the behavior of the workers drafted from farm to factory. Segregated in the working-class slums, thrown together in the factories, sharing a common lot and a common fate, the urban working class in every industrializing country began to experiment with organization and collective bargaining. The very demands of rational production encouraged such a development, for literacy and technical competence, organization and organizational skills, were taught in the processes of work. The new common culture of working-class man was thus created, to be articulated by the emerging working-class leaders, the craftsmen of physical and social organization. It was a culture which incorporated the norms of self-control, parsimony, planning: it accompanied a social character oriented towards work, security, and equality. Its consequences were apparent in the increasing control the workers exerted over the conditions of production. Out of common fate had evolved a common culture; with common enemies came the creation of a social class. All of the differences in life situation came together under the generalizing term "the working class," and Victorian polemics are studded with references to the "labor problem." Economic weakness, common enemies, the life of factory and slum provided the organizational leverage; a family culture based upon traditional kinship, religion, and thrift provided common folk values; individual weakness and inability to play public roles provided the basis for a corporate protest (Perlman and Taft, 1935; Greer, 1955).

The effects of the emerging industrial working-class culture were not confined to the situation on the job. As the society was increasingly committed to the complex interdependence of the urban factory and the urban market, it became increasingly dependent upon the orderly performance of tasks by the workers. Their technological monopoly was translated into political pressure through the strike; their organizations, resting on common fate, brought increasing pressure on the party organizations. They fought for two resources beyond trade unionism: formal education and the vote.

In their victory they achieved the most important social revolution of all time. They forced the society to treat them as citizens, through their achievement of the political franchise; and to treat them as responsible actors, through their achievement of the intellectual franchise, universal education. But their success was complementary to the inexorable demands of developing industrial society, a society that could not be operated without the assurance of proper behavior from its vast work force of manual workers whom the political franchise involved organically in the status quo. Nor were illiterate workmen capable of the increasingly complex work roles that the productive system kept throwing up; mass education was a necessary working tool for the entire economy.

The end result was a vast increase in the "internal inclusiveness of the society," as noted by Wendell Bell (Bell, 1967). The various forms of partial citizenship decreased in their actual distribution and were condemned in principle, though they persisted in the differential handicaps of the poor, the illiterate, the rural, and the ethnic. At the same time, other blessings and burdens of citizenship were more widely distributed. Universal manhood conscription may not seem an increase in citizenship—until one remembers how many regimes could never have dared trust weapons in the hands of the entire male citizenry. Universal taxation is another ambiguous gain, yet it forces the political beneficiary to look at the price of benefits—just as it ties the taxing power more closely to the consent of the citizens.

These immense changes were hastened along by crises in the over-all structure of the large-scale societies. In the twentieth century, modern warfare twice demonstrated the intricate interdependence of the polity and the economy, increasing that interdependence in the process. The great economic collapse of the 1930s made clear to all the political vulnerability of a large-scale society which could not provide economic security for its population. The Full Employment Bill of 1946 was a major symbolic act, for it stated authoritatively the principle that every worker had a right to a job, the basis for economic citizenship. The trend is clear, from the struggle for popular education and the franchise back in the early nineteenth century to the fight for the Civil Rights Bill in 1964. It is in one direction and that direction is towards the equality of citizens before the state and the public order.

The Speed of Change

The society of the United States was a relative latecomer to Western history. Emerging precisely at the point in time where scale was rapidly increasing, it was itself one aspect of increasing scale in western European society. From the beginning it was a dependent part of international markets and empires. Its closest approximations to a peasantry, the chattel slaves of the South and subsistence farmers of the frontiers, were really a far cry from the remnants of feudal agrarian society. Its class system, weakened by distance from Europe and the opportunities of the frontier, never resembled the harsh outlines of government based on feudalism and conquest and, with early independence from the British system, the feudal concept of estates evaporated. The society of the United States thus maximized those aspects of increasing scale which destroyed the age-old agrarian society and exalted the rational producer.

"Americanization" has been a derogatory term for the changes which have occurred at a rapidly accelerating rate in the western European countries. The process of increasing internal inclusiveness is not, however, a characteristic unique to the United States. It occurred here earliest, and progressed most rapidly, because fewer aged structures constrained the process. The lack of hereditary ruling and taxing elites elevated the role of the entrepreneur in the cities, while the availability of land on the frontiers allowed millions the opportunity to become free and rational producers. The political norms invoked by the Declaration of Independence and the Constitution led easily and logically to the political and intellectual enfranchisement of the total population. This, in turn, led to the economic enfranchisement won, at least in principle, in the 1930s and 1940s.

But such is the irony of history, that the society of rational producers was hardly realized before its radical transformation into something new and strange became evident. World War II energized and activated the

American economy to an enormous extent. In the process the technologies of production, given a chance by the unlimited demand and the shortage of manpower, raced ahead towards the maximum application of nonhuman energy to work. In the postwar years the results became obvious: American society was not only the wealthiest in the world, it was also far wealthier than it had ever been before. That wealth, distributed through collective bargaining between corporations, unions, the free market, and the government, raised the resource level of millions of American households. Leisure increased, as the forty-hour week and the three-week vacation became the norm. The average income was more than double that of the early years of the twentieth century. Higher levels of formal education, made easier by a late start at work and increasing educational facilities, marked each succeeding generation. The goods of the market, the pleasures of leisure, and the rich and novel symbolic worlds of the mass media became part of the "American way of life."

The society of rational producers accepted all this as its due. The enormous spurt of prosperity was a just reward for self-control, parsimony, and labor. The American people expressed its values through the major investments of the postwar years: the deification of the family was evident in the rapid spread of home ownership. Appetite for movement and privacy was satisfied by the flood of automobiles which carved new concrete channels through fields and city neighborhoods. Commitment to the children was evident in the increasing "child market" for commodities, the "adolescent culture" of the mass media, anxieties and plans for higher education, and, always, the preference for the single-family house in the neighborhoods of the likeminded (Greer, 1965).

The suburban move did not create these values. The suburbs have been felicitously and accurately called "new homes for old values." What occurred was the result of release from those constraints of poverty and space which had prevented the average American from living as he had wanted to do all along. Now with new consumer freedoms the old working-class culture could express itself in many new ways. That culture was evident in the conservatism of the "new middle classes"—their focus upon the child population, their pious religious participation, their concern with earning, buying, and planning to buy.

David Riesman has called them the "nouveau riche" of leisure (Riesman, 1950). He has pointed out their great new opportunities for learning, for development, for the creation of a new social character appropriate to the economies of plenty. But it is important to note certain concomitants of the new society which actually prevented learning, in old ways, important norms required for life in the society of increasing scale and internal inclusiveness. The knowledge, skills, and norms of good "consumership" are hardly adequate for a round of life; taste is no substitute for morality. And what was happening to morality?

Morality is that aspect of the common culture which emphasizes duties rather than rights. But the new affluence provided little in the way of guidelines to responsible public action. Indeed, through its cushioning effects, it tended to pull the teeth of older protest movements. Labor unions, their jurisdictions firm and their members' paychecks increasing, found little cause or profit in militancy. The socialist movements, committed to a reevaluation of work and social class, found the workers content with their "fair share" and uninterested in radical change. Feminism virtually disappeared, as the female became the captain of consumption and director of child-rearing in a child-oriented society. Aside from the continual pressure of colored ethnics for fuller inclusion, little action in the public domain reflected the duties, as against the rights, of citizenship.

In reality, the inherited social character of the rational producer had never had more than slight relevance to the demands of the public interest. Oriented to the maximization of profit at the entrepreneurial level, to parsimony and security at the level of the rank and file, the public purpose was assumed to be automatically fulfilled through individual aggrandizement—even the protest movements were powered by a concern with equal opportunity to aggrandize. No wonder the vast increase in energy, leisure, and symbolic communication has not resulted in the education of adults to a concern with public affairs and the high culture.

The Gross National Product is shared out among millions of households, where it is consumed in private. Much is undoubtedly being learned in the process—styles of dress and furniture change; child-rearing and sex practices are exposed to questioning and conscious thought; many of the peripheral crafts and skills of the society are diffused in the do-it-yourself manner. But the hard core of responsibility for the public affairs of society and one's action in them is not an area where adult education has flourished. "Public affairs" programs on the mass media remain public charges because there is little effective market for the dramatization of dilemmas and promises in the larger society.

This weakness in the political culture is maximized by the processes which are transforming the organizational shape of the society. The continuing changes in the space-time ratio (the cost in time of traversing space) result in a continuing process of national integration. The corporations safeguard market and resources through continuing mergers. As this occurs, the effective center of control shifts from the city, where the major industry is now a branch plant, to the national headquarters, where real decisions occur. Parallel changes take place in labor unions. (A labor leader described, ironically, a dozen bargaining sessions around the country waiting the word from New York—where the management of the telephone company and the president of the union were settling the issues.) Increasingly, even at top levels of local control, the industrial-commercial empires are manned by salaried workers.

The local political community is also changing, *para passu*. While the nation becomes overwhelmingly urban in its residence, the city loses its governmental form. The increasing command of space incident to the diffusion of the automobile has allowed the development of endless tract housing on the peripheries. These settlements, separately incorporated, live within the ecology of the metropolis but are not subject to any public powers at the local level. Typically, small residential enclaves and suburban municipalities are stewards for highly local interests; they are little concerned with the great issues of the metropolis as a whole and, like dogs in the manger, prevent any broader power from acting. Thus the governmental fragmentation of the metropolitan area prevents the generation and solution of significant issues at the place where they occur—the local political community (Greer, 1962).

Public action is learned through participation in the near-at-hand. It is learned through membership in a group, where one's private vocabulary is measured against the common culture, and where one's individual enthusiasm or grievance can be turned into social fact through communication and collective action. But study after study has shown that Americans are poor participators in the social groups accessible to them. They are most apt to participate in the voluntary organizations of suburbia—those groups devoted to the problems of household, family, and neighborhood. And of those who do participate, some must learn at least the ABC's of public action. But they are a minority and their public affairs tend to the trivial and the parochial.

For the rest, true significance is no longer local. The shifts in space-time ratio have radically changed the meaning of space and it is more useful now to speak, not of statute miles, but of what John Friedman calls "interactional space." The very concept of space is reduced to its effects as a barrier to and a channel for social interaction. In this sense, many of the most significant leaders of American thought and action are not primarily citizens of any local community. With national and international roles, the nation is their community, O'Hare Airport their crossroads, and the airstrips from Boston to Norfolk their Main Street. Even at the bottom of the occupational pyramid, where men engage largely in routine jobs seldom taking them beyond a plant or neighborhood, some dimensions of the world are supralocal. Each evening when they turn on the Big Screen their attention moves through interactional space to the national society. It is the locus of true significance, but it is far away and it is not experienced as personal action in a concrete social group.

While the organization of work and distribution of consumption goods have been radically changed, a more basic dynamic has continued to revolutionize the *process* of production. We have seen the origins of intensive urbanization in the progressive mechanization of the extractive industries, which released workers from the rural areas. We have noted that agriculture is the most automated of our industries. But the process has not stopped there. The "secondary" industries of fabrication are increasingly staffed, not with men, but with machines operated and controlled by other machines and powered by nonhuman energy resources. Production soars while the blue-collar labor force declines. As this occurs, more labor has moved into the white-collar jobs of sales and clerical tasks (the processing and diffusion of orders), into service jobs and the professions. Men increasingly work, as Riesman points out, not with "hard" materials but with "soft" symbols and social structures (Riesman, 1950).

Many of these jobs, however, are now in danger. The development of electronic data processing has provided a new kind of machine, one which can process orders at lightning speed with a far lower rate of error than the fallible human being could ever achieve. Digital computers with "canned" programs perform analyses in one minute which took, only a few years ago, several hundred man-hours on hand calculators (and let us recall that the computer is only about a decade old). Meanwhile, the service industries are increasingly applying new machines and sales activities are being revolutionized by prepackaging. Even the teacher is experimenting with teaching machines—devices which minimize error and improve learning through the abolition of the "human relationship" between pupil and mentor. The revolution which began with agriculture bids fair to permeate the traditional worlds of human work.

The world of the rational producer is working itself out of a job. The society based upon the economy and logic of scarcity becomes a monster cornucopia of production; the world focused upon cities, hinterlands, and regions, becomes involved and almost dissolved in the giant national system; the economy exalting the value of hard work and self-control produces a set of tools which threaten to make work as we have known it obsolete. The results are a set of massive problems, a fierce tension between the common culture, the social character, and the politico-economic situation of Americans.

THE PROBLEMS OF PLENTY

Each year production in the United States increases by two or three percent and personal income moves steadily upward with it. The vast array of consumer goods spreads further: to color television, pastel sports cars, power-driven reels for deep sea fishing. The number of millionaires passes 100,000. Yet the unemployment rate hovers around 5 percent; it is 14 percent for the youngest entrants to the labor force, 30 percent for those who did not finish high school, and 50 percent for those in the latter category who are colored. "Silent firing" becomes the rule. The author recently visited one of the major steel plants, economic resource for a populous valley, where no one had been hired for a couple of years and no one was going to be hired for several more. A large proportion of the stock of conventional jobs is disappearing.

These are the results of substituting machines for routine human work, for *drudgery*. Norbert Wiener believed that anything which could be done better by machines should be, for machines allow "the human use of human beings." The difficulty is that human beings can be used in American society only in a job, and jobs are not multiplying as fast as would-be workers. Then, since the job is one's claim to economic citizenship, the society dichotomizes into the relatively skilled, honored, and prosperous holders of increasingly technical jobs, on one hand, and the unemployed on the other. Subsisting on inadequate doles, the latter are "social basket cases," casualties of increasing scale.

The unemployed are a minor proportion of the citizenry at present, but there is no assurance this will remain true. By Adam Smith's definition, less than half the labor force is now employed in "productive" work, and some economists believe that in two decades it will be more like 15 percent. The accumulated labor force, meanwhile, is accelerating, as the child crop from the war and postwar years makes ready to marry and procreate. The society faces more than a temporary problem: as one in which the right to economic citizenship is affirmed it must generate millions of roles to confer that citizenship. The political rights of the unemployed (as well as the vulnerability of complex orders to sabotage) will force that duty upon whoever holds political authority.

In a global perspective, it does not seem a grim or tragic predicament. When one considers the problems of nations whose wealth per capita is less than one-twentieth of ours—the energy-poor and inefficient producers who dominate world society—it seems no problem at all. And, indeed, certain solutions to the problem seem clear and feasible. These solutions would require either a change in the assignment of work, a change in the nature of the role which guaranteed one economic citizenship, or a change in the nature of work. Given our certainty of production, any of the three would have the major effect of distributing economic citizenship to the increasing population of the republic.

The sheer number of human hours required by our productive plant is decreasing faster than our standard work week. (And probably faster than we can see from statistics, for featherbedding is a concomitant of silent firing.) It is not difficult to see that shortening of work weeks and the outlawing of "overtime" could easily effect a redistribution of jobs. The cost of production would increase somewhat in the short run, but the long-run human costs of multiplying the unemployed would be greatly minimized. Further, the resulting increase in leisure could be counted as a social good.

To go further, the very requirement that economic citizenship depends upon the job could be amended. The guaranteed household income is a distinct possibility and, as the authors of *The Triple Revolution* point out, the total cost of guaranteeing $3,000 a year for every American household would run less than two percent of the Gross National Product (Perrucci and Pilisuk, 1968). Such a minimal level would not attract many people who had the opportunity of earning the average income for the nation—over twice as much. But it would have the advantage of shoring up broken households where middle-aged women are busy raising a significant proportion of our next generation, of removing some of the stigma of failure from the older men whose skills are obsolete, of providing some kind of base on which the unemployed youth of the poor might lay the foundations for a rise to useful employment. In short, those bred to a society which once demanded menial, casual, and heavy physical labor would not have to bear alone the burdens of transition to a world where such labor was of decreasing value. Even though they might remain net charges upon the society, the effects upon the middle-aged miners in the worked-out coal fields of Illinois or West Virginia could be counted as a suitable social investment.

The foregoing are means of adjusting to the decline in our conventional stock of jobs relative to our burgeoning population. More important, however, is the long-run possibility of using labor, released now from manual drudgery, in a wide variety of spheres where the chief resource demanded is simply human action itself. From a strictly economic point of view, what is needed is work which is highly labor intensive, which produces negotiable goods, and produces goods which do not compete with themselves in future market situations. From a social point of view, what this writer prefers is work which enhances the quality of human life, for producers and consumers alike. The kind of work that is immediately apparent is that focusing upon the human services: education, health, the arts and sciences.

Indeed, we can already see a shift of investment towards these areas of production. The recreational industries, from tourism to fly-tying, are booming; the most important generator of new jobs in the economy today is education; even health is an increasingly big business. But the shift is not fast enough to accommodate the new generations of job-hungry youth and it is unlikely to accelerate fast enough to provide work for the millions of new households that will form in the next decade. This is in large part because the fields of health, education, welfare, and the arts, at best supplied by a very imperfect market, have been wards of the government. As such, they have been as stunted as most charity cases.

The obvious solution is a massive increase in governmental invest-ment in these areas of production. Where the market is incapable and the task is crucial, the public sector must act, as even the late Senator Taft acknowledged. Education is a public task by general acknowledg-ment, and so, increasingly, is research. The massive increase of resources in these areas could produce a rapidly professionalizing labor force with increasingly powerful tools for solving human problems.

Research, justified by a concern for all of mankind as well as the national interest, could face other crucial problems than that of ex-ploring space. These include, at least (1) the discovery of new sources of nonhuman energy, to take the place of our depleting reserves of fossil fuel and to make this power available to people now the victims of the erratic distribution of coal and oil; (2) the delineation of the social and physical causes of overfertility and the implementation of population control in the variety of human societies; (3) the discovery of the basic principles of learning and the development of a variety of educational techniques, suited to the varieties of persons and cultures and the dif-ferent capabilities required; and (4) perhaps the most important of all, the delineation of the nature and constraints of social organization in our rapidly expanding and increasingly complex society, with a concern not only for inexorable constraints on collective action, but also for the conditions of increasing freedom to choose. In short, our abundance of material goods and services could subsidize an increase in knowledge and techniques which would help the entire global society to achieve "the American standard of living," a goal impossible at present.

The above policies have all been suggested by reasonable men, yet they have a wildly utopian ring. Emphasizing the interdependence of the total society and, in the process, the necessary interaction of govern-ment and the economy, they violate the common culture of the American as a rational producer. They sound immoral to him and, therefore, impossible to the observer. To pay people more for not producing, to pay an adequate livelihood whether people work or not, is anathema. Further, to increase the amount of the wealth distributed by the federal government and then to invest that wealth in the "nonproductive" work of health, education, welfare, research, and the arts is to violate both the norms concerning who should have power and those concerning what should be done with it.

The social character of Americans is based upon the discipline of poverty and the religion of work. Their moral armature depends upon the mortification of the flesh through toil, a debt paid to the self-controls which constitute conscience. Leisure itself is a problem for such a character, and the prevalence of moonlighting on the one hand and do-it-yourself tasks on the other testify to the use of make-work as a means to security. The harsh character suited to the subsistence job or the subsistence farm, inappropriate though it is to the soft life of routine employee and aggressive consumer, continues full force in the absence of a replacement. For the threat that one's character is obsolescent is also a threat that one's self is obsolete: hence the anxiety over work, the threat in leisure.

Leisure for others, particularly for those who cannot find a job at productive labor, is the same threat doubled. Used to privatizing his economic life, the rational producer has only a personalistic vocabulary for achievement or success; the failure of others is proof of their incompetence and hence their lack of character. Even as his own life is organized around the armature of threat, scarcity, and work, so he cannot believe men will work hard without these whips—and he cannot accept the morality of men who do not work for a living. His harsh judgments of others are the mirror images of his own concept of self.

His privatization of public issues is simply a continuation of his heritage, the common culture of the merchant, farmer, and laborer. It is evident in his alienation from public responsibility and in his suspicion of the political process and public affairs. Since he is involved only peripherally, through the ritual of the vote and his spectatorship of the big screen, government is unreal and far away. Where he lives dwell only consumers of goods and compliers with order. Only in the small scale world of the local polity does he have access to a concrete political process; its trivial issues generally fail to arouse him to public action, save for sporadic efforts to impose a veto where his minor interests are considered in danger.

Democracy is an aristocratic concept, and the ideal political norms of the United States imply a common culture stressing noblesse oblige, the duties as well as the rights. The duties begin with the obligation to understand, take positions, and contend. They continue through the obligations to serve the public interest and to pay the price in the form of goods, services and powers surrendered to the public purpose. Democracy is, then, the socializing of political responsibility.

Judging from our data on American politics, the common culture has diffused these duties only as vague desiderata. The average citizen has not integrated them in the essential armature of his social character. His knowledge of the high culture, including his own political history, is typically vague and inaccurate. His knowledge of public affairs, even the burning issues of his politics, is hardly any better. (In one recent referendum for metropolitan government the slogan of the opposition was: "If you don't understand it, don't vote for it!") His education is typically already obsolete by the time he takes his place in the ranks of householders and citizens; it is not kept up by lifelong learning. Under the circumstances, it is easy for him to lose all perspective on the vast issues of the continental nation. He has no idea of the relative share of the Gross National Product going into governmental expenditures, or the relative importance of armaments in those expenses, much less the share spent by local, state, and federal governments. Illiterate of statistics, he is unable to read the alphabet, much less the language necessary to understand the world of national policy.

He translates these issues, then, into his own vocabulary of everyday action. The federal government is defined as a small business man, forever on the edge of bankruptcy. With the imperative of thrift and parsimony held sacred, he hardly understands, much less appreciates, the importance of research and development, risk capital, and the long view that attempts to predict and control the future. It would help if he could improve his economic notions to take account of, at least, the imperatives of big business enterprises, but he does not understand big business. His economic folk-thought omits the most important aspects of the contemporary society: rapid technological change, the complexity of organization, and the interaction of political and economic goals.

He confronts opposition, from the world without and from ideological opponents within, in the crude dichotomy of chauvinism. All that threatens is inherently evil. His ethnocentrism is so pronounced that he continually underestimates the power of other nation states and overestimates the importance of his domestic enemies. His political illiteracy is perhaps most dangerous in the areas where he should be competent—the values behind the Bill of Rights and the history of governmental oppression which gave rise to that bill (Mack, 1955–56). His inability to accept the problematic nature of the real world blinds him to much of the reason for controversy and, therefore, to the basis for protecting the person with a minority opinion. Life to him is simple in principle: thus the anxiety generated through his blurred awareness of the Communists as radical critics of his way of thought. His response is a religious reaffirmation of what he takes to be his "way of life"; the deification of small business (though 200 corporations produce 80 percent of the economic values in the society), the decrial of the federal government's spending (though most of it goes for the wars of past and future which he supports in principle), opposition to "growing federal power" (though most of his security is a by-product of the welfare programs and economic stewardship of the national system).

But he is not really given to political contention. In his everyday social relationships, he avoids conversation about politics if there is any genuine difference of opinion, for it is "controversial." (He imagines a politics without controversy.) His chief source of political information is in the mass-media figures who agree with him, and his outlet for political opinions is the circle of kin and friends upon whom he can count to share his assumptions and pieties (Greer, 1963). But political questions do not really limit his friendship circle, for he tempers the winds of conversation to the company, excising if necessary all subjects of general import. (In an unpublished study of a middle-class Oregon population, Robin Williams and his associates found no relation between friendship and similarity of values.) While such behavior probably reflects, rather than creates, the lack of significance found in public issues, each opportunity lost perpetuates the existing situation.

Half-in and half-out of the large-scale society, the "typical" social character sketched in above is a changeling. One can see traces of the peasant villager, the vague fear of the unknown and the lack of confidence that the world is in any way subject to one's choice and efforts. One can see, in many cases, a "daemonic universe" in which the President of the United States is a "conscious agent of the Communist conspiracy," while fluoridation of the water supplies is a plot by Communists to weaken the bone structure of American bodies. One can see also the hard carapace of the rational producer's social character: the suspicion of political leaders and the public enterprise, hatred of positive government of all sorts and especially taxes, contempt for controversy and the political process. The common culture has not produced a social character adequate for a broadly based democratic polity; it has produced a society of employees, spectators, and consumers who think they are free enterprisers.

Yet so constituted is the American polity that its ability to act rests finally upon the consent of the average citizen. The local political community is based upon their agreement and must return to them for changes in taxes, in powers, and in its formal structure. The rules for the local community are, in turn, frozen into the constitution of the states, while the latter are given conditions for the integration of governmental action in the society. At each level the political leadership must have the assent of the citizens. Only thus can government action be legitimated through the common political culture, and the law which is that culture be frozen into statutes and charters.

One might well ask how, under the circumstances, the country is governed at all? And indeed, the history of the United States includes some vast hiatuses in which little governmental direction was evident—whether we speak of the lawlessness of the western territories before statehood, the "lynch law" of the South and the Indian "wars," or the uncontrolled development of our giant corporations and our vast and ragged cities (Wood, 1961; Josephson, 1934; Kroeber, 1961). In the past, the society, simpler in its organization and protected from its enemies, could live with a modicum of governmental responsibility. Today this becomes less possible by the minute: the anxieties of the cold war with its threat of thermonuclear holocaust, and the anxieties of economic change with its threat of disastrous depressions inevitably increase the responsibility of the federal government and the national political leadership.

National leaders dominate the big screen and the issues they confront are the most salient in modern life. But they are far away from the social presence of the citizens and they achieve support only through the delegation of trust to party or person in the forced choice of a two-party election. But indeed, this distance from the voters is probably the only reason they can act at all. When we look at the states and their politics, we are struck with their incapability to act with respect to their legitimate problems. This inability of state governments to organize consensus probably rests, in turn, upon their very exposure to the rank and file of their constituencies. We hear much about the overrepresented rural vote as the cause of state incapacities, yet the only careful studies of the problem indicate that urban delegations to the capitols get what they want—they simply cannot even agree among themselves on what it is. The doctrine of states' rights has foundered in our complex society upon the inability of the states to act as semi-sovereign governments. They have been, instead, veto groups—brakes upon the policies generated at the national level.

Equally rigid has been the hold of popular democracy upon our city governments. Limited in their abilities to tax, their abilities to expand their jurisdictions and powers, and their abilties to reformulate their structure, they have been passive victims of the powerful transformations associated with expanding scale. Their limits are, in turn, due to their exposure to the population through the referendum, that plebiscite which assumes competence and concern on the part of everyone aged twenty-one [now eighteen] or more. Unable to act under these limits, unable to reorganize themselves (so they could act) under the state constitutional limits, cities have increasingly turned to devices which evade the vote of the electorate. Special district governments with their own taxing power can integrate jurisdictions and increase governmental control—at the expense of being virtually invisible to the citizens. State and federal grants-in-aid for new purposes break the deadlock of local indifference and stalemate, but at the expense of being administered by professional bureaucracies hardly exposed to the citizenry. Positive government evaporates from the local democracy in the process, leaving the mayors of our cities in the role of "caretakers." As such they try to update the services legitimatized in the past and to increase the flow of nonlocal funds into their bailiwicks. Prisoners of the common political culture, they attempt to "wire around" the dead cells of the local democracy (Greer, 1963).

THE UBIQUITY OF CHANGE

To recapitulate, social character has been identified as typical ways of acting in important social situations. Based upon a culture created to handle the everyday situations that must be confronted, social character perpetuates that culture as individuals attempt to adapt the new to the framework of the familiar, applying wonted behavior to the emerging world. Thus the social character appropriate to the rational producer, the laborer, the small businessman, and the peasant, has been applied to the rapidly urbanizing society of the twentieth century. In the process, its inadequacies are evident; it fits neither the situations of the individual actor nor the demands of the large-scale system. It is perpetuated in the rhetoric of politics, the folk theory of economics, and the cliches of popular morality. Yet one suspects that it can give lip service in these areas only because of their lack of salience to the ordinary citizen (as burial rites are among our most conservative customs largely because of their unimportance to the ongoing society). Let us examine, then, the changes in those situations where Americans *must* be competent and concerned with outcomes.

The typical American worker is becoming a white-collar employee and his work is changing to the control of symbols and people. Further, he is apt to work within a large-scale formal organization, one which integrates the behavior of hundreds of men with that of hundreds of machines on one power grid and one time schedule. This means that the work he does is demanding, for error can cumulate geometrically. What is more, the action demanded is *rational choice* in respect to the larger system. It rests upon a precise knowledge of abstract theory applied to the concrete facts at issue; it encourages rationality in the formulating and resolving of the question at issue.

The increasing scale of the organization within which the individual acts has other consequences. At the bottom of the skill hierarchy the workers are conscious of the sheer complexity and integration of behavior in the corporation. At the top, the managers are aware of this complexity as it persists, thrives or fails within a complex organizational environment, national in scale. The very scope of their roles is conducive to wider horizons; the North Carolina textile industry is integrally related through the world market to those of Japan and Hong Kong, while many major American corporations do a large minority, or even a majority, of their business overseas. With jet aircraft, the executive life can literally be lived in an international network of organizations. This is a far cry from the squires of the Pennsylvania mill towns still described by nostalgic novelists.

Meanwhile, back at the plant, the squires have given way to the experts at social engineering. David Riesman (as so often) first underlined the significance of the "human relations in industry" approach to the problems of authority in economic organization (Riesman, 1950: 302–327; 330–338). The solution of brute mechanical problems of production has been accompanied by an increasing awareness of the problems of social coordination, integration, and morale. Perhaps a decline of the social character called the "rational producer" among routine workers has accompanied the postwar prosperity and the increase in security. At any rate, "labor commitment" is a problem not only in the underdeveloped countries (Moore and Feldman, 1962). The role of the organizational engineer is increasingly one which requires an understanding of the varieties of humanity which, together, constitute "the firm." Labor leader, personnel man, arbitrator—all are in the same profession, and provide major reference groups for management.

The changing nature of everyday life is evident also in the world of leisure. Here it is important to remember that, for the first time in history, the whole range of men has the right of *choice,* and in many different areas. Increased formal education and access to the mass media mean a broadening of cultural equipment, for many different vocabularies run through the collage of noise and images on television and, when they are new, allow alternate definitions of known events. The increase in household incomes means an improved power to act; it is evident in the growth of what some have called the "ardent amateur" (Foote, 1960). This wealth is invested in fields as diverse as sports, movie-making, and the arts and crafts. Perhaps most important of all, the increase in leisure has increased our life-space, allowing action in a variety of realms.

In a recent national poll it was reported that six percent of the adults interviewed had taken an active part in a theatrical production within the past year. This finding is to be read along with a recent statement that there are now over 10,000 little theaters in the United States. Galleries for the arts multiply in the metropolitan areas and spring up in the smaller cities, while the sale of books—both soft and hard cover—has increased faster than the population.

All in all, it seems possible that the release of man from the iron role of the laborer is beginning to produce an efflorescence of man as a maker and man as a social actor. It is, to be sure, a phenomenon broadcast throughout the population. It is most evident in the hobbies and crafts, pursued and consumed in the privacy of the household. It is least evident in social action, the significant role in public space. Yet the consistent finding that a large minority of the citizens in the suburban municipalities is involved in their local community at a number of levels may indicate an increasing preference for social and political action as leisure pursuits. Equally important is the finding that public life in the suburbs is accessible to and engaged in by women as frequently as by men.

Another realm of everyday life that is not amenable to the old norms of the rational producer is that of child-rearing. The authoritarian norms of the past assumed a clear congruence between the world of the fathers and that of the sons; only the most obtuse can believe that this holds true today. Instead, children are given the most general norms and discover for themselves how they are applied in the large-scale, formal group such as the junior high, the high school, or the university. Nor do the norms of self-control, parsimony, and work fit very well in the relations between parents and child; there is so little real work for the child in the ongoing round of the household, that it penalizes the parent more to find it than it does the child to perform it. Indeed, the work of the household is not the proper task of the child. With the widespread realization that formal education is the key to the future, the pressure on children is calculated to ensure commitment to the goals of the educational system. With this achieved, the child is rewarded with his "fair share" of the consumables, a share calculated by comparison with his peers. For the parents, this is an expected cost of rearing children.

The major cost in rearing children, however, is the burden of uncertainty. With the breakup of the scarcity economy and its ways, parents are involved in the enterprise of inventing a rationale for child-rearing. The thorniest problems in learning theory, authority relationships, and depth psychology are innocently posed and somehow settled by these amateur social scientists who struggle with the unknown. Grappling for certainty, they swing between the discarded norms of their own childhood and the efforts of social scientists to generalize about the complex and delicate process which transform the neonate into the American citizen of tomorrow. Their effort to be rational and their consequent uncertainty are, again, not likely to reinforce the norms of the authoritarian social character.

The everyday life situations which the contemporary American must handle show certain recurring attributes. One is the pervasiveness of the *problematic:* on the job, in the children's bedroom, or facing the big screen. The intellectual answer is demanded and it cannot be intuited or remembered; the social answer which resolves the impasse is required yet it does not come "naturally." Both kinds of uncertainty can lead to what Riesman calls "the other-directed character," the person without any intrinsic standards for the good or the true. It can also lead, however, to belief in the possibility of rational consensus, a solution to the problems of the intellectually uncertain. And it can lead to a belief that one must take the standpoint of the other in order to understand him and solve the problems of the socially uncertain.

Perhaps a new American social character is emerging from these recurrent problems of everyday life. It would be one organized around the armature of intellectual control and socially created agreement. It would emphasize the necessity to think, in abstract terms, of a larger and more problematic world than was ever assumed by the rational producer. Particularly in respect to facing, on television and elsewhere, the variety of social worlds, pluralism and scale would require that an immense value be placed upon taking into account the role of the other person. Projecting these demands upon the events revealed by the big screen, the public world in which one is totally involved (through the bomb, conscription, taxes, the danger of depression or inflation), such a social character would require a general education and source of information far beyond what has ever been available in the past to either common men or privileged elites.

Such an education is possible in the United States today and is approximated for some of the oncoming generation. Should the above speculations be correct, that generation would be the first to realize and formulate a new American character type. It would be congruent, not with Americanism but with the human world of large-scale society. Freed from the older constraints of poverty, parochialism, and authoritarianism, our first postwar generation is still an enigma to its parents. It has not known the depression of the 1930s, a catastrophe which unnecessarily reinforced and prolonged the dominance of a scarcity culture, nor has it known the appalling experience of watching a Hitler dominate the proudest societies on earth. At the same time it has been educated in schools immensely superior to those of older generations (schools which Dr. Conant says have much that is right about them and, generally, only minor arrangements which are wrong). Finally, it is a generation which has grown up with the world in its living room, with the White House, Little Rock, Khrushchev and de Gaulle before it on the big screen. Its perspectives should be broader, its pieties more relevant to reality, and its questions more significant.

In the meantime the American society is not filled with either the "ideal type" of rational producer nor with the new character type sketched in above. What seems the likely case is a complex mix of social characters, with old styles, new styles, and hybrids galore.

(Anyone's social character may vary greatly between the realms of work, politics, leisure, kinship, and the high culture.) One would expect the new style to predominate where the task was most inexorable and the new norms most requisite, while the older style would be common where it could be maintained without difficulty.

The fundamentalists of religion, politics, and work should be found in the remnants of the smaller-scale society and in the roles of small scope within the larger world. The small towns of the rural areas, the open country neighborhoods, the South, should be heavily loaded with the older types; they should be common among small businessmen, farmers, ranchers, miners, and common laborers. They should also be found among Negroes and other ethnic groups cut off, by segregation, from full participation in the wider society.

The new social character should be most common in the metropolitan areas, in the most rapidly expanding and large-scale economies of the Middle Atlantic and the West Coast. They should be common among such workers as those employed in mass communications, entertainment, education, government, and distribution. They should be most common in those jobs requiring broad decisions and exceptional technical expertise, though one would expect them to appear in force among the ranks of the service workers—maintenance men, restaurateurs, landscape gardeners, and the like. For it is in jobs where the intellectually and socially problematic are most crucial that one would expect a major alteration in the ethic of hard work, parsimony, and self-control.

But both are extreme types, and it is not likely that either will be found to dominate the social positions indicated. Between the old style and the new, lies the tolerant middle, the rational producer whose carapace of habit and character is softening in the sun of prosperity and leisure, the new-style American who still commits himself erratically to the grim conscience and religion of work. The middle range is made up of the changelings: arbitrating between the extremes, it is the cushion which prevents the war of norms from utterly hamstringing the society. It is sorely pressed today in mediating between the southern sheriffs and the Student Nonviolent Coordinating Committee. It is that part of a generation torn between mutually irreconcilable commitments. Its bad conscience and its overconstrained leisure, its fetishism of commodities and privatization of action are alike, symptoms of a social character no longer adequate to its world. The tensions will probably not be resolved in this generation, however; for that resolution we must look to the next crop.

Meanwhile, the mix is changing. The present generation controlling this country is one which remembers the great depression, a bench mark of poverty. Like children who never had enough to eat and thus become, as adults, compulsive eaters, this generation has been obsessed

with the consumption goods of the private market. But as new generations come on, we shall find a differing hierarchy of values and a new
set of norms. The passing of the depression generation will be accompanied by the declining importance of those who spent their earliest
years in small towns and open country. (The true meaning of urbanization is obscured by their presence for, so rapidly have our cities grown,
that a large proportion of our "metropolitanites" is really made up
of country boys in the suburbs.) Increasing quantities and qualities
of formal education should radically alter the cultural equipment of
these new, city-bred, post-depression citizens.

Perhaps, from all these trends, one could hazard the prediction
that the people of the United States are busy inventing the social
character appropriate to the large-scale society. As they do so, they
will be laying the foundations for the first truly democratic civilization
in the history of mankind. No effort is more important than this, for
we are committed, willy-nilly, to a democratic solution to our problems.
This means that our public policy cannot long remain far above the
common culture and the social character of the usual citizen.

REFERENCES

Bell, Wendell (ed.) (1967) The Democratic Revolution in the West Indies.
Cambridge, Mass.: Schenkman.

Cottrell, Fred (1955) Energy and Society. New York: McGraw-Hill.

Foote, Nelson N. (1960) Housing Choices and Constraints. New York:
McGraw-Hill.

Frank, Lawrence K. (1948) Society as the Patient. New Brunswick:
Rutgers Univ. Press.

Greer, Scott (1955) Social Organization. New York: Random House.

———— (1962a) Governing the Metropolis. New York: John Wiley.

———— (1962b) The Emerging City, Myth and Reality. New York: Free
Press.

———— (1963) Metropolitics: A Study of Political Culture. New York:
John Wiley.

———— (1965) Urban Renewal: A Sociological Critique. Indianapolis:
Bobbs-Merrill.

Hauser, Philip M. (1960) Population Perspectives. New Brunswick: Rutgers Univ. Press.

Hughes, Everett (1943) French Canada in Transition. Chicago: Univ. of
Chicago Press.

Josephson, Matthew (1934) The Robber Barons, The Great American
Capitalists, 1861–1901. New York: Harcourt, Brace and World.

Kroeber, Theodora (1961) Ishi in Two Worlds: A Biography of the Last
Wild Indians in North America. Berkeley: Univ. of Calif. Press.

Mack, Raymond W. (1955-56) "Do we really believe in the Bill of
Rights?" Social Problems 3 (Winter): 264-267.

Moore, Wilbur, and Arnold Feldman (1962) Labor Commitment and Economic Development. Princeton: Princeton Univ. Press.

Perlman, Selig, and Philip Taft (1935) Labor Movements (History of Labor in the United States, 1896–1932). New York: Macmillan.

Perrucci, Robert, and Marc Pilisuk (compilers) (1968) The Triple Revolution: Social Problems in Depth. Boston: Little, Brown.

Riesman, David, Reuel Denny, and Nathan Glazer (1950) The Lonely Crowd. New Haven: Yale Univ. Press.

Turner, Ralph E. (1941) The Great Cultural Traditions. New York: McGraw-Hill.

Williams, Raymond (1960) Culture and Society, 1780-1950. Garden City: Doubleday.

Wilson, Godfrey, and Monica Wilson (1945) The Analysis of Social Change. London: Cambridge Univ. Press.

Wood, Robert (1961) 1400 Governments. Cambridge: Harvard Univ. Press.

CHAPTER 6

TECHNOLOGICAL MAN

VICTOR C. FERKISS

Time, said Saint Augustine, is a threefold present: the present as we experience it, the past as a present memory, and the future as a present expectation. According to that criterion, suggests sociologist Daniel Bell, the world of the future has already arrived: "The future is not an overarching leap into the distance; it begins with the present . . . for in the decisions we make now, in the way we design our environment and thus sketch the lines of constraints, the future is committed." In contrast, many of our contemporaries, in forecasting the marvels of even the most proximate decades, depict the future in a manner that renders it bewitching, remote, and detached.

Isaac Asimov, an eminent biochemist, foretells that by the year 2000 man will be exploring the limits of the solar system and living underground. Marshall McLuhan has predicted that by the same time the wheel and the highway will be obsolete, having totally given way to hovercraft. Biologist Bentley Glass has stated that artificial production of children will probably be realized by the end of the current century. Physicist Herman Kahn predicts that, before the turn of the twenty-first century, science will have achieved almost complete genetic control of man and acquired the means for the creation of new species. Even more startling and intellectually remote are the forecasts of astronomer Arthur C. Clarke and paleontologist Pierre Teilhard de Chardin. Clarke has prophesied a man-machine symbiosis in which artificial sensors will make it possible for man to feel he is present wherever his creations are. Teilhard de Chardin sees the evolutionary development of humankind soon to eventuate in a superorganism, a collective being, a "single, hyper-conscious arch molecule," a "stupendous thinking machine."

In *Technological Man: The The Myth and the Reality,* from which the following two essays have been drawn, Victor C. Ferkiss offers a compendium of the apocalyptic visions that have been be-

held in recent times by such varied seers as Bell, Asimov, Mc-
Luhan, Glass, Kahn, Clarke, Teilhard de Chardin, and others.
More importantly, his work surveys the coming age of advanced
technology and man's place in it.

Ferkiss asserts that modern technology has made "human society
a seamless web," and he attempts to define the direction mankind
must take if it is to deal capably with the new challenges posed to
society by technological change. Ferkiss claims that humanity has
reached a turning point, an *existential revolution,* where it is "on
the threshold of self-transfiguration having attained power over itself and its environment." This existential revolution, manifested in
a system of ideas, techniques, and machines, Ferkiss expects, will
put us, in terms of power, about where God is—or used to be.

In his description of this new revolution, Ferkiss systematically
details the scientific and technological predictions and break-
throughs that will threaten the persistence of civilization as we
have come to know it. He discusses the psychological shocks
and practical problems that might be encountered with the realization of such probabilities as solar conquest, gene banks and artificial brains, transmutation of base into precious metals, undersea
colonies, cyborgs, teaching machines, computers with IQ's of 150,
brain rejuvenation, biological and pharmacological weaponry, breaking of genetic codes and development of fetal therapy, and urbanization of the world. This partial list of probabilities, Ferkiss warns,
ought not to be viewed as melodramatic predictions derived from
fiction and fantasy. Not all may come to pass, he admits, and
others will take longer than predicted, but the speed of change is
increasing exponentially, and the scientific bases of the predictions will become technologically feasible within the next seven
decades, and a significant portion is already within our grasp.

To deal with this existential revolution, Ferkiss proposes that we
not only "invent" our future but, first and foremost, create a
"technological man" who will replace industrial man and manage
our future. Technological man will not be a new biological type
but, rather, a new cultural type with a new philosophy. This
philosophy, Ferkiss suggests, would require the guidelines of three
fundamental elements: a new naturalism, a new holism, and a new
immanentism. The *new naturalism* asserts that man is in fact part
of nature, rather than apart from it. The *new holism* involves the
realization that in the total system of mind-body-machinery-society-
nature everything connects and interacts. The *new immanentism* expresses the recognition that life exists within systems and that systems create themselves. The shape of the total system derives from
what happens within it, not from the external action of Fate, For-
tune, or some "cosmic watchmaker."

Finally, Ferkiss suggests that, if the new vision of man is valid,
it cannot come into being without a reorientation of human cul-

ture. Such a reorientation would require radical changes in our economic and political systems, with new standards for social as well as biogenetic controls. Echoing the words of Saint Augustine and Daniel Bell, Victor C. Ferkiss sees the future as beginning with the present. The technological revolution, though still in its infancy, has forced mankind to deal immediately with the world of tomorrow in order to survive the consequences of the new technology.

Victor C. Ferkiss is Professor of Government at Georgetown University.

THE EXISTENTIAL REVOLUTION

Mankind, it is alleged by the prophets of the new man, is on the threshold of a new age. He has, so they tell us, within or almost within his grasp new powers over himself and his environment that will radically transform the whole character and meaning of human existence. But before we can affirm or deny the reality or extent of this existential revolution we need to be more specific about the changes technology is making possible that threaten the persistence of civilization as we have known it or that herald the coming of the new technological man.

Trying to understand what is happening to man today is difficult for several reasons. Many of the new scientific and technological break-throughs, like the development of the atomic bomb or the circumnavigation of the earth by astronauts, are or appear to be isolated events. It is not at once apparent what effect they are having on man's social life and self-image; most of us go about our daily business as if they had never occurred. We may once have thought of building a fallout shelter or we may have stayed at home to watch the first manned rocket launchings on television, but soon we are once again caught up in the daily routine of bills, promotions, vacations and lawns to mow. Other triumphs of science, like the successful transplantation of the human heart, strike us as novel and possibly important to a few humans with medical problems, but they seem like more of the same thing: further steps in a long upward spiral of medical progress, added conveniences like faster cars and color TV. Isn't it wonderful, we say, and then belie our words by going on about our business.

"The Existential Revolution" by Victor C. Ferkiss, pp. 92–103 in *Technological Man: The Myth and the Reality*, 1969, is reprinted by permission of the publisher, George Braziller, Inc. "Toward the Creation of Technological Man" by Victor Ferkiss, pp. 202–23 in *Technological Man: The Myth and the Reality*, 1969, is reprinted by permission of the publisher, George Braziller, Inc.

Still other additions to man's power over nature, such as the synthesis of DNA, involve such esoteric scientific problems that to most of us (though not necessarily to our more alert offspring) they are largely meaningless. Not understanding the scientific issues involved, we soon lose interest (though we many feel guilty about this if we are middle class and college trained, for today not being interested in science is not unlike admitting to being bored by classical music). Having no philosophical or scientific context within which to place these discoveries, we soon forget about them.

Finally there are a great number of possibilities that never enter our consciousness at all simply because through lack of background knowledge and interest we never hear about them or, if we do, we unconsciously dismiss them as mere speculation or even fantasy. Gene banks and artificial brains, extrasensory perception and the ability to derive atomic energy from ordinary rocks may crop up in the headlines of our newspapers, but they become a kind of background noise to the stock-market reports and the war news, filtered out like the television program our children are watching in the next room. If we do notice these items, we may simply suppress them, as many of us do with information relating to the dangers of nuclear war or a world population that will more than double in the next generation. The power of the ordinary to reclaim our attention is enormous, and is in part a necessary condition of our sanity. It also may represent a healthy acceptance of fate. An early modern saint is famous for his reply to a question about what he would do if he knew that God was going to bring his life to an end within the hour. His reply was that he would go on playing billiards. But his faith in the state of his soul and the beneficence of the Almighty may not be an appropriate response for those whose civilization is threatened by developments all of which might not be beneficent (in part because the present civilization is not as morally healthy as it might be), developments that it still has some power to affect.

There exists today a sizable literature about the foreseeable future (the period from today until the era of our great-grandchildren) in which the leading experts in various fields set forth their views as to what technological developments are likely to occur. Ability to predict technological change is far from absolute, but usually the unanticipated event occurs in addition to the anticipated rather than as a substitute for it, so most of what is predicted probably will occur. Many predictions necessarily rest on assumptions about how much effort will go into certain lines of research as well as about what appears to be intrinsically impossible, but increasingly the prophets take this complication into account. Some predictions are to a certain extent mutually incompatible, in practice even if not in theory. Thus improvements in communications technology might lead to a slackening of efforts to improve transportation or vice versa, or an increased ability to convert ordinary substances such as sand and rock into scarce minerals might make interplanetary mining uneconomic; but this does not negate the possibility of any of the alternatives or the need to take cognizance of them.

While not all futurists agree on details—and today every competent scientist, businessman, military leader or government official is continually involved in predicting the future through sheer necessity to plan ahead in his own activity—there is considerable consensus on basic trends in technological development.[1] (In part, of course, this may be due to common orientations or to the fact that there is developing a futurist Establishment that dominates most studies and conferences.) Most disagreements are about probabilities rather than possibilities and about timing. When one realizes the magnitude and probable impact of the events forecast, one is struck by the wide measure of agreement rather than by the minor disagreements. If only a small fraction of the developments predicted take place, the existential revolution will present humanity with psychological shocks and practical problems on a scale unknown to recorded history.

THE EXTENSION OF ENVIRONMENT

Because of its remoteness from ordinary human life, progress in the conquest of space presents perhaps the fewest immediately disturbing elements for contemporary civilization to assimilate. We are already getting used to the intercontinental missile and its cousin, the satellite that can observe or destroy any part of the earth's surface unless prevented from doing so. Mechanical contact with or electronic observation of the surface of the moon and Venus is already a reality. What does the future hold? Some predictions are so certain that a consensus exists as to the actual date of their probable occurrence—a permanent lunar base by 1975, permanent manned stations on some planets by 1990—given certain assumptions about budgetary commitments on the part of the governments concerned.

There is nothing very startling about these predictions. Less expected by most of us, however, is the probable discovery of an antigravity drive on a principle other than rocket propulsion, which one panel of experts expects soon after the year 2020.[2] Such an event would open the door to travel beyond the solar system, in addition to being a contribution toward nullifying the force of gravity (rather than merely overcoming it) here on earth. Some predictions such as competition for the raw materials of other planets and extraterrestrial farming by about the same time would have important economic and psychological effects if fulfilled.[3] But even if they came to pass they would simply mean that man's conquest of the solar system was essentially Europe's conquest of the earth in the colonial era writ large: colonies, bases, plantations, economic exploitation.

More significant are those technological developments associated with the conquest of space that have direct implications for the nature of man himself. Journeys into outer space—especially beyond the solar system—would take vast amounts of time with any immediate foreseeable techniques. Scientists therefore predict placing voyagers in a state of coma from which they would automatically recover at a set time. An even more significant alternative would be multigeneration missions in which those who arrived at their destination would be the descendants of the original crew. Should this occur, man would really have left earth behind, scattering his seed far into the universe. Those born and reared in space would be in sense a different kind of man. They might never be able to communicate with the planet that sent them forth. But the impact of their going on the consciousness of those who remained behind would still be immense.

The difficulties of operating in and adjusting to the physical conditions of outer space and strange planets have led to speculation that the astronauts of the future would be Cyborgs, men who would have many artificial organs and thus would be better able to cope with harsh and novel surroundings. An alternative or supplementary means of exploration (at least within shorter distances where something like real-time communication was possible) would be a kind of machine-man symbiosis, in which there would be direct electromagnetic connection between the human nervous system and equipment that was receiving transmissions from sensors elsewhere in space. Those humans involved would control the exploring machines and receive impressions (muted, if necessary) as if they were actually physically experiencing the exploration themselves. Space would thus become part of the human environment, since even those not in the direct symbiotic relationship would be part of a culture that knew the sights and sounds of the expanses of space firsthand.[4]

Not only in space but also on earth itself is the environment about to be radically extended. The oceans will in a generation or two become part of the human habitat.[5] They will not merely be crossed by travelers, fishermen or the world's navies, or explored by a few aquanauts for scientific, military or recreational purposes; they will become as domesticated as the land surface of the planet. Men will farm the waters, breed and herd fish, and mine the bottom of the high seas. The conquest of the 70 per cent of the earth's surface that is under water will mean changes in man, society and nature. Permanent undersea colonies will be established; individuals and even whole families may eventually spend most of their lives under water. Cetaceans, many of whom exhibit a high level of natural intelligence, will be bred and trained as helpers; already the U.S. Navy is using dolphins in undersea recovery work.[6] Man himself will learn to breathe water through medical alteration of his lungs or other means; the U.S. Navy's leading expert's target for the creation of "gillmen" is 1972.[7] Extensive research in breathing water impregnated with compressed gas is currently underway at Duke University under the direction of Dr. Johannes Klystra. Whether or not any particular developments now foreseen actually will take place, man's over-all relation to the oceans is about to change inexorably and irrevocably. Just as we soon will no longer see the moon primarily as an aid to romance but rather as a revolving mining camp or military base, our children standing on the shores of the Pacific will see not a vastness of untamed water stretching far beyond the horizon to Cathay, but a pond full of derricks, mines, ranches and perhaps even suburbs.

What of man's economic life? Some predict that the race between technological progress and population growth will be won by the former. How likely this is we must judge in due course. Certainly there seems to be increasing consensus among scientists that new weapons will soon be available for the war on hunger and scarcity. Most startling and important, it is even hoped that the alchemist's ancient dream of transmuting base metals into precious ones will be fully realized at last. Man already can create new sources of energy and new elements through his mastery of the atom. But this ability is so far restricted by the need to use naturally unstable radioactive minerals as a point of departure. If man can unlock the energy in ordinary iron or hydrogen and use it to turn the common elements of the land and seas into mechanical or electrical energy or into other elements, scarcity would lose most of its meaning. Some predict that the world's need for fresh water soon could be remedied by economically feasible desalination using radioactive materials; if ordinary minerals could be substituted this would remove all obstacles to unlimited water supplies. It is already technically possible to create synthetic protein from petroleum; once we are able to do this on a large scale no one need ever go hungry or suffer the physical or mental defects caused by lack of protein; for petroleum itself can probably be made available without limit through chemical alchemy. In time man should be able to use any part of the earth's surface or interior for any purpose he wishes; through recycling he could use it over and over again.

Today natural forces still get in the way of man's productive activities, especially in agriculture. This, too, will soon be a thing of the past. Completely accurate prediction of the weather over the globe is almost unanimously expected in a relatively short time; many foresee control of the most significant aspects of the weather within a generation.[8]

The single factor that most distinguishes the coming civilization, whatever one chooses to call it, is the substitution of "communication" processes for traditional "work" as man's primary activity. That automation in one form or another will be the basis of the new civilization is generally held by futurists. Teaching machines will become the norm, and in time information will be directly transmitted to the human brain electronically. Use of the computer will lead to what, in effect, will be a universal language for some purposes, based on the computer's needs. By 1990, many confidently predict, computers will be available with the equivalent of IQ's of 150 in terms of their ability to respond to directions, understand their environment and initiate activity. Routine labor will be taken over by robot household servants (though many see as an alternative the breeding of intelligent animals, particularly primates, for low-grade routine labor on the land as well as in the sea). The climax of this process will come when machine-man symbiosis begins to play its role on earth; a median date predicted for its large-scale practicability is 2010.[9]

The progress of technology will increase vastly the means available to men to control other men. New biological and pharmacological weapons will be available that will coerce without destroying men or property, largely through their direct effect on the will. Electronics will increase greatly the means of centralized surveillance available to ruling groups (a national data bank is already a subject of controversy in Washington, and it could be instituted tomorrow, Congress permitting).[10]

The Impact of Biology

But neither the extensions of man's effective environment into the depths of space or the oceans, nor the vision of automated affluence, nor even the greater social controls that are predicted for the near future most radically affect man's existential situation. He has always sought knowledge, ease and power over his fellows. The coming of the new man is foreshadowed most by the contemporary revolution in the biological sciences.[11] We have noted already the extent to which man's biological integrity could be affected by various kinds of symbiosis with the machine, whether through increased use of artificial organs or by being literally plugged into a computer. But increasing understanding of the processes underlying biological activity will also make it possible to subject organic processes to human control. Drugs may become widespread not only as means of social control but as accepted means of self-realization. General and permanent immunization against most diseases is considered increasingly feasible. Physical and chemical treatment for psychological and psychotic states may soon relegate the Freudian analyst to the role of witch doctor that many scientists feel is only appropriate. New contraceptive techniques are constantly being developed to bring fecundity under control, and increasingly the aspiration of researchers is something (a capsule implanted in the body that permanently inhibits formation of appropriate cells unless neutralized, for instance) that would make breeding, rather than prevention, require a special medical act. New medical discoveries lead researchers to expect the lengthening of the human life span fifty years, which in their view would only be a return to the normal. It is already virtually certain that even the brain can be rejuvenated by injections of DNA, thus making it possible to maintain memory and problem-solving ability unimpaired into old age.[12]

However, it is not the curing of disease but the control of genetic processes and the shape of man that most excites speculation. Man's physical shape will be alterable by new and radical forms of medical cosmetology; the nose job and the paraffin-inflated breast of today will be succeeded by a variety of techniques to alter color of hair, skin or eyes or to change contours or even sex, with only the basic skeletal structure constituting any limitation. Mental states will be alterable as well: intelligence and character affected by chemical means, dreams stimulated or even preprogramed. Biochemical processes may make possible the growing of new organs to replace old ones; the year 2007 is predicted by some as the date for this breakthrough.

But at best the human mind and body, once formed, present a difficult problem for the biologist. Far better to "adjust" them beforehand. The breaking of the genetic code will in the reasonably near future make it possible to predetermine not only sex but other characteristics. Genetic defects could be countered by excision or addition of genes in embryo; if suitable artificial wombs being worked on at present are perfected, "foetal therapy" is well on the way. New knowledge of the mechanisms of heredity, storage of genetic materials and artificial insemination will make it possible for women to order the kind of child they wish as they would order a new car. For parents with higher self-esteem, techniques are being developed that will make it possible to produce exact duplicates of the father or mother by substituting the cell nuclei of the desired parent for that in the fertilized human egg. This has already been done with frogs.[13] Alternatively, society could breed subtypes of men as it now does dogs for various roles and functions. Biologist Bentley Glass predicts artificial production of children "will probably be realized by the end of the 20th century." [14]

What do all these discoveries in biology and the increasing symbiosis of man and machine, even if only on the social and intellectual rather than on the physical plane, add up to? Physicist Herman Kahn, in these respects more conservative than other futurists, perhaps because he is not a biologist, lists two "far-out" predictions that, he holds, nevertheless deserve serious consideration. One is the almost complete genetic control of man, wherein he still remains, however, *Homo sapiens;* the other is the end of *Homo sapiens* and the creation of a new species by man's own actions.[15] If in time, as some predict, man is able to create new species of plants and animals directly in the laboratory rather than through the more time-consuming process of selective breeding, just as he already can create live viruses from inanimate matter, why not a new species built up from human genetic materials? But whatever the specifics, man is about to enter upon a new plane of existence. "The logical climax of evolution can be said to have occurred when, as is now imminent, a sentient species deliberately and directly assumes control of its own evolution," is the way a leading medical researcher describes man's new status in the cosmos.[16]

Probably not all of these things will come to pass. Many of them will take longer than predicted; the conservatism of scientists in the past is being replaced rapidly by a euphoria in the present, which many would justify by claiming that the speed of change seems to be increasing exponentially. But the central core of these predictions will become technologically feasible within the next seventy-five years —advances in space travel, exploitation of the oceans, new sources of energy and new resources, increased substitution of communication for physical labor, a great increase in the technological means of social control, and above all the ability of man to affect his own biological and mental composition and that of his descendants. Together these changes constitute an existential revolution that poses a new challenge for mankind. If man can do or be whatever he wishes, how shall he choose? What should be his criteria of choice? In the past, nature and ignorance set limits to man's freedom and his follies, now they need no longer stand in his way, and technological man will be free even to destroy the possibility of freedom itself.

THE POPULATION EXPLOSION

But these scientific advances do not tell the whole story. For while man through science and technology has been extending his power over the universe and himself, another force has been at work that alone would have brought modern civilization to the brink of existential revolution—the population explosion. Here is a case where increase in quantity has clearly resulted in a change in quality; the population explosion has meant that man while gaining more power over nature and himself has also largely overwhelmed nature and is forced to live cheek by jowl with his fellow man. Teilhard de Chardin and others

are certainly correct in holding that the new civilization—call it
Noosphere or technological civilization or what you will—would have
been impossible as a result of advance in communication or other
technologies alone. Increased human interaction is a function of human
density as well as of the technical means for interaction. As a sober
demographic periodical states: "These next twenty-five years form part
of a process which began 200,000 years ago and which is about to
culminate in man's full possession of the earth." [17]

The human population increase in recent centuries has been both
a result of technological advance and a cause of it. New sources
of wealth have made it possible to support more people, new medical
techniques have kept many from dying young. At the same time large
population densities have provided the "critical mass" necessary for
economic, political and scientific development. The result has been a
radical change in the human environment and a new challenge to
human technology and wisdom.

It is almost impossible to understand the magnitude of the population problem without a cursory look at its origins. Demographers
estimate that there were five million human beings alive at the time
of the invention of agriculture, two hundred million at the birth of
Christ. By 1650 there were five hundred million, by 1800 some nine
hundred million. By the beginning of the twentieth century the number
had risen to one and a half billion and in the last seventy years has
more than doubled so that there are more than three and a half
billion humans today.[18] In short, the first great population explosion
followed the invention of agriculture. Then there was a leveling off
until the Industrial Revolution, at which time another explosion
ensued, which is still going on, with population increasing not arith-
metically but geometrically according to the laws of compound interest.
Some even predict a world population of fifteen billion, more than four
times the present number, by the end of this century, some three
decades from now.[19] Technological man must find some way of causing
population to at the least start leveling off again, a feat of large-scale
rational social control unparalleled in human history. Individual
societies have brought death, birth and resources into balance by various
means throughout history, but never has the race as a whole faced
this task.[20]

For whatever the possibility of increased resources becoming
available through technological advance, this will not solve the population crisis. Even if the rise in population does not itself inhibit technological advance through competition for the resources, the seed money,
necessary to finance new technologies, the problem is increasingly not
one of food or even shelter but of simple living space. At present rates
of increase there would literally be standing room only in time,

with the world like a culture of bacteria in a laboratory ready to burst out of its receptacle. Space travel, of course, provides no solution; even if habitable planets were available, the cost of planetary colonization would be too high in any foreseeable future; even here on earth migration has proved only a temporary palliative to population pressures.

The problems posed by the population explosion can be put in perspective by a consideration of urbanization. As late as 1800, only fifty cities in the whole world could boast a population of more than 100,000 but urban concentration increased until there are today more than 1400 such cities, and over 140 metropolitan areas with at least a million inhabitants which contain 11 per cent of all the world's population.[21]

One can argue that a totally urbanized world (however much one might or might not like to live in it), making full use of the resources of the seas and the polar regions, to say nothing of resources drawn from other planets, is conceivable, and that such a world could support many times the world's current population, with food and other needs all produced artificially through the transmutation of elements and the synthesis of organic molecules. Therefore even if the earth's carrying capacity is limited, why not go to fifty billion before stopping?

Such an argument, of course, assumes that the new technologies needed to provide for such masses can be developed before world famine engulfs us. But it also neglects the fact that the new technologies themselves consume resources; the modern American with his house or apartment, automobile, food, office, schools and so on consumes and wastes an increasing amount of resources and requires a large amount of living space. Technological advance itself crowds the very men it sets out to save. Everything humanity needs might be created by science—even air and water could be depolluted and reused forever if enough energy were available—but space cannot be created. Only some inconceivable breakthrough into another dimension—the discovery of a coexistent universe in which, in effect, two or more systems of interacting energy could occupy the same space, analogously to the way frequency modulation permits a single radio wave or laser transmission or telephone wire to carry many messages simultaneously—could make it possible for human procreation to go on unchecked indefinitely.

In any event, the kind of civilization capable of supporting a significantly larger number of men through technological advance would necessarily have to be a new civilization, one based completely on rational calculation, maximum social discipline, recycling of resources and so on. Its institutions and culture would be utterly at variance with the blind procreative urges that have led to the population explosion as well as with most of man's customs and attributes as they have hitherto existed. Whether world population is stabilized at the present or a higher figure, the population explosion has already set the precondition for existential revolution by populating the earth to an extent where man cannot forgo using his new powers.

Power over man and nature, power that both limits human freedom and gives it new meaning, coexists with a density of interaction and interdependence among men that also both limits freedom and gives it new meaning. The existential revolutions caused by technology and population, though different in their origin and history, lead to the same climax at the level of the species. Beneath the surface of twentieth-century civilization the rumbling can be heard clearly and the earth is already starting to move.

NOTES

1. In assessing the future I have leaned most heavily on Herman Kahn and Anthony J. Weiner, *The Year 2000;* T. J. Gordon and Olaf Helmer, *Report on a Long-Range Forecasting Study;* Daniel Bell and his associates who prepared the special issue of *Daedalus,* "Toward the Year 2000; Work in Progress" (Summer, 1967); William Gilman, *Science: U.S.A.;* Nigel Calder (ed.), *The World in 1984;* Arthur C. Clarke, *Profiles of the Future; Wall Street Journal, Here Comes Tomorrow;* Sir George Thompson, *The Foreseeable Future;* Foreign Policy Association, *Toward the Year 2018;* and Sergei Gouschev and Michael Vassillev, *Russian Science in the 21st Century.* Not all of these prophets are in agreement, of course. See also Stuart Chase, *The Most Probable World,* and Harrison Brown, James Bonner and John Weir, *The Next Hundred Years.*
2. Gordon and Helmer, *Report on a Long-Range Forecasting Study,* p. 25. Clarke's estimate is between 2050 and 2060 (*Profiles of the Future,* p. 235).
3. Gordon and Helmer, *Report,* p. 25.
4. For early and somewhat timid looks at the impact of space travel on humanity see Lincoln P. Bloomfield (ed.), *Outer Space: Prospects for Man and Society;* Lillian Levy (ed.), *Space: Its Impact upon Man and Society;* Harold Leland Goodwin, *Space: Frontier Unlimited;* and Howard J. Taubenfeld (ed.), *Space and Society.* But see also Arthur C. Clarke, *The Promise of Space.*
5. On the oceans see Harris B. Stewart, Jr., *The Global Sea;* Marine Technology Society, *Exploiting the Ocean;* John Bardach, *Harvest of the Sea;* Elisabeth Mann Borghese, "The Republic of the Deep Seas"; and Athelstan Spilhaus, "Oceanography: A Wet and Wondrous Journey."
6. "Dolphins Operate Sea Lost and Found," New York *Times,* March 23, 1967.

7. "Breathing Water Seen in 5 Years," Washington *Post*, November 12, 1967.
8. See D. S. Halacy, Jr., *The Weather Changers;* Thomas F. Malone, "Weather Modification"; and W. R. Derrick Sewall, "Humanity and the Weather."
9. Gordon and Helmer, *Report*, p. 21.
10. Alan Westin, "The Snooping Machine."
11. On man's future biological self-control see John D. Roslansky (ed.), *Genetics and the Future of Man;* Jean Rostand, *Peut-on Modifier l'Homme?;* Max Gunther, "Second Genesis"; Kurt Hirschorn, "On Re-Doing Man"; Dwight J. Ingle, "The Biological Future of Man"; Hermann J. Muller, "The Prospects of Genetic Change"; and Albert Rosenfeld, "Will Man Direct His Own Evolution?"
12. "Brain Renewal Object of Science," Washington *Post*, May 3, 1968.
13. "Genes Are Held Able to Cure Disease," New York *Times*, October 22, 1967.
14. "There Is Peril, Too, In Growing Technology," New York *Times*, March 24, 1968.
15. Kahn and Weiner, *The Year 2000*, p. 56.
16. John Heller, quoted in Max Gunther, "Second Genesis," p. 117.
17. *Population Bulletin*, 15 (March, 1959), p. 21, quoted in Alvin M. Weinberg, *Reflections on Big Science*, p. 4.
18. Edward S. Deevey, Jr., "The Human Population."
19. For instance, Harrison Brown as quoted in the New York *Times*, April 23, 1967. Estimates differ radically, in part because base figures are uncertain in many areas. The official United Nations estimate is about seven billion by 2005. See also Philip M. Hauser, "Population," in Foreign Policy Association, *Toward the Year 2018*.
20. By 1967 the American birth rate had dropped to 17.9 per thousand; our lowest on record, but far above the replacement rate. "U.S. Birth Rate Drops to New Low," Washington *Post*, February 26, 1968. The white American rate, however, is close to the replacement level, as are those of Sweden, Norway, Japan, Great Britain and France. "Birth Rate Decline," New York *Times*, April 29, 1968.
21. William B. Shore et al., *The Region's Growth*, p. 16.

TOWARD THE CREATION OF TECHNOLOGICAL MAN

Technological man is more myth than reality. . . . Bourgeois man is still in the saddle. Or, to put it more accurately, things are in the saddle, since bourgeois man is increasingly unable to cope with his problems. At the same time, an existential revolution is under way that may destroy the identity of the human race, make society unmanageable and render the planet literally uninhabitable. Bourgeois man is incapable of coping with this revolution. The race's only salvation is in the creation of technological man.

But what does this mean? What can it mean? Will technological man be a new ruling class, performing a new role based on new sources of power? For the most part, no. Science confers power, but ruling classes perform political roles, not scientific roles as such. Technological man will not be a new ruling class in the usual sense of the term. Will technological man then be a new personality type—hyperrational, objective, manipulative? Not noticeably so. The link between certain types of society and certain kinds of dominant personality types is easily oversimplified, and in any event we have had rationalistic, instrumental, hard-nosed human beings dominating Western society since the beginnings of the modern era; the economic man of the classical economists was such a type. Nor will technological man be a new biological type, created either by manipulation of man's genetic structure or by carrying man-machine symbiosis to the point of altering human integrity. Such a development would mean that technological man had failed to come into existence, and bourgeois civilization had fallen prey to the monsters of its own creation.

Technological man will be man in control of his own development within the context of a meaningful philosophy of the role of technology in human evolution. He will be a new cultural type that will leaven all the leadership echelons of society. Technological man will be man at home with science and technology, for he will dominate them rather than be dominated by them; indeed he will be so at home that the question of who is in charge will never even arise. To state that man should rule technology rather than vice versa is almost a truism, of course. It serves no intellectual function save implicitly to deny the contention of those who argue that man cannot control technology and of those who argue that he should not. But otherwise it is an empty exhortation to virtue, fit more for the political stump than as a basis for serious discussion of human problems. Control technology yes, but in whose interest, in accordance with what norms?

Any useful definition of technological man must therefore include within it some definition of what his outlook on life will be. For to control technology, to control the direction of human evolution, we must have some idea of where we are going and how far, else we will be mere passengers rather than drivers of the chariot of evolution. We are thus forced to try to do two difficult things, simultaneously to predict the future and to develop a new philosophy of society based on the future's needs. But though technological man will create himself and cannot be programmed in advance, the needs that call him forth go far toward defining both his task and the world view he must bring to it.

How can one possibly lay down a future philosophy for general acceptance? Even if such dominant world views as traditional Christianity, orthodox Marxism and classical liberalism have clearly failed to provide a rationale for dealing with the existential revolution, may they not simply be replaced not by a new philosophy but by a variety of conflicting value systems determined by individual histories, whims and tastes? Have we not defined lack of a common value system in the declining period of bourgeois civilization as part of our problem? Will not any new philosophy be intellectually arbitrary, capable of being spread, if at all, only through coercion or an irrational persuasion, which would be self-defeating since a unifying world philosophy for technological man must, above all, be based on shared perceptions and values?

Technological man, by definition, will be possessed of the world view of science and technology, which will themselves provide a standard of value for future civilization. At this point many readers may be tempted to throw up their hands. Those enamored of certain versions of Greek and medieval philosophy and of traditional religious systems will snort that values are either transcendent in nature or are derived from an analysis of the natural world which is essentially deductive and nonempirical in nature. Others will simply object that part of the whole mission of philosophy from Kant to Wittgenstein has been to show that values cannot be derived from natural philosophy: the belief that the "ought" cannot be derived from the "is" is now an elementary commonplace in every primer in ethics or the social sciences.[1]

But the matter is not so simply resolved. Many leading modern philosophers, such as John Dewey, have argued from what man is to what he should do and be,[2] and many who formally deny that the data of existence provide ethical imperatives sneak their values in through the back door by appeals to common sense as a standard when all is said and done. Various subterfuges are used to get around the problem. Psychologists decide what is proper conduct through application of the concepts of "deviance" and "mental health," which are clearly based on the "is" of common experience. Skinner has been faulted by critics such as Joseph Wood Krutch for assuming in his utopia, *Walden Two,* that the problem of social values could be easily solved, since survival and health are universally acknowledged as values.[3] But what is the alternative to Skinner's position (in essence, that of Aristotle) save to locate values in a transcendent source communicating through mysterious forms of revelation that all men may not accept, in the irrational desires of the individual or in some innate knowledge implanted in the individual brain and available through individual introspection?

Fortunately, we do not have to answer all the fundamental questions about ethics that this discussion raises. The problem is not finding a sanction for values but simply defining them, which though a difficult problem is at least one capable of rational discussion. That is, we can assume we ought to do what is good for us if we can decide the latter. If our doctor tells us smoking will cause cancer this does not prove we should stop smoking. We have the option of preferring an earlier and possibly more painful death. If someone tells us the arms race is suicidal, he does not thereby prove that collectively we should eschew suicide.

In this sense, the "ought" can never be derived from empirically grounded predictions about the consequences of actions. Any preference for pleasure over pain, knowledge over ignorance, health over disease, and survival over destruction is incapable of justification unless we first agree that there is some inherent reason for respecting the order of nature that impels all creatures toward survival, activity and growth. Stated thus, the proposition that science cannot be the source of values is irrefutable.[4]

But what practical consequences does this have for most of mankind? Whether we choose to restrain the suicidal or masochistic is a problem in civil liberties, but few would deny that we should restrain the murderer or torturer. Problems arise from the fact that even if we admit that survival or happiness is desirable these may require different conditions for different people, since what makes me prosperous may make you poor. Not the nature of "goods," but their scarcity, allocation and occasional incompatibility present difficulties. So, too, at a general social level the problem arises of priorities among goods: granted that health and survival are both desirable, what happens if society must risk the health of all, or even just of some, in order to ensure its survival?

But these problems, however complex, may be more amenable to analysis and solution than we assume. Jeremy Bentham's hedonistic calculus may have to be rejected as simplistic, but Bentham did not have the resources of modern science (including the social sciences) to provide data as to what the effects of alternative policies might be, and he lacked computers to manipulate this data. Whether science can help us to reconcile conflicting values is a question that must be decided on the basis of experience and experiment, and the idea that it can help us cannot be dismissed out of hand through essentially irrelevant assumptions about the differences between the descriptive and normative orders. Dewey is certainly right in saying that a culture that permits science to destroy its values without permitting science to create now ones is a culture that destroys itself.[5]

The increasing knowledge of the order of nature provided by contemporary scientific discovery, the increasing power over that nature given to man by his technology and the fact that increases in population have raised the amount and intensity of human interaction to a new plane that bespeaks an evolutionary breakthrough, all combine to present technological man with the outlines of a new philosophy of human existence, a philosophy that can provide general guidelines that he can and must take advantage of if he is to retain control of his civilization.

BASIC ELEMENTS OF A NEW PHILOSOPHY

A basic element in this new philosophy is what might be called the *new naturalism*, which asserts that man is in fact part of nature rather than something apart from it, but that nature is not the rigid, mindless, deterministic machine that earlier eras conceived it to be. The totality of the universe is a dynamic process, a constant movement and becoming. Some scientists have gone so far as to contend that some form of mind exists in even nonliving matter,[6] but such an assumption is not necessary to the belief that the universe is, in a sense, a moving equilibrium of which man is a part.

However, man is not merely a part of nature, but the highest part, an element in a semidetermined system of nature with himself, for all practical purposes, private and undetermined, his mind the most complex thing in the universe. "If this property of complexity could somehow be transformed into visible brightness," writes a leading molecular biologist, "the biological world would become a walking field of light compared to the physical world . . . an earthworm would be a beacon . . . human beings would stand out like blazing suns of complexity, flashing bursts of meaning to each other through the dull night of the physical world between." [7] Man gains in dignity as he is seen as part of physical nature, while his most complex mechanical creations pale into insignificance.

Closely related to the new naturalism is the *new holism*, that is, the realization of how interconnected everything is. From the evolutionary philosophies of the nineteenth century has come the idea of becoming, which destroys the traditional distinctions between being and nonbeing, thus paving the way for the rejection of the Newtonian view of the world as matter in motion, a complex of forces exerted on objects, and of analogies based on leverage and weight and anything else associated with the primitive machinery of the early industrial era. The image of the mechanical universe must give way to the idea of process.

The basic concepts of process and system imply a recognition that no part is meaningful outside the whole, that no part can be defined or understood save in relation to the whole. There are few closed or isolated systems in nature and none in society, save for the desert islands of legend. Gestalt psychologists have always regarded the mind-body relationship as that of an integrated whole, but it is really mind-body-society-nature that is the totality.[8] All men are linked with each other and with their social and physical environment in a fantastically complex moving equilibrium, so that in thinking about social questions we must, in the words of M.I.T. president Julius Stratton, "advance from the anatomy of components to the physiology of the organic whole—which indeed is now the society itself." [9]

But this whole, the universal as well as the social, is a new kind of whole, determined not from outside but from within. For another element in the new world outlook is the *new immanentism*. Eastern philosophies have always stressed the immanent, leading to pantheism not unlinked to the panpsychism of some modern biologists. But for the Western world, especially the Judaic-Christian tradition, God, the principle of order and change, was primarily outside. Though in theory He was everywhere, He was envisioned as "up there" or "out there." [10] A civilization whose world view was dominated by the physicist and the mechanic could think of the Deity as a cosmic watchmaker, of the universe as in some sense having been created and set down. But the modern world view increasingly rejects this viewpoint as the biological sciences come to the fore. However physicists may look upon the development of the physical universe as a whole, the world of living things is somehow different. Nature here works another way, life is antientropic. "The factory that makes the parts of a flower is inside, and is not a factory but a development. . . . The creative principle of the universe," John Rader Platt writes, "is not an external but an internal one." [11] Nothing is isolated. Life exists within systems. And systems create themselves.

These three principles—the new naturalism, the new holism and the new immanentism—provide the necessary basis for the outlook that must come to dominate human society if man is to survive the existential revolution already under way. Technological man must so internalize these ideas and make them so much a part of his instinctive world view that they inform his personal, political and cultural life. They in turn lead to certain further principles. If man and nature are one, then society and the environment are one. Therefore, meaningful social policies must be ecological in character, that is, they must be based on a recognition that the interrelationship of men to each other and to the total environment means that any decision, any change, affects everything in the total system.

Thus, in a sense, nature has rights as well as man, since its activity and that of man are inextricably intermingled. The new holism, with its emphasis on process, means that not only must every decision be seen in ecological perspective, but it must be recognized that there are no individual decisions any more than there are actually geometric points in the empirical world. Decision-making is part of a seamless process.

Man cannot become free by being outside or apart from the process. He is affected by what others do—that is, he is the subject of power—and he exercises power because his actions affect others. For in this holistic process every action of the whole passes through and is modified by the state of every cell or particle. Freedom consists in responding autonomously and authentically to the currents of life and action passing through one; the loss of freedom is not the loss of an impossible complete self-determination—which would necessitate standing outside the universe—but is a synonym for being bypassed and being allowed to play one's part in shaping the whole.

For the whole shapes itself. This is the meaning of the new immanentism. Order is not imposed from outside in accordance with a predetermined plan of man or nature, it is a structure of interrelationships created by the constant activity of its own elements, which somehow always form a pattern as long as the whole survives. Men's actions, men's ideas and the technological forces that they set in motion are all part of this whole, and their activity leads to further development. Freedom is not outside but within nature, Dewey has said.[12] So, too, freedom does not exist apart from society. Planning is the self-consciousness of the human element in developing patterns of interrelation—a self-consciousness that alone makes control and therefore freedom possible. Control over the elements in the total system—human and nonhuman—is effected by a constant process of adjustment, pressures and signals. As in nature, cells die or are destroyed; sometimes as in cancer they multiply out of control until checked; often signals are blocked or short-circuited rather than amplified. But there is no need for postulating an overseer who directs from outside; every part of the whole has power and influence, every living particle is a source of direction and life. This diffusion of power runs the risk of becoming a dissipation of responsibility as well,[13] unless each participant constantly holds himself responsible not only for the immediate result of his particular acts but also for their ultimate impact upon the shaping of the whole.

Technological man, imbued through education and constant experience with the conviction that this is what the universe is like, will discover techniques and construct guidelines for dealing with the problems created for humanity by the existential revolution. From this basic world view he can derive ethical norms that, channeled through reformed institutional structures, can become the basis for policies that will make survival possible.

What norms can guide technological man in this task? They are not all derived directly from his basic outlook, but are nonetheless compatible with it and rest upon the same sets of data about the universe. The first of these norms is that man is part of nature and therefore cannot be its conqueror, that indeed he owes it some respect. As Albert Schweitzer said, a morality that deals only with the relation of man to man and not of man to nature is only half a morality.[14] Human self-knowledge is impossible in a world in which nature has been destroyed or so altered that it cannot speak to men. "Our goal," in the words of biologist Roger Revelle, chairman of the U.S. Committee for the International Biological Program, "should not be to conquer the natural world but to live in harmony with it." [15]

Secondly, ecological perspective dictates that man's economic and social life demands co-ordination if he is to survive, and his exploitation of natural resources must be determined by what is optimum for the total system. At the same time, the ability of the system to respond demands maximum freedom. Therefore, in purely cultural or individual matters where the linkage of behavior to the system is least direct, maximum freedom should be allowed. What this amounts to is combining economic and physical "planning" with cultural pluralism to the maximum extent possible.[16]

On an even more basic level, man must maintain the distinction between himself and the machines of his creation. Since man is superior in complexity to the physical universe, some presumption exists that this complexity has an evolutionary meaning that should be preserved. Linkages of man to machines and technologies that would make him irrevocably dependent on lower orders of reality would be antievolutionary. The great strength of man throughout his evolutionary history has been the flexibility that has resulted from his variety and his complexity. He has triumphed not merely because of his intelligence but also because of his allied versatility. Human flesh is weak, but man avoided the "error" of the crustaceans in protecting themselves in a way that made future development impossible. The human individual is weak, but man has avoided the dead end of the social insects, who have created a marvelous structure in which the nothingness of the individual and the inability to change are opposite sides of the same coin. Man's destiny lies in continuing to exploit this "openness," rather than entering into a symbiotic relationship with the inorganic machine that, while it might bring immediate increments of power, would inhibit his development by chaining him to a system of lesser potentialities. The possibilities of man as a "soft machine" are far greater and as yet little explored.[17] Man must stand above his physical technologies if he is to avoid their becoming his shell and the principles of their organization his anthill.

But not only must man stand above the machine, he must be in control of his own evolution. Those who think of man's destiny as a mindless leap forward forget that man is not only the sole creature capable of being conscious of evolution but the only one capable of controlling it, and this control must include the power to slow down and stop evolution if he so desires. Actually, some elements of physical technology may be already peaking, at least as far as their effect on society and man is concerned. If the population explosion is brought under control we may enter what might be called a "steady-state" form, wherein the unplumbed future would lie in biological science, and in man's mind. The final step to man would have been taken.[18]

In such a civilization man will have the task of finally finding himself, of fulfilling his roles in the universe by becoming fully man. In the Old Testament, Yahweh reveals essentially nothing of Himself to the Hebrews save that "I am Who I am." [19] Man if he is in any sense akin to divinity has as his role becoming himself, doing his own thing. This means that the conquest of outer space should take second place to furthering man's forward movement to the conquest of "inner space."

How man can best explore himself remains a question. Some see mind-expanding drugs as the way [20] (a minor Hippie organ is called *Inner Space*). Arthur Koestler sees the primitive ape-brain as still existing as a "layer" of man's developed brain, and holds that only through drugs can the savage within us be sufficiently controlled so that we can avoid destroying ourselves,[21] just as the Hippies hold that only thus can the *bourgeoisie* be "turned on." A score of mystic and cultural traditions argue otherwise. But one thing is certain: in a world in which man controls his environment so as to provide for his physical needs and to conquer hunger and disease, the new frontier will be within.

Genetic engineering may have a role to play in perfecting the human body, but the untapped frontiers of knowledge and action lie in the mysterious and versatile computer that is the human brain. Much of what it can do in relation to the body and the external environment by the use of tools we already know through existent technology, but of what it can do directly we may have only an inkling. Newton was the last of the magicians, it has been said; in the world of technological man everyone would be a magician even by Newton's standards.[22] But the basic point is that man's role is not to create a new creature, a new mutation of himself physically, but to exploit this still-unleashed marvel of flesh and bone and synapses that we hardly know.

THE REORIENTATION OF CULTURE

If this new vision of man as the intelligent self-conscious part of the universe, with full responsibility for himself and the universe, is valid, certain consequences for society must follow. Obviously, technological man cannot come into existence as the dominant human type without the reorientation of human culture. The new naturalism, the new holism and the new immanentism must become as much the dominant and energizing themes of this new civilization as the world views of medieval

Christianity or bourgeois mechanistic materialism were in earlier eras. Education, art, relations between the sexes and the generations, literature, philosophy and religion—all elements of culture—must reflect the new world view not only explicitly but in terms of their own internal processes and styles.

How can this be achieved? Save for education (and here only to a limited extent), none of these components of culture is subject to centralized control. One can decide that all children deserve an education that frees their minds from mechanical forms and constraints and sensitizes them to their parts in mankind's constant interaction with the total universe, but one cannot prevent parents and painters and preachers from reflecting a sterile past if they choose. Yet it does not matter that it is not possible to centralize control over cultural activities, for the new immanentism itself should tell us that change and restructuring must come from within, and that the points of leverage are everywhere. Unless the new outlook spontaneously permeates civilization, mankind will fail in any event.

But how can this new world view become dominant while the cultural pluralism that appears to be both the emerging pattern of tomorrow and, to some degree, an innately desirable one, also exists? The answer is that the level of integration is the totality. Uniformity is not necessary to unity any more than every piece of a mosaic must be the same color and texture or every cell in a body must have the same function. What is required is that all participants in technological civilization recognize that there is a whole that they do not totally represent, and that the one intolerable action is the claim of any individual or group within it to dominance and universality, for this would quite literally short-circuit the total cultural process.

Individuals or groups contribute by being themselves while recognizing that although their "selfhood" is relative yet the very tenuousness of its identity must necessarily be maintained. Political groups in democratic societies are coming to realize slowly that they can and must tolerate and encourage differing viewpoints, that the interest of the whole demands that each group holds to its own views and interests. In the ecumenical age of the West, religious groups are slowly coming to the same conclusion. Tolerance of ambiguity and diversity in culture is a cultural recognition of the fact that it is the absence of entropy that makes activity possible; homogeneity cannot lead to a higher harmony, but only to that cessation of activity we call death.

But to say that only by arising spontaneously can the new vision of the world arise at all is not to deny that everyone who possesses it must seek to share it. In many areas of life, such as international relations and control of environmental pollution, the fact that bourgeois civilization still persists is a pressing and immediate danger. The men who will be national rulers or citizens, intellectual leaders or consumers in the year 2000 are in school right now, so the time for reform is now.[23] It may be that only outside formal educational processes can the job be done: perhaps we should hope that McLuhan is right in his insistence that electronic media have already superseded the schools and are re-orienting human consciousness to the total environment.

A new culture will have to be reflected in radical changes in our economic and political systems. Traditional societies distribute goods and make economic decisions with reference to traditional norms rather than rational bargaining for the most part. If these norms are based on experiences with the physical and social environment that still hold valid, they survive; if not, they die. The market system of bourgeois capitalism is much more self-conscious, rational and flexible. Supply and demand are adjusted to each other and production therefore tends to come into equilibrium with needs, at least of those individuals with any economic power. But the decision-making process of the market suffers from a fatal flaw: it is individualistic and antiholistic. Only the immediate economic interests of the buyer and seller are used as standards. Consequences for other parties—employees or suppliers, persons in other industries or nations, taxpayers and the unemployed—are all neglected. It is assumed that an "invisible hand" will direct everything to the common good.

But this assumption becomes less tenable as the growing complexity of a society based on technological advance and increased population density creates an ever-thicker pattern of interaction and interdependency, one which requires means for consciously taking the interests of others into account. Someone must clean up the tin cans when deposit bottles are no longer used, someone must clear the polluted air, find jobs for the technologically unemployed or alternative uses for products no longer in demand. The faster the rate of change, the larger the increments of change—the less breathing space between decisions, so to speak—the more difficult life becomes. Until now we have managed to live with the results of market decisions; someone has come along to clean up the wreckage. But, even so, problems of equity remained. Why should all clean up the debris left by a few? Or, since quite often the few pay for adjustments without realizing it, would they rationally and freely choose to have their party in the first place if they knew the real cost of the fiddler?

In any event, the pace of technological change is increasing and population continues to grow so that it is less and less possible to rely on serendipity. Man must take over control of his society. But the problem of making decisions so that they reflect the total needs of the system rationally considered and distribute gains and losses with some equity cannot be solved by the simple substitution of purportedly socialist regimes for capitalist ones. Though in principle socialist governments represent the interests of the whole, in practice decisions are made in terms of immediate expediency, the interests of particular leaders or departments and the same uncritical acceptance of any technological change that promises growth in productivity that applies in capitalist societies. The struggle against polluting Lake Baikal is in principle the same struggle as that against polluting Lake Tahoe, and the socialist USSR has, on the whole, perhaps done less well with its ecological problems than has the capitalist United States. Military needs are preferred to human needs in socialist as well as in capitalist nations, and interest groups go their own ways to virtually the same extent.[24]

What all societies need is a system of social accounting that will make clear the total costs to the system of each possible outcome of the decision-making process (including, of course, failure to change) and the incidence of gains and benefits to all concerned.[25] Such accounting is no longer impossible, thanks to refinements in data collecting and computerization of results, but there are still those who would argue that it would be meaningless or undesirable. It can be held, for instance, that there is no way of structuring the outcome of decision-making to give optimum benefit to all, no possibility of acceptable compromise. A sophisticated, logical argument demonstrates that no standard of measurement can represent the desires of all conflicting elements adequately.[26] Combining individual orders of preference into common standards of social priorities is extremely difficult. So, too, it may be argued that value choices—including such matters as the desire for fresh air or the avoidance of ugliness—cannot be reduced to common terms with such economic matters as taxes, wages and profits. Finally, it can be held that individuals and groups will be unwilling to accept less than total satisfaction of their specific demands upon the society.

These objections to the possibility of an acceptable level of agreement on common social priorities and activities are weighty but hardly conclusive. Legislative bodies and private groups using formal decision-making processes have for generations arrived at decisions that, while perhaps blurring the logic of choice, have been psychologically acceptable to participating individuals and interests, in part because preferences themselves change in the process of discussion and decision. Nor is it impossible to devise means for taking into account and weighing the importance which individuals and groups attach to "noneconomic" goods. By actually or hypothetically forcing a choice between them and intrinsically quantifiable values, the desirability of such goods can be measured. Real-estate agents have rough ways of determining clients' preferences among architectural styles and the value attached to a "good address" or a good school district; economists are able to weigh the monetary value of leisure by testing under what circumstances workers will work overtime; and voters often express their preferences for lower taxes over additional amenities.

What stands in the way of making society more rational in its choices is less the intrinsic difficulty of the task than the lack of the will and the techniques necessary to make overall social decisions. Some possible techniques for decision-making already have been advanced; an example is the "mixed scanning" that the sociologist Amitai Etzioni holds will be necessary in the "active society," the society that consciously controls itself.[27] But above all there must be a willingness to exercise self-control. To say that rational planning by sharpening our perception of clashes of interest will make compromise difficult calls attention to an important characteristic of the politics of the future, but to conclude that compromise will become impossible is to foreclose discussion; if human nature is unchangeable then social systems are likewise unreformable. But if technological man comes into existence he will necessarily have to recognize that individuals and groups cannot always get all that they want from the totality, and he will necessarily be rational enough and sufficiently cognizant of the absolute importance of keeping the total system in equilibrium to render even the most difficult problems of social choice solvable. If this sounds utopian, one can only agree with the biologist John Rader Platt, who has observed that utopia may be the only viable social system in the world to come.[28]

What applies to domestic politics applies to international politics as well. But here the clash of interests is not only more overt and intense than it is domestically, but the common psychological identifications that help to make solutions possible on the domestic level are less available. Yet room for hope exists. Man may yet come to accept a holistic view of the world community. Lack of international communication is no longer primarily a function of technology but of how society chooses to use it; world-wide communication is inherently feasible, and technology presses toward universalism. Various political devices have been suggested for making world government possible—from international political parties that would engage in struggles for delegates to world bodies across national lines, thus restructuring emotional identifications,[29] to various improvements in the power of currently existing bodies such as the United Nations. The gradual breaking up of many larger nations may, paradoxically, make world government easier to achieve: an independent Flanders, Scotland or Quebec might be more inclined to world citizenship than larger or more nearly self-sufficient nations.

But however it may be implemented institutionally, basically the change will be one in attitude. An ecological outlook on the world will see all problems as interdependent; an immanentist view will recognize that significant change in the nature of the world can result from intensification of incremental changes that go on all the time —what some students of world politics refer to as a "functional" approach to international unity. A hopeful straw in the wind is the increasingly international style of youth and the identification with other persons across national lines that they increasingly manifest.[30] The joint exploration of the oceans offers possibilities for co-operation as well as conflict; so does the conquest of space that, symbolically especially, holds forth the image of humankind as a unity engaged in expanding its frontiers. As man increases his controls over biological processes, more thought will have to be given to mankind as a species, which should redound to feelings of political solidarity. Science itself —despite nationalism and careerism—possesses elements of a functioning international community whose attitudes could and would have to become part of the character of technological man if he is to come into being.[31]

If it is clear that a new philosophy involves new norms for decision-making, and that new social and political institutions are needed to convert these into policies and practices so that education, the economy and the domestic and international political orders can become the social tools through which technological man can develop his self-awareness and exercise his powers, it is less clear what precise policies are best suited to deal with the crisis presented by the existential revolution. This in part is as it should be, since the future will remain open as long as man is man.

But certain lines of policy suggest themselves as flowing from all we have been saying so far. Man's greatest need is not to transcend his species as such but to develop it fully. We want to envision great-great-grandchildren who will resemble us, not because we aim at a symbolic immortality as individuals, or because we feel that the human race is perfect, but because we do not yet know what this race can do, and can only talk meaningfully of its fullest development if it retains its basic identity. Man is not a superape; he is no longer an ape at all. Before we abandon man for a machine-man or a genetic mutant, we should learn what he can do in his present form once liberated from hunger, fear and ignorance. Nor should we forget Pascal's warning that in seeking to become angels we may become less than men.[32]

THE NEED FOR CONTROLS

Continuity of the species means some continuity of social and cultural institutions and processes. Too rapid change leads to disorientation. If the future is absolutely unpredictable, any meaningful activity becomes impossible, and perhaps we should seek to slow down the rate of social and cultural change, as men such as Arnold Toynbee have advocated.[33] On the other hand, certain things are changing inevitably anyway: short of sterilizing half of those now living we cannot prevent a substantially larger population in the near future. Since civilization is an interrelated whole, if we wish to retain other elements of human culture we must make some adjustments to the changes we cannot prevent. This need to adjust in order to preserve is something a wise conservatism has always known, and is what has distinguished it from sheer inertia and obscurantism.

Certain controls may be necessary if we are to preserve any freedom at all. Of paramount importance is the control of technological and economic innovation. Control does not mean that new techniques will not be introduced, but rather that they will be channeled in such a way as to serve the general rather than simply a private good. A society where talent produces new goods for sale and new means of destruction while cities decay and children baffle the educational system is no more innovative than one in which technological resources are devoted to the development of the depressed segments of the population and to enhancing the environment. Means must be found to channel technological advance into areas where it has the greatest potential for social usefulness.

This may not be as difficult as might be imagined. Government already directly or indirectly controls most research and technical innovation even in capitalist nations; the problem is to put technological men in power rather than men of a previous breed who do not have any sense of how these scientific resources might best be used. Paradoxically, the control of technological change might be the supreme opportunity that technology affords for human progress. If technology compels men "to be more men" and "reveals the nature of nature more clearly," as one philosopher of science puts it, it does so by calling forth our highest powers, forcing us to use reason to decide what nature is and what it is for. But this is a challenge that the race cannot shirk. "To despair of reason is to despair of man."[34] Controlling technology in all its ramifications may be the supreme test of our species' adulthood.

Several conflicting priorities exist in the use of space and the oceans. Some access to nature in an untouched state is a scientific as well as a spiritual need. Both space and the oceans—especially the latter— must be used in such a way that they are not turned into mere dump heaps.[35] Economic exploitation of both must serve the common good of the race. The oceans must be used in a way that benefits not alone the richer nations, best equipped technologically to exploit them, but the poor as well. Treaties for international control must aim not merely at orderly exploitation but at the principle that the oceans are a common world resource, to be used to equalize living standards rather than to perpetuate or accentuate conditions of economic inequality.[36]

The economic problem of space exploration does not stem primarily from the need to distribute its potential economic benefits, which have been grossly exaggerated at least as far as any immediate future is concerned, but rather lies in the alternative use of resources now devoted to space exploration. A less feverish and costly endeavor would make possible diversion of resources—including scarce scientific talent—elsewhere. A planet that spends billions to put one or two men on another planet while children starve, not only in India but within the borders of the major powers, has carried the antientropic drive too far and perhaps should consolidate before moving onward.

Population control, conservation not of natural resources but of nature itself, and biogenetic policy are closely interrelated issues. The problems presented by the population explosion are so dramatic as to have already excited widespread popular concern throughout the world. It is quite possible that total world population could increase several times over and high living standards in terms of food and material artifacts be maintained within the developed areas of the world. Severe famines and widespread poverty can exist in the poorer nations without necessarily disturbing living standards elsewhere. The notion that the "Third World," the "nonwhite" races or the "underdeveloped" will rise up in wrath against the rich is largely a propaganda cliché. In a world of nuclear weapons, population size loses most of its meaning as a factor in national power and the rich would undoubtedly defend themselves against despoliation to the death.

But even if most or part of the world can keep on multiplying without famine becoming universal, sooner or later growth must stop. Even if the world becomes a mere anthill, using the most advanced technology imaginable to recycle every bit of air for breathing, creating food out of rocks and energy out of sea water, the sheer mass of flesh will ultimately make further growth impossible. We will have reached "standing room only," and interplanetary or even interstellar migration offers little hope of a solution. Growth will have to stop and a steady state be achieved wherein death and birth rates are equal, as they have probably been throughout most of human history. But long before this point is reached, man will have destroyed every vestige of his natural environment, completely lost touch with his animal heritage and changed from an individual into a social insect in all but appearance.

Since putting an end to growth is inevitable, the only question is when.[37] Given the laws of compound interest, it will not be too many generations before stoppage becomes mandatory. The problem therefore is one of whether we can halt population growth prior to the total destruction of man's relationship with nature and before his historic culture becomes meaningless. There is a "wisdom in wildness," writes Charles Lindbergh (himself a distinguished contributor to science and technology), and technological man would agree.[38] If wilderness is necessary to the human spirit, we face a problem of crisis proportions. But even if the problem is reduced to one of simply carrying off wastes that pollute water and air and endanger life, health or economic efficiency, it is still a serious one, all psychological and aesthetic questions aside.

Yet it is easy to understand why resistance to controls exists. The more fundamental habits of behavior are the more resistant they are to change. Procreation, especially, involves intimate individual concerns. Any social policies in this area will mean, for modern Western man, a sharp break with tradition. Advocates of population control have suggested a variety of ways in which this might be accomplished. Some would use punitive sanctions such as a negative income tax or, in the case of those too poor to pay taxes, sterilization after they produce children beyond their quota. Others look to positive means, such as a bonus for not having children, on the theory that it is less onerous to choose between two goods—a child or financial gain—than between a child and financial loss—a good and an evil. The solution advanced by the economist Kenneth Boulding, as we noted earlier, is that each human being at birth should be given the right to have one child, and that these rights could be used, bought or sold.[39] This proposal would maximize choice, but Boulding ignores the problem of those who produce outside the system and the punitive sanctions necessary to underpin it.

It has also been suggested that technological means could be used, such as putting contraceptive substances into the water supply, thereby making the having of a child require special permission by placing control of the antidote under public auspices.[40] These suggestions are not all as outlandish as they seem. Most human societies, including our own, arranged marriages until recently. In the West the combination of the tradition that no one married until he could support a wife —which meant owning land in some areas—with severe penalties for illegitimacy, were an effective social mechanism of population control. In Victorian England mass infanticide was practiced by consciously tolerating and even encouraging high infant mortality rates, especially in foundling homes.[41] In recent years large numbers of

couples in Western society who have adopted children have accepted
the intrusion of social inspection and decision with regard to their
fitness to be parents with minimal aftereffects.

Yet there is no question that a general and rigorous and open
policy of population control would be regarded by most people as
revolutionary, especially since many of them do not yet find the
consequences of unlimited growth impossible to bear and have little
regard for or knowledge about the future. Present evidence indicates
that most prosperous Westerners now want families of about three or
four children which would constantly refuel the population explosion.[42]
Therefore family planning, to be an effective check on growth, will
require some degree of social control.[43]

If population growth is not checked, then every other aspect of
life will necessarily have to undergo revolutionary change simply to
insure human survival over the next several generations. Societies
that refuse to change their breeding habits will have to change how
they eat, dwell, work and use their leisure, and freedom of procreation
will be paid for by a loss of other freedoms. Here is an area where
even an enlightened conservative might feel that one alteration in
existing patterns was a cheap price to pay to prevent the total restructuring of human life.

If population growth in the developed nations posed an obvious
threat to economic growth and material living standards, it might
be relatively easy to elicit popular support for measures to curb the
birth rate. But what if the result of uncontrolled growth is instead
the overcrowding of cities, highways and recreational facilities, and
the destruction of humanity's ageold contract with the natural environment that gave our species birth? Then the political problem becomes
more difficult. An aesthetic attachment to privacy, solitude and the
wilderness is a minority position in bourgeois civilization. In any
democratic system, these values will have to be maintained by com-
plicated political maneuvering—through convincing the majority that
minority tastes have economic benefits for the whole, by trading off
concessions in some areas of policy for preservation of what cannot
be replaced and similar strategems.[44] But these are stopgap measures.
Unless technological man assumes a steady state as an optimum for
population growth and manifests a reverence for wilderness and history
as necessary elements in total culture, postindustrial society will become
an anthill society. Fortunately, the scientific community has been
generally ardent in its support of pollution controls and conservation,
and an increase in scientific comprehension by the public may cause
this attitude to spread.[45]

Feelings about genetic controls, however, are more divided. The scientific community, even more perhaps than other professional groups, is suspicious of lay controls; this despite the many scientific activities that are supported by public funds. The medical profession, especially, enjoys an elite status that in capitalist nations has led them to try to maintain control not only of the content but of the financing and distribution of medical care. Most scientists have rejected suggestions—inspired by recent publicity over the synthesis of DNA and the rash of heart transplants—that in the United States a commission be set up on the ethical and social aspects of biological research.[46] This is in partial contrast to the widespread support that scientists have given to American participation in the International Biological Commission,[47] which is concerned with maintaining the quality of the world environment.

This apparent inconsistency in scientists' attitudes stems from the fact that scientific discovery and its consequences are separated in the thinking of most scientists. Research must remain under the control of scientists rather than laymen. But for obvious economic and legal reasons the consequences of research may be subject to social controls; some scientists have even taken the position that what the military do with their discoveries is none of the scientists' concern. But the distinction between discovery and its application may be an unreal one in practice, even if we deny the conclusion of men such as Ellul that all knowledge will eventually be used.

If human beings are involved in biological research—having their organs transplanted, being administered new drugs—the very act of experimentation has social consequences,[48] the first test-tube baby will be a human being with a claim on citizenship. Biological research can enable mankind to determine its own genetic future. Obviously, a society that does not control these developments has lost control of itself. Just as war is too important, in Clemenceau's oft-quoted phrase, to be left to the generals so the future form of the race is too important to be left to the professionals in the life sciences.[49]

Technological man has yet to emerge. Bourgeois man still dominates the world—just as much in nominally socialist as in capitalist nations. Industrial society is not so much being transformed into a postindustrial, technological society as it is breaking down—economically, politically and culturally. Rigidities in social institutions and attitudes create a society comparable to a geological formation with fault lines where slippage is inhibited and great earthquakes therefore necessarily build up. The existential revolution is building up pressures that can lead to cataclysm, or it can be converted into what Platt calls a "cultural shock-front," after the passage of which man will enter upon a new and stable plateau of existence where he can finally become Man.[50] If technological man comes into existence not only among scientists and technologists but in all walks of life in all advanced nations—and there are signs that he is emerging, like the seed beneath the snow—the existential revolution can become an instrument for liberation rather than destruction.

A world society could be based upon a realization that man is part of nature, yet something special in it—a mere reed, in Pascal's words—but a thinking reed, and that his problem is not to overcome nature but to live in a more subtle and conscious harmony with it, not to transcend his animal nature but to recognize that spirit and flesh are one and that the total human being must be activated and developed to new intensities and planes of activity. Such a world could become the launching pad for the next and final step in man's evolutionary process, where he becomes not a new creature but finally fully himself. For his destiny is not to become enslaved by his own creations or to lose himself in some cosmic nirvana, but to exploit fully all the intricacies of his individual self. It is to complexity, to individuation and to a new and more inclusive unity that the universe moves—to the transfiguration rather than the loss of identity of the individual human and the species.[51] If technological man can create a world society wherein man and his environment are in balance, man can abandon the age-old fight against nature for survival and accept nature as a companion, just as an adolescent can abandon the struggle against his parents to assert his adulthood and in time can become their friend. Then man can turn to his real purposes, which are play and cultivation of the deeps of the inner space of the individual and society.

Technological man will be his own master. Prior to his emergence, the outlines of technological civilization must remain dim save for the knowledge that it will have to rest upon a unified view of the universe, on ecological balance and on fidelity to the essential identity of the human species. Technological man will create his own future, and it may contain some surprises even for him. The Dominican mystic Meister Eckhart wrote at the beginning of the long journey that brought Western man from the cocoon of medievalism through industrial civilization to our own day and its choice between chaos and transfiguration, but his words have timeless meaning: "There is no stopping place in this life—no, nor was there ever one for any man, no matter how far along his way he'd gone. This above all, then, be ready at all times for the gifts of God, and always for new ones." [52]

The new gifts are all about us today, and the newer ones in store are unpredictable in their nature and their timing. Upon man's ability to recognize them for what they are and to convert them into what his development requires rests not only his future but, for all we know, that of all of creation.

Notes

1. For example, Eugene J. Meehan, *The Theory and Method of Political Analysis,* p. 47. For some recent critiques of the effects of this attitude see Kenneth Boulding, "Philosophy, Behavioral Science, and the Nature of Man," and Christian Bay, "Politics and Pseudopolitics." See also T. H. Weldon, *The Vocabulary of Politics.*
2. Cf. especially Dewey, *The Quest for Certainty.* His views are criticized in Morton White, *Social Thought in America,* pp. 203–219.
3. *The Measure of Man,* pp. 90–91. Marx, of course, had to struggle with a similar problem. See Howard L. Parsons, "Value and Mental Health in the Thought of Marx."
4. A more subtle problem arises in defining health, happiness or even survival, which we cannot go into here save to note that it is a problem for all men, not for technical philosophers alone.
5. Paraphrased by Henry H. Villard in Morse and Warner, *Technological Innovation and Society,* p. 197.
6. Cf. the discussion in Theodosius Dobzhansky, *The Biology of Ultimate Concern,* pp. 12–34.
7. Platt, *The Step to Man,* p. 151.
8. See Roszak, "The Counter Culture," Part IV. For some approaches to the total problem of man in nature see Marston Bates, *The Forest and the Sea;* Nigel Calder, *Eden Was No Garden;* Lynton C. Caldwell, *Planned Control of the Biophysical Environment;* William R. Ewald, Jr. (ed.), *Environment for Man;* Aldous Huxley, *The Politics of Ecology;* S. Dillon Ripley and Helmut K. Buechner, "Ecosystem Science as a Point of Synthesis"; Paul B. Sears, "Utopia and the Living Landscape", Paul Shepard, *Man in the Landscape;* and Philip L. Wagner, *The Human Use of the Earth.* On man himself see Jacob Bronowski, *The Identity of Man;* Alexis Carrell, *Man, the Unknown;* and P. B. Medewar, *The Future of Man.*
9. M.I.T. commencement address, 1964, in Burke, *The New Technology and Human Values,* p. 94.
10. This traditional attitude is under severe attack by contemporary theologians even in orthodox churches. See Leslie Dewart, *The Future of Belief.*
11. Platt, *The Step to Man,* p. 183.
12. Paraphrased by Herbert J. Muller in Burke, *The New Technology and Human Values,* p. 44.
13. Cf. Warner R. Schilling, "The H-Bomb Decision."
14. Quoted in Bates, *The Forest and the Sea,* p. 254.
15. Quoted in "How Man Changes His World," New York *Times,* September 24, 1967.
16. As Joseph Rosenfarb points out, "An economy being planned does not necessarily involve a planned culture," *Freedom and the Administrative State,* p. 87.

17. The term comes from a different context, William Burroughs' novel, *The Soft Machine,* but is relevant here.
18. Platt, *The Step to Man,* p. 187.
19. Exodus, 3:14, *The New Jerusalem Bible.*
20. William Braden, *The Private Sea;* Timothy Leary, *The Politics of Ecstasy;* also Rev. George B. Murray, S.J. and Jean Huston, "LSD: The Inward Voyage."
21. This is the general thesis of Koestler in *The Ghost in the Machine.*
22. For an interesting if controversial approach to this point see L. Pauwels and J. Bergier, *The Morning of the Magicians.*
23. On suggested reforms see Lynton C. Caldwell, "Managing the Scientific Super-Culture"; Robert S. Morison, "Education for Environmental Concerns"; and E. V. David, Jr. and J. G. Truxal, "The Man-Made World."
24. On specific problems of controlling the effects of science and technology on society see Barry Commoner, *Science and Survival;* H. Wentworth Eldredge, *Taming Megalopolis;* Nigel Calder, "Tomorrow's Politics"; LaMont C. Cole, "Can the World Be Saved?"; Rene J. Dubos, "Scientists Alone Can't Do the Job"; Amitai Etzioni, "On the National Guidance of Science"; Wilbur H. Ferry, "Must We Rewrite the Constitution to Control Technology?"; Julian Huxley, *The Human Crisis;* Henry Jarret (ed.), *Environmental Quality in a Growing Economy;* John Lear, "Policing the Consequences of Science"; Roger Revelle, "Outdoor Recreation in a Hyper-Productive Society." For basic perspectives see Joseph Wood Krutch, *And Even If You Do;* Yves R. Simon, *Philosophy of Democratic Government,* pp. 260–322; Oswald Spengler, *Man and Technics;* Andreas G. Van Melsen, *Science and Technology;* also Denis de Rougemont, "Man *v.* Technics"; Lynton C. Caldwell, "Biopolitics"; and Richard L. Means, "Why Worry About Nature?"
25. On problems and techniques of decision-making see Raymond A. Bauer, *Social Indicators;* David Braybrooke and Charles E. Lindblom, *A Strategy of Decision;* Robert A. Dahl and Charles E. Lindblom, *Politics, Economics and Welfare;* Bertram Gross (ed.), *Action Under Planning;* also Todd A. La Porte, "Politics and 'Inventing the Future' "; and Roger Starr and James Carlson, "Pollution and Poverty."
26. Kenneth Arrow, *Social Choice and Individual Values.* For a critique see James Coleman, "The Possibility of a Social Welfare Function."
27. Amitai Etzioni, *The Active Society,* pp. 282–309 and "Mixed-Scanning."
28. Platt, *The Step to Man,* p. 200.
29. *Ibid.,* p. 51. Something similar has been suggested by Arthur I. Waskow. See "Peaceful Strife Expected by '99," New York *Times,* February 12, 1968.
30. Keniston, "Youth, Change and Violence," p. 233. This is perhaps less true in the developing nations than the developed. Most developing

nations are currently going through a kind of xenophobia not unlike that exhibited by the developed nations in the nineteenth century.

31. Michael Polanyi, "The Republic of Science."
32. See also the warnings of Carlyl P. Haskins, "Organ Transplants Bring Warning on Life's Values," Washington *Post,* January 29, 1968.
33. "Toynbee Urges Man to Slow Rapid Pace of Change," New York *Times,* March 14, 1967.
34. Van Melsen, *Science and Technology,* Vol. II. pp. 306–308.
35. On the problem presented by space travel see Carl Sagan *et al.,* "Contamination of Mars."
36. A U.N. committee on the subject was convened by U Thant on March 18, 1968. See also Luther J. Carter, "Deep Seabed" and J. V. Reistrup, "Davy Jones' Locker Tempts the World."
37. As the distinguished conservative economist Wilhelm Ropke puts it, "If it has to stop eventually, why not now? Why must the earth be first transformed into an anthill?" *A Humane Economy,* p. 44.
38. Charles A. Lindbergh, "The Wisdom of Wildness."
39. Kenneth Boulding, "Where Are We Going If Anywhere?" pp. 166–167.
40. For various suggestions see Platt, *The Step to Man,* p. 105; "Annual Bonus Is Urged For Not Having Babies," New York *Times,* March 2, 1968; "Zoologist Urges Taxes On Diapers," New York *Times,* May 29, 1968. Institution of a form of easily dissoluble childless marriage, in addition to more permanent procreative unions, has also been urged. "Overcrowding Crisis Due in 1970's, According to Experts on Population," Washington *Post,* July 15, 1967.
41. William L. Langer, "Europe's Initial Population Explosion."
42. "The Irrepressible Family," *The Public Interest,* 3 (Spring, 1966), pp. 127–128.
43. Kingsley Davis, "Population Policy"; also Margaret Snyder, "Behavioral Sciences and Family Planning."
44. See Aaron Wildavsky, "Aesthetic Power or the Triumph of the Sensitive Minority Over the Vulgar Mass."
45. The pages of *Science* and the *Bulletin of the Atomic Scientists* reflect this. The American Association for the Advancement of Science recently set up a committee on human-environmental relations. See Dale Wolfle, "The Only Earth We Have."
46. Joshua Lederberg does so in "Legislation on Transplants Should Begin With Specifics," Washington *Post,* January 28, 1968. See also "Transplant Controls Urged," Washington *Post,* February 28, 1968; " 'Genetic Engineering' Fears Discounted," Washington *Star,* March 8, 1968; "Scientist Doubts Genetic Abuse: Calls Research the Best Defense," New York *Times,* March 9, 1968; "Naive Howls on Medical Research," Washington *Star,* March 14, 1968; "Dr. Bernard Rejects Curbs on Doctors," Washington *Post,* March 9, 1968.
47. Despite this support American participation has been less than adequate, even though spurred on by the House Subcommittee on Science,

Research and Development, chaired by Representative Daddario. See "House Panel Asks U.S. Aid for World Study of Man's Effect on Earth," New York *Times,* March 20, 1968; and Philip M. Boffey, "International Biological Program."

48. On experimentation on humans see M. H. Pappworth, *Human Guinea Pigs;* Bernard Barber, "Experimenting with Humans"; Walter Goodman, "Doctors Must Experiment with Humans"; P. B. Medewar, "Science and the Sanctity of Life"; and Edward Shils, "The Sanctity of Life."

49. Some scientists such as Lederberg realize this, as in his "Society, Not Science, to Decide When to Cure Some Diseases," Washington *Post,* December 30, 1967, though he is less than enthusiastic that this is the case.

50. Platt, *The Step to Man,* p. 195.

51. Cf. George Gaylord Simpson, *The Meaning of Evolution,* pp. 307–308.

52. Quoted in Huston Smith, "The New Age," p. 18. Eckhart lived circa 1260–1328.

CHAPTER 7

THE FUTURE OF CRIME

RICHARD QUINNEY

The work of Richard Quinney has been notably influential in providing sociology with a reorientation of the study of deviance and crime. Traditional conceptions have viewed deviance and crime as *objectively given,* suggesting the existence of some set of *fundamental norms* that represent taboos against acts that are intrinsically "evil." Deviance is a negative quality attributed to a particular act a person commits. From this point of view, the typical questions for inquiry have been (1) who is the deviant? (2) how did he become a deviant? (3) what conditions are likely to produce deviants? and (4) what can be done to change deviant conduct? Such a conception of deviance, however, especially with respect to complex modern societies, fails to account for the varying nature of social norms. As a result, sociologists have been looking more and more upon the processes of social interaction that may result in forms of deviance coming into being and have been trying, finally, to define it.

Within this perspective, Professor Quinney begins his reinterpretation of deviance and crime from a nominalistic position: A thing exists only when it has been given a name; any phenomenon is real to us only when we can imagine it. This suggests that deviance and crime are *social* constructions. More specifically, Quinney's notion of the social reality of crime flows from his beliefs that social groups create deviance by making rules whose infraction constitutes deviance and that crime is a definition of human conduct that is created by authorized agents in a politically organized society. People and behaviors, then, become "deviant" because social groups label them as such, and they become "criminal" because of the formulation of criminal definitions and their application by the legal system. Thus, crime is *created.* The greater the number of criminal definitions formulated and applied, the greater the amount of crime.

In *The Problem of Crime,* a chapter from which follows, Quinney describes how American criminal law has been shaped around our basic American values. Much of our criminal law, for example, has been formulated for the purpose of publicly enforcing moral principles. Many times, conduct that is labeled as criminal does not involve an injury to another person (for instance, prostitution, homosexuality, drunkenness, the use of drugs, vagrancy) but merely disturbs the community's sense of public morality. Quinney notes, however, that more and more of what is viewed as pathological or deviant is political in nature. This "politicality" of crime is made apparent in two ways: The actions of many so-called criminals are politically motivated behaviors such as protest and dissent, and the labeling of the behavior as criminal is also politically motivated.

"The Future of Crime" reflects upon both the social and the political realities of crime in our rapidly changing social system. Professor Quinney points out how these realities are altering the character and conceptions of crime and, more importantly, how crime is and will continue to be an essential part of American society.

Richard Quinney received his Ph. D. degree in sociology at the University of Wisconsin. Having served on the faculties of Saint Lawrence University, the University of Kentucky, and New York University, he is currently teaching at Brooklyn College and the Graduate Center of the City University of New York. His major areas of concentration include criminology, sociology of law, and political sociology. In addition to making numerous contributions to various scholarly journals, he has written several books, including *Criminal Behavior Systems: A Typology* (1967, 1973), *Crime and Justice in Society* (1969), *The Social Reality of Crime* (1970), *Criminal Justice in America* (1974), and *Critique of Legal Order* (1974).

Given our understanding of the ethos of American society, and the relation of crime to that ethos, we can venture into a brief discussion of the future of crime in America. Two things seem certain: first, crime is undergoing change in American society; and second, the problem of crime will always be with us no matter how much change takes place. It is within this framework of change and continuation that the future of crime can be considered.

THE CHANGING CHARACTER OF CRIME

. . . Crime is becoming more political in American society. That is, the behaviors of the criminally defined are increasing in their

"The Future of Crime," by Richard Quinney, chapter 5 in *The Problem of Crime,* 1970, is reprinted by permission of the publisher, Dodd, Mead & Company, Inc.

politicality, and the actions of the state in labeling behaviors as criminal are becoming more political. This is also to say that crime is becoming more relevant to society. At stake, as well, are the fundamental issues of governmental control and individual rights.

Another trend that seems to be well under way, in addition to the increasing politicality of crime, is the decrease in the use of the criminal law for the regulation of certain other behaviors.[1] The criminal laws that are primarily involved are those that pertain to the control of public morality: the laws that sanction prostitution, homosexuality, drunkenness, and vagrancy. There is also some indication that laws on drug use will change after we pass through the current period of public and legal hysteria. In regard to some of these forms of conduct, however, sanctions even more repressive and punitive may replace the criminal sanction. Nevertheless, the result will be a major reduction in the amount of crime. Perhaps up to 90 percent of our known crimes will be eliminated by a simple change in the use of the criminal law.

Some criminal laws affecting these offenses against public morality are already in the process of being changed or eliminated. For example, in 1966 the United States Court of Appeals for the District of Columbia ruled that a person cannot be convicted of the crime of public drunkenness. The reasoning was that an intoxicated person lacks the necessary criminal intent to be guilty of a crime. Vagrancy statutes have been similarily questioned. In 1967 the New York Court of Appeals ruled that a vagrancy statute of 1788 was unconstitutional because it punished persons for merely having no visible means of support. In addition, legal reforms regarding the regulation of homosexuality are currently under consideration. Thus, through various court rulings and model penal codes, legal control of morality is being questioned and eliminated. Old statutes are being declared unconstitutional on the ground that they interfere with the liberty of a person to conduct himself as he sees fit as long as he does not harm or interfere with the rights of others.

The sanctions that are attached to the existing criminal laws are also undergoing change. There has been a progression in the history of American criminal law from the use of punitive sanctions to sanctions that are more oriented to treatment. The traditional punitive philosophy that punishment deters criminals from repeating their offenses and deters other persons from committing crimes is gradually being replaced by less punitive measures and by treatment programs of various kinds. As a result, probation is increasingly being used instead of prison sentences. Within the prison, group therapy programs are being instituted. And upon release from the prison, inmates are being integrated into the community by such facilities as the halfway house.

In addition, capital punishment is finally nearing its end in the United States.

All of this is not to say that the punitive sanction is vanishing from American criminal law. Indeed, part of the rationale for criminal law is, and always will be, making the offender suffer for his transgressions. It will probably be some time, also, before punitive sanctions will be used to any advantage, if this is at all possible. Our legal system tends to punish most severely those persons who are least deterrable and punishes least severely those persons who are most deterrable.[2] Punitive sanctions thus appear to fulfill social functions other than the intended purpose of deterrence.

Although the trend may be to a decrease in the intentional use of punishment, the replacements for punishment may not be as nonpunitive as they seem. Already the results of the implementation of the "rehabilitative ideal" have not been especially lacking in punitiveness.[3] In fact, many of the programs that have emerged have led to more severe penal measures. Finally, that which is practiced in the name of treatment may actually deny or conflict with individual civil rights. An increasing awareness of this problem may do much to change the character of crime in the United States.

INCREASING CONCERN ABOUT CRIME

The amount of public attention that is devoted to crime varies considerably from one time to another. Throughout this century there have been periods in which crime has been an acute concern. When these periods occur, investigation committees are appointed, lawenforcement activities are heightened, and the public's attention is focused on the problem of crime.

We are currently engaged in another crusade on crime. Only this time the concern is likely to be with us for some time. This appears to be the case because our increasing concern about crime is a reflection of some radical changes that are taking place in American society. For instance, a rising expectation of what constitutes a just society is creating in the many persons who suffer from injustices the motivation to behave in ways that may be labeled as criminal. The established society, in attempting to maintain its hold, reacts by making and enforcing criminal laws. Furthermore, our expectation of a peaceful (and crime-free) society makes us more conscious of crime, whatever amount of offensive conduct there may be in the society. In addition, the label of crime is being used as a last resort to handle those conflicts in society that have not been dealt with more imaginatively through basic structural and cultural changes in American society. All of these conditions are producing a concern about crime.

In response to the increasing concern about crime, the President's Commission on Law Enforcement and Administration of Justice was established in 1965.[4] One part of the commission's task was to investigate the nature of the public's anxiety about crime. Through several surveys and public opinion polls, the commission did indeed find that crime was perceived by the public as one of the most serious of all domestic problems.[5] It was found that crime was mentioned by the public as the second most pressing problem in the United States, second only to the problem of race relations. Most persons also thought that crime in their own community was getting worse. Moreover, the commission found that personal *fear* of crime was especially great. The fears involve an anxiety about personal safety and, to some extent, the fear that personal property will be taken. Persons, according to the findings, have an intense fear that they will be accosted by a stranger on the street or that a stranger will break into their homes to attack them. These fears have brought about a change in the lives of many persons.

Realizing that crime also affects lives economically and that economic factors relating to crime are important in the formation of public attitudes, the President's Commission attempted to assess the economic costs of crime in the United States.[6] The commission roughly divided the economic costs of crime into several categories. It was estimated that about $815 million was spent by individuals annually as a result of crimes against person, $4 billion as a result of crimes against property, $8 billion as a result of traffic in illegal goods and services, and $2 billion as a result of other crimes. In addition, governmental expeditures for the control of crime—for police, courts, and corrections—were estimated at more than $4 billion a year. Finally, private costs as a consequence of crime (including protective services, burglar alarms, and insurance) amount to about $2 billion annually. Such figures, however, are as difficult to interpret as they are to comprehend. Estimates of the economic costs of crime are fallacious in their assumption that crime and its costs can be separated from other activities in the whole of society. They also ignore the fact that to maintain a society with little crime, if at all possible, would likely cost much more, in terms of money as well as individual human rights. The money spent on crime, given the ethos of our society, may actually be a bargain for the society.

The President's Commission on Law Enforcement and Administration of Justice paved the way for legislation of the crime problem. In June 1968, the United States Congress enacted a law called the Omnibus Crime Control and Safe Streets Act.[7] As originally conceived, the bill was to assist state and local governments in reducing the incidence of crime by increasing the effectiveness of law enforcement and criminal justice. But back of the bill were the growing fears of what it is to be living at this point in American history. An attack on crime became the scapegoat for all these fears. The result was a Crime Bill that was filled with the emotions of the times: the cry for "law and order," the demand for a "war on crime" and a concern about "crime in the streets." In many ways the slogans, and the resulting Crime Bill, were euphemisms for the fears brought about by a society that was at the same time deep in conflict and undergoing wide-ranging social changes.

In essence the Crime Bill attempts to control crime by placing the power of the state above the rights of the individual. Through several controversial titles in the bill, basic rights heretofore guaranteed by the Bill of Rights, constitutional amendments, and Supreme Court decisions were either overthrown or reinterpreted. Among other things, privacy can be invaded by allowing eavesdropping and wire-tapping; voluntary confessions and eyewitness identifications can be admitted in federal trials; and suspects can be interrogated without counsel. We are thus experiencing an American tendency of sub-ordinating the right of the citizen to the power of the state.

The story has not yet ended. The conflict between those forces that would restrict human rights in the name of government and those that would provide for individual autonomy no matter what the social consequences will always be with us in the struggle for a just society, a society that allows decent lives to be lived in the presence of others. This conflict is dramatically being played out in the problem of crime.

CONTINUATION OF THE CRIME PROBLEM

A common assumption in the study of crime has been that crime is abnormal—abnormal from the standpoint of both the individual and the society. Such an assumption has led to the search for abnormal personal and social factors which might be related to crime. Crime has, in turn, been commonly regarded as an indicator that something is wrong with society. The famous dictum of Lacassagne, one of the leaders of the French environmental school of criminology, that "societies have the criminals they deserve" reflects this belief. Vivid descriptions have been presented, and theories have been propounded, on the belief that crime is a result of maladjustments in society. One recent description reads as follows:

> The social function of crime is to act as a notification of maladjustments. Just as pain is a notification to an organism that something is wrong, so crime is a notification of a social maladjustment, especially when crime becomes prevalent. Crime is a symptom of social disorganization

and probably can be reduced appreciably only by changes in social organization.[8]

Any phenomenon, however, can be viewed in terms of both its functional and dysfunctional elements. Crime is no exception. Behavior that is defined as criminal in any society serves various functions for certain segments and aspects of society and serves, at the same time, as a disruptive agent for other parts of the society. Also, whether one chooses to investigate either the functions or dysfunctions of crime depends to a considerable extent on his own assumptions about crime in society.

The conception that crime is a normal and functional part of society has its modern sociological expression in the writing of Emile Durkheim. To Durkheim, there is "no phenomenon that presents more indisputably all the symptoms of normality, since it appears closely connected with the conditions of all collective life." [9] Since crime is bound up with the fundamental conditions of social life, he argued, crime is indispensable to the normal development of society. Crime allows for individual expression and, ultimately, for the moral evolution of society.

> To make progress, individual originality must be able to express itself. In order that the originality of the idealist whose dreams transcend his century may find expression, it is necessary that the originality of the criminal, who is below the level of his time, shall also be possible. One does not occur without the other.[10]

From a limited time perspective, then, crime might be narrowly construed as disruptive to a society. From a broad perspective, however, crime may be more accurately conceived of as behavior that is essential to the welfare of the society. It may be argued that crime is necessarily created in a society. That is, behavior and persons are defined as criminal in order that a sense of appropriate and proper conduct may be established.[11] In such a manner, crime is not alien to society but contributes to the organization of the society. Crime, according to this conception, preserves social order; it does not disrupt society. Crime does not necessarily reflect social maladjustments, nor does it necessarily create instability.

Among the functional aspects of crime are the ways in which crime is economically related to society. Karl Marx noted this interdependence some time ago:

The criminal produces not only crime but also the criminal law; he produces the professor who delivers lectures on this criminal law, and even the inevitable text-book in which the professor presents his lectures as a commodity for sale in the market. There results an increase in material wealth, quite apart from the pleasure which . . . the author himself derives from the manuscript of this text-book.

Further, the criminal produces the whole apparatus of the police and criminal justice, detectives, judges, executioners, juries, etc., and all these different professions, which constitute so many categories of the social division of labour develop diverse abilities of the human spirit, created new needs and new ways of satisfying them.[12]

The economic and occupational functions of crime are readily apparent in the United States. For example, between one and two million persons find full-time employment in jobs and occupations that depend upon the existence of crime. Included in this labor group are approximately 277,000 policemen, sheriffs, and marshals, 213,000 lawyers and judges, 136,000 persons engaged in social welfare and recreational work, 48,000 staff members of federal and state prisons, and 6,000 professors involved in teaching and research on crime, criminal law, law enforcement, and related subjects.[13] In addition, over 430,000 persons are annually confined in prisons, jails, workhouses, reformatories, training schools, and detention homes. A sizable portion of these persons find economic security in such confinement. Their confinement has the additional function of lowering the unemployment rate of the nation. One can be certain also that of the two and one-half million major property offenses reported in 1965, a considerable proportion provided economic support for those who committed the offenses. It is not facetious to argue that crime pays in an economic sense for many individuals and for the society as a whole. As Marx observed, in very modern terms, "Crime takes off the labour market a portion of the excess population, diminishes competition among workers, and to a certain extent stops wages from falling below the minimum, while the war against crime absorbs another part of the same population." [14]

Some time ago in a critique of the Wickersham report on the costs of crime, Hawkins and Waller observed that crime is an integral part of the economic system in still other ways.

Without in the least apologizing for crime as a moral phenomenon, we are forced to the conclusion that it is an industry like other industries, bound together in inextricable interdependence with all the other institutions and activities by means of which man makes a living. . . . As an industry, it gives direct employment to thousands of persons who would otherwise be in competition in the labor market; indirectly, it contributes to the financial welfare of those who supply it with equipment and those who benefit by the spending of the spoils. Most immediately it supports the manufacturers and sellers of the weapons and tools of criminals and policemen, the landlords who rent houses of prostitution and offices of private detective agencies, and a host of others. More remotely, the most diverse and respectable industries are involved through our delicate interlocking exchange mechanism.[15]

In our capitalistic, private-profit economy, several forms of crime depend for their existence on the demands of legitimate business. Some forms of crime, if they did not exist, would have to be invented in order to supply various business enterprises with services and supplies that could not be obtained through any other means.

The existence of crime also serves a number of humanitarian causes. Many organizations, for example, find their rationale for expounding and perpetuating human values in the fact that persons violate the criminal law. Some criminal laws possibly originate among these organizations for the purpose of providing a rule that will be violated. The standard of living of the population has, in addition, been raised through the assistance of criminals. In particular, much of the progress in medical science has been possible because prisoners have been available to serve as "volunteers" in potentially dangerous medical experiments. Much of the progress in the development of antimalarial drugs, for example, can be attributed to the experimental programs conducted in federal and state prisons. As one medical researcher involved in the malaria test program at the federal prison in Atlanta commented, in reference to the inmate volunteers, "Without these guys we'd be dead. We couldn't do anything." [16]

In conclusion, then, crime can be viewed as a normal part of society. From this perspective, crime is important to the functioning of society. Much of a society's crime initiates, as well as represents, important social changes, changes without which a society might otherwise cease to have any semblance of order. If our search for an understanding of crime is preoccupied with a model of crime as abnormal, we will fail to understand many essential aspects of crime in American society.

Crime is such an essential part of society that a society without crime is inconceivable. As long as men make laws, there will be crime. The forms of crime, to be certain, will change as human values change. But as long as men continue to value and preserve, condone and condemn, behaviors will be labeled as criminal. And as long as a society includes as one of its cherished values some measure of individual freedom, there will be violations of the criminal law. A crimeless society could only be one that is static and unchanging, one in which persons cease to value and to aspire, and a society more totalitarian in control than we would want to imagine.

NOTES

1. See Herbert L. Packer, *The Limits of the Criminal Sanction* (Stanford: Stanford University Press, 1968).
2. William J. Chambliss, "Types of Deviance and the Effectiveness of Legal Sanctions," *Wisconsin Law Review,* 1967 (Summer 1967), 703–19.
3. Francis A. Allen, "Criminal Justice, Legal Values and the Rehabilitative Ideal," *Journal of Criminal Law, Criminology and Police Science,* 50 (September–October 1959), 226–32.
4. President's Commission on Law Enforcement and Administration of Justice, *The Challenge of Crime in a Free Society* (Washington, D.C.: U.S. Government Printing Office, 1967).
5. See President's Commission on Law Enforcement and Administration of Justice, *Task Force Report: Crime and Its Impact: An Assessment* (Washington, D.C.: U.S. Government Printing Office, 1967), pp. 85–95.
6. President's Commission on Law Enforcement and Administration of Justice, *Task Force Report: Crime and Its Impact,* pp. 42–59.
7. See *The New York Times* (June 20, 1968), pp. 1 and 23; Richard Harris, "Annals of Legislation: The Turning Point," *New Yorker* (December 14, 1968), pp. 68–179.
8. Edwin H. Sutherland and Donald R. Cressey, *Principles of Criminology,* 7th ed. (Philadelphia: J. B. Lippincott, 1966), p. 24.
9. Emile Durkheim, *The Rules of Sociological Method* (Chicago: University of Chicago Press, 1938), p. 66.
10. Durkheim, *The Rules of Sociological Method,* p. 71.
11. See Robert A. Dentler and Kai T. Erikson, "The Functions of Deviance in Groups," *Social Problems,* 7 (Fall 1959), 98–107; Kai T. Erikson, "Notes on the Sociology of Deviance," *Social Problems,* 9 (Spring 1962), 307–14; Lewis A. Coser, "Some Functions of Deviant Behavior and Normative Flexibility," *American Journal of Sociology,* 68 (September 1962), pp. 172–81; Roger Nett, "Conformity-Deviation and the Social Control Concept," *Ethics,* 64 (October 1963), 38–45.

12. Karl Marx, *Selected Writings in Sociology and Social Philosophy*, trans. by T. B. Bottomore (New York: McGraw-Hill, 1956), pp. 158–59.

13. Approximate figures from U.S. Bureau of the Census, *Statistical Abstract of the United States, 1965* (Washington, D.C. 1965).

14. Marx, *Selected Writings in Sociology and Social Philosophy*, p. 159.

15. E. R. Hawkins and Willard Waller, "Critical Notes on the Cost of Crime," *Journal of Criminal Law, Criminology and Police Science*, 26 (May–June 1935), 692–93.

16. *New York Times Magazine* (September 25, 1966), p. 47.

THE AUTHORS

JAMES A. INCIARDI is currently an assistant professor in the Department of Epidemiology and Public Health, University of Miami School of Medicine, and Vice-President of the Resource Planning Corporation of Washington, D.C., and Miami, Florida. He has published widely in the areas of drug use, organized crime, juvenile delinquency, and corrections.

HARVEY A. SIEGAL is at present a faculty member in the Department of Epidemiology and Public Health, University of Miami School of Medicine, and a senior research associate at the Resource Planning Corporation.